365 PARTY FOOD RECIPES

365 PARTY FOOD RECIPES

EASY RECIPES FOR THE BUSY KITCHEN

MARY B. JOHNSON

STERLING INNOVATION
An imprint of Sterling Publishing Co., Inc.

New York / London
www.sterlingpublishing.com

STERLING and the distinctive Sterling logo are registered trademarks of Sterling Publishing Co., Inc.

Library of Congress Cataloging-in-Publication Data Available

2 4 6 8 10 9 7 5 3 1

Published by Sterling Publishing Co., Inc.
387 Park Avenue South, New York, NY 10016
© 2007 by Sterling Publishing Co., Inc.
Distributed in Canada by Sterling Publishing
c/o Canadian Manda Group, 165 Dufferin Street
Toronto, Ontario, Canada M6K 3H6
Distributed in the United Kingdom by GMC Distribution Services
Castle Place, 166 High Street, Lewes, East Sussex, England BN7 1XU
Distributed in Australia by Capricorn Link (Australia) Pty. Ltd.
P.O. Box 704, Windsor, NSW 2756, Australia

Food Styling by Susan Vajaranant & Victoria Granof with Art-Dept Agency
Prop Styling by Phyllis Asher

Design by Leah Lococo Ltd
Photographs by Theresa Raffetto

Printed in China
Sterling ISBN-13: 978-1-4027-4792-2
ISBN-10: 1-4027-4792-6

For information about custom editions, special sales, premium and corporate purchases,
please contact Sterling Special Sales Department at 800-805-5489 or specialsales@sterlingpub.com.

CONTENTS

INTRODUCTION

PARTIES ARE A TIME TO CATCH UP WITH family and friends—a time to cherish and enjoy the people who are most important in our lives. There's no better way to enjoy the company of the ones we love than with good food, and we've got 365 ways to do just that! Here are dozens of appetizers for informal gatherings, from dips to finger foods to mini pizzas; "small plate" first courses for more formal, sit-down affairs; even abundant platters that look and taste great passing around at larger parties. We also offer a section on drinks, if you are looking to go beyond the usual wine, beer, and soft drinks. And finally, the desserts chapter has tons of sweet little nibbles.

Throwing a party can be a labor of love, but it does not need to be a stressful event. And though there are lots of easy recipes inside (check out Easy Onion Bread Sticks, page 175, or Piglets in a Blanket, page 144), the true key to an easy, stress-free successful party is organization. Plan out your menu in advance, and make as many dishes as you can ahead of time. (Remember, pâté and terrines often taste amazing when they've been made in advance since the flavors can really meld together.)

Here are a few tips to keep in mind when planning the menu for your party: Try to choose a variety of flavors, textures, and types of foods to have a well-rounded menu. For example, if you want to serve the Tuna Niçoise Tartlets (page 120), you should avoid also serving the Hot Cheese Olives (page 76) and Easy Olive Focaccia (page 199)—the olive flavor would be too overwhelming. Keep the size of your kitchen in mind when picking recipes; your refrigerator will only hold so many dips and pâtés until party time, and your oven can only cook a limited number of hot dishes. And be sure to limit the amount of appetizers you plan on serving that require last minute preparation. Your best bet is to include some of the simple items, such as Cocktail Nut Mix (page 147), that you can prepare ahead, place in a bowl, and forget about. Dips with chips, vegetables, or pita bread are also easy to prepare (precut vegetables reduce prep time and look great around a dip bowl). We've included plenty of recipes for homemade pizza dough, pastry shells, aïoli, and other from-scratch components that you should try when you have a chance. But if you're short on time, there's no reason you shouldn't head to the store for premade doughs, condiments, and sauces. They cut down on prep time while still allowing you to assemble a fantastic spread. And one last tip: Knowing your head count is helpful in planning how much food to prepare. If you're throwing a cocktail party or any party with no main course, a good rule of thumb is ten to thirteen appetizers per person.

So get ready, and get planning for your next party, whether it's an intimate dinner with your best friends, or a big bash for the entire neighborhood. No matter what your taste, you'll find a wide variety of recipes here with origins all over the world, including Vietnam, Italy, the Caribbean, Mexico, China, and the good old USA. Feel free to pick and choose among different cuisines to keep the taste buds delighted. Whichever dish you decide to try, it's sure to be a hit.

DIPS & SPREADS

TRI-COLORED CHEESE TORTE

PREP: 15 minutes plus chilling

Makes 16 servings

1 (11-ounce) log goat's milk cheese

½ cup mascarpone cheese

¾ cup Classic Basil Pesto (page 427) or store-bought pesto

⅓ cup marinated sun-dried tomatoes, chopped, plus 2 teaspoons of the marinating oil

¼ cup pine nuts, toasted and roughly chopped

Crostini (page 166) or crackers for serving

1. Line an 8-inch round cake pan with plastic wrap, extending the plastic well beyond the sides of the pan. Spray with nonstick cooking spray.

2. Combine the goat cheese and mascarpone in a bowl and mix well. Scoop ½ cup into another bowl, add the pesto, and mix well. Scoop ½ cup of the remaining plain cheese mixture into another bowl, add the sun-dried tomatoes, and mix well.

3. Spread one-third of the remaining plain cheese over the bottom of the prepared pan using the bottom of a spoon that has been sprayed with nonstick cooking spray. Top with the pesto mixture, then with half of the remaining plain cheese. Top with the tomato mixture and then the remaining plain cheese. Cover the torte with the extended plastic wrap and refrigerate at least 4 hours or overnight.

4. To serve, unfold the plastic wrap from the top of the torte and place a flat serving dish, top side down, on top. Invert the torte onto a serving dish and remove the pan and plastic wrap. Pat the pine nuts around the sides. Drizzle the tomato-marinating oil around the torte. Serve with crackers or crostini.

CURRIED CHEESE SPREAD WITH ALMONDS AND CHUTNEY

PREP: 40 minutes plus chilling

Makes 8 servings

1 (8-ounce) package cream cheese, softened

½ teaspoon hot curry powder

¼ teaspoon dry mustard

½ cup hot mango chutney, cut into small pieces

¼ cup golden raisins, chopped

¼ cup slivered almonds, toasted and chopped

Swedish gingersnap cookies for serving

1. Stir the cream cheese in a bowl until fluffy. Add the curry powder and mustard and stir until blended. Stir in the chutney and raisins. Scrape into a serving bowl. Cover with plastic wrap and refrigerate at least 2 hours before serving.

2. To serve, let stand at room temperature to soften, about 30 minutes. Just before serving, sprinkle with the almonds. Serve as a spread for the gingersnaps.

TRIPLE RED-PEPPER CHEESE SPREAD

PREP: 15 minutes

Makes about 2 cups, about 16 servings

½ cup crème fraîche or mascarpone cheese

2 tablespoons mayonnaise

2 teaspoons fresh lemon juice

1 teaspoon finely minced garlic

½ teaspoon freshly ground black pepper

8 ounces extra-sharp yellow cheddar cheese

1 freshly roasted or jarred piquillo or other red pepper, drained, patted dry, and finely chopped

1 large red bell pepper, finely chopped

1 canned chipotle pepper in adobo sauce, finely chopped

½ cup finely chopped celery

Combine the crème fraîche, mayonnaise, lemon juice, garlic, and black pepper in a mixing bowl and whisk until smooth. Grate the cheese into the mixture using a microplane. Add the piquillo pepper, bell pepper, chipotle, and celery. Mix well. Serve the spread at room temperature as a sandwich spread or a dip for crackers, chips, bread.

GINGER-CARROT SPREAD

PREP: 10 minutes COOK: 25 minutes

Makes 10 servings

2 ⅓ cups thinly sliced peeled carrots

2 cups water

2 tablespoons grated peeled fresh ginger

1 tablespoon butter

1 tablespoon honey

1 teaspoon grated lemon zest

1 tablespoon lemon juice

¼ teaspoon fine sea salt

⅛ teaspoon white pepper

2 tablespoons sliced almonds, toasted

1. Combine the carrots, water, ginger, butter, and honey in a medium saucepan over medium-high heat; bring to boiling. Cover, reduce the heat, and simmer 7 minutes or until the carrots are tender. Increase the heat to medium-high; uncover and cook 12 minutes or until the liquid is absorbed.

2. Combine the carrot mixture, lemon zest, lemon juice, salt, and pepper in a food processor and process until smooth. Scrape the carrot mixture into a bowl and sprinkle with the toasted almonds.

ROASTED-PEPPER PARMIGIANO-REGGIANO SPREAD

In this savory spread for crackers, if you prefer, you can use a 10-ounce jar of roasted peppers instead of roasting, peeling, and seeding fresh peppers.

2 egg yolks
1 teaspoon grated lemon zest
1 tablespoon lemon juice
½ teaspoon salt
¼ teaspoon freshly ground black pepper
½ cup olive oil
3 roasted yellow bell peppers, peeled, seeded, and cut into 1-inch pieces
1 cup grated Parmigiano-Reggiano cheese
1 tablespoon chopped fresh parsley

1. Place the egg yolks, lemon zest, lemon juice, salt, and pepper in a food processor and process until blended. With the machine running, pour in the olive oil through the feed tube in a steady stream until thick. Scrape down the sides of the work bowl.

2. With the machine running, add the peppers, a few pieces at a time, and process until thick. Scrape the mixture into a medium bowl and stir in the Parmigiano-Reggiano and parsley. Cover and refrigerate at least 1 hour before serving.

TOMATO JAM

PREP: 15 minutes   COOK: 30 minutes

Makes about 1½ cups

8 ripe plum tomatoes, diced

1 large garlic clove, crushed through a press

½ lemon, juiced

1 cup fresh carrot juice

2 tablespoons brown sugar

1 tablespoon soy sauce

1 tablespoon grated lemon zest

1 teaspoon kosher salt

1. Combine all the ingredients in a food processor and process until blended.

2. Transfer the mixture to a saucepan; heat to boiling over medium-high heat. Reduce the heat to medium-low and simmer until the mixture is thickened, not watery, about 20 minutes, stirring occasionally.

3. Transfer the mixture to a food mill placed over a bowl and press out all the tomato and garlic puree. Pour the puree into a clean saucepan; simmer over medium heat until no liquid remains, just a roasted-smelling jam. Cool to room temperature before serving.

HERBED OLIVE SPREAD WITH PRESERVED LEMON

PREP: 10 minutes

Makes about 1 1/2 cups, about 12 servings

1 cup pitted oil-cured black olives

1/2 store-bought or homemade (page 53) preserved lemon, peel only, cut into 1-inch pieces

1/2 cup capers packed in salt, rinsed, and patted dry

1 cup fresh flat-leaf parsley leaves

1/2 cup loosely packed fresh basil leaves

2 tablespoons lemon juice

1/8 teaspoon kosher salt or more to taste

1/8 teaspoon freshly ground black pepper or more to taste

1/2 cup olive oil

Combine the olives, preserved lemon, capers, parsley, basil, lemon juice, salt, and pepper in a food processor and pulse to combine. With the motor running, add the olive oil through the feed tube in a slow, steady stream and process until emulsified. Taste and add more salt and pepper if needed.

TAPENADE

PREP: 10 minutes

Makes about 1 cup

1 cup pitted niçoise or other imported black olives

4 to 8 anchovy fillets (to taste)

1 garlic clove, crushed through a press

2 tablespoons capers packed in salt, rinsed and patted dry

2 tablespoons extra-virgin olive oil

2 tablespoons lemon juice or more to taste

½ teaspoon freshly ground black pepper or more to taste

Combine the olives, 4 anchovies, garlic, capers, olive oil, lemon juice, and pepper in a food processor or mortar and process or crush to a paste. Taste and add more anchovies, lemon juice, and/or pepper if needed.

YELLOW SPLIT PEA PUREE

PREP: 20 minutes   COOK: 45 minutes

Makes 6 servings

1 cup yellow split peas
2 garlic cloves, unpeeled
¼ teaspoon turmeric
1 tablespoon extra-virgin olive oil
¾ teaspoon salt
¼ teaspoon ground cumin
Lemon-Onion Salsa (page 53)
Lavash or other soft flat bread for serving

1. Place the split peas in a bowl and pick over to remove any discolored peas or small pebbles. Rinse the peas in several changes of water until the water is clear. Drain in a colander.

2. In a medium saucepan, combine the peas, garlic, turmeric, and 3 cups water. Heat to boiling over medium heat (watch so it doesn't boil over); simmer until the peas are soft, about 40 minutes. Drain the peas in a colander, reserving the cooking liquid. Fish out the garlic and discard the skins.

3. Transfer the peas and garlic to a food processor. Add the oil, salt, and cumin and process until a thick, coarse puree forms, adding a little cooking liquid to help churn the mixture but not enough to make it soupy. Spread the puree in shallow bowls, using the back of a spoon to create very shallow trenches.

4. To serve, spoon the salsa evenly over the puree. Serve with the lavash for dipping.

SPICY MIXED-OLIVE MAYONNAISE

PREP: 10 minutes
Makes about 1½ cups

¾ cup mayonnaise
½ cup pitted niçoise olives
½ cup pitted green olives
2 tablespoons fresh parsley leaves
1 tablespoon capers packed in salt,
   rinsed and dried
2 teaspoons grated lemon zest
½ teaspoon red pepper flakes
⅛ teaspoon freshly ground black pepper

Combine all the ingredients in a food processor and
pulse until coarsely mixed.

CHIPOTLE-OLIVE SPREAD

PREP: 10 minutes

Makes about 1 1/2 cups, about 12 servings

1 cup Spanish olives stuffed with pimiento, halved

1/3 cup packed coarsely chopped fresh cilantro

1/3 cup extra-virgin olive oil

1 1/2 canned chipotle peppers in adobo sauce
   or more to taste

1 garlic clove, crushed through a press

1 tablespoon grated lemon zest

1/2 teaspoon freshly ground black pepper

Combine the ingredients in a food processor and pulse until finely chopped. Taste and add more chipotles if needed.

CHIPOTLE-AVOCADO SPREAD

Makes about 1 1/4 cups, about 10 servings

1 ripe avocado, pitted, peeled, and cut into chunks
2 canned chipotle peppers in adobo sauce
    plus 2 teaspoons of the adobo sauce
1/4 cup homemade or store-bought mayonnaise
2 tablespoons lemon juice or more to taste
1/2 teaspoon salt
1/4 teaspoon ground white pepper

Combine all the ingredients in a food processor and process until smooth. Taste and add more lemon juice if needed.

GARLIC-HERB CHEESE SPREAD

PREP: 10 minutes

Makes about 1½ cups, about 12 servings

8 ounces farmer's cheese or ricotta cheese

2 large garlic cloves, crushed through a press

¼ cup fresh parsley leaves

½ teaspoon chopped fresh thyme or ¼ teaspoon
   dried thyme leaves, crushed

½ teaspoon salt

¼ teaspoon freshly ground black pepper

2 teaspoons finely snipped fresh chives

Place the cheese in a food processor and pulse until smooth. Add the garlic, parsley, thyme, salt, and pepper and pulse until the parsley is finely chopped. Scrape out the mixture into a bowl and stir in the chives.

THREE-CHEESE SPREAD FOR A CROWD

PREP: 15 minutes plus chilling   COOK: 5 minutes

Makes 32 servings

1 tablespoon unsalted butter

1 small onion, chopped

1 garlic clove, crushed through a press

2 (10-ounce) packages sharp cheddar cheese, shredded

1 (8-ounce) package cream cheese, cubed

4 ounces blue cheese, crumbled

¼ cup dry sherry

1 teaspoon Worcestershire sauce

1 teaspoon dry mustard

2 tablespoons chopped fresh parsley

1 teaspoon paprika

¼ cup toasted sesame seeds or more if needed

½ cup toasted chopped walnuts or more if needed

1. Place the butter in a large microwave-safe bowl, cover with plastic wrap, and microwave on high power 30 seconds. Add the onion and garlic, cover, and microwave on high power 1 minute. Add the cheddar cheese, cream cheese, and blue cheese, cover, and microwave on medium power until softened, 3 minutes, stirring every 1 minute.

2. With an electric mixer, beat the sherry, Worcestershire sauce, and mustard into the cheese mixture.

3. Spread one-third (about 1¼ cups) of the mixture into a 9- by 6-inch rectangle on a sheet of parchment paper. Sprinkle with the parsley and roll up jelly-roll fashion starting from a short side. Wrap the parchment around the roll and twist the ends to seal. Repeat with another third of the mixture, sprinkling with paprika instead of parsley. Roll the remaining third of the mixture into a ball and wrap in plastic wrap. Refrigerate the cheese logs and ball until slightly firm, about 1 hour.

4. Spread out the sesame seeds in a shallow bowl, roll a cheese log in the seeds to coat, and wrap in plastic wrap. In the same way, coat the remaining log and cheese ball with the walnuts and wrap. Refrigerate until serving.

HUNGARIAN PAPRIKA CHEESE SPREAD

PREP: 15 minutes plus chilling

Makes 16 servings

1 (8-ounce) package cream cheese, softened

1 small onion, grated

¼ cup beer

4 oil-packed anchovies

1 tablespoon Hungarian sweet paprika

1½ teaspoons Dijon mustard or more to taste

1¼ teaspoons capers packed in salt, rinsed and patted dry

½ teaspoon caraway seeds

Melba toasts, matzohs, or crackers for serving

Combine the cheese, onion, beer, anchovies, paprika, mustard, and capers in a food processor. Place the caraway seeds in a mortar and crush with a pestle or place on a cutting board and mash with the side of a knife or cleaver. Add the caraway to the cheese mixture and puree. Taste and add more mustard if needed. Scrape into a bowl, cover, and refrigerate overnight. Serve as a spread for melba toasts, matzohs, or crackers.

RUMAKI REDUX SPREAD

PREP: 10 minutes   COOK: 7 minutes

Makes 6 to 8 servings

One of the most popular hors d'oeuvre of the 60s was rumaki, a broiled, skewered bacon-wrapped chicken liver with a water chestnut inside. It can be prepared before the party and kept in the refrigerator; let it stand at room temperature for 30 minutes before serving for the best flavor.

2 tablespoons plus ½ cup unsalted butter, cut into 1-inch chunks and softened

8 ounces chicken livers, cleaned of ducts and stringy matter, rinsed, and patted dry with paper towels

¼ teaspoon kosher salt or more to taste

⅛ teaspoon freshly ground black pepper or more to taste

1 tablespoon soy sauce

½ teaspoon dry mustard

⅛ teaspoon freshly grated nutmeg

⅛ teaspoon cayenne or more to taste

6 slices bacon, cooked and crumbled

½ cup finely chopped drained and rinsed canned water chestnuts or ½ cup chopped peeled fresh water chestnuts

2 green onions, thinly sliced

Crackers for serving (Japanese rice crackers are nice)

1. Melt 2 tablespoons butter in a large skillet over medium-high heat. Add the chicken livers and sprinkle with the salt and pepper. Sauté until browned on the outside but firm and still pink on the insides, about 4 minutes.

2. Scoop the livers and cooking liquid into a food processor. Add the remaining ½ cup butter, the soy sauce, mustard, nutmeg, and cayenne and process until smooth, scraping down the sides of the bowl with a plastic spatula once or twice. Taste and add more salt, pepper, and/or cayenne if needed.

3. Scrape the mixture into a bowl; stir in the bacon and water chestnuts. Spread the mixture in a wide serving bowl and sprinkle with the green onions. Serve with crackers.

MANGO-MINT DIP

PREP: 15 minutes plus chilling

Makes about 2 1/2 cups, about 20 servings

2 ripe mangoes
2 green onions, minced
2 tablespoons fresh mint leaves, shredded crosswise
2 tablespoons lime juice
2 tablespoons orange juice
1 tablespoon finely snipped fresh chives
1/4 teaspoon salt
1/4 cup toasted flaked coconut
Corn chips for serving

1. Cut the mangoes in half and remove the pit. Scoop out the flesh and place in a food processor; process to a chunky puree. Transfer to a medium bowl and add the green onions, mint, lime juice, and orange juice. Mix well, cover, and refrigerate until chilled, about 1 hour.

2. Just before serving, add the chives and salt and mix well. Transfer to a shallow serving bowl and sprinkle with the coconut. Serve as a dip with corn chips.

CRUNCHY CHICKEN SALAD SPREAD

PREP: 10 minutes

Makes about 2½ cups

2 cups finely shredded cooked chicken breasts

½ cup diced celery

½ cup quartered seedless red grapes

½ cup chopped toasted pistachios

½ cup mayonnaise

½ cup sour cream

2 tablespoons snipped fresh dill

1 tablespoon grated onion

1 tablespoon red wine vinegar

½ teaspoon salt

¼ teaspoon freshly ground black pepper

Combine the chicken, celery, grapes, and pistachios in a medium bowl and mix well. In another bowl, combine the mayonnaise, sour cream, dill, onion, vinegar, salt, and pepper and whisk until blended. Pour the dressing onto the salad and mix until coated.

Serve as a spread for bagel chips.

CHILI CRAB SALAD

Makes 6 servings

2 (5½- to 7½-ounce) cans crabmeat
   or 1 pound lump crabmeat, picked over for shells
1 cup sour cream
¼ cup chopped green onions
3 tablespoons store-bought cocktail chili sauce
2 teaspoons prepared horseradish
Celery sticks for serving

Combine the crab, sour cream, green onions, chili sauce, and horseradish in a bowl and mix well. Transfer to a shallow serving bowl and cover. Refrigerate at least 2 hours before serving. Serve with celery scoops.

GREEN-AND-GOLD
AVOCADO-MANGO SALAD

PREP: 15 minutes

Makes about 3 cups, about 24 servings

2 ripe Hass avocados, halved, pitted,
  and flesh cut into ½-inch dice

1 ripe mango, peeled, pitted, and cut into ½-inch dice

2 jalapeño chile peppers (taste to make sure they are hot),
  halved, seeded, and finely chopped
  (wear gloves when handling)

1 large plum tomato, seeded and chopped

2 tablespoons minced red onion

2 tablespoons chopped fresh cilantro

¼ cup lime juice or more to taste

1 teaspoon dry wasabi (Japanese horseradish)

1 teaspoon salt or more to taste
  or more to taste

2 tablespoons olive oil

Combine the avocados, mango, jalapeños, tomato, onion, and cilantro in a bowl and mix gently. Mix the lime juice, wasabi, and salt in a cup to dissolve; stir in the oil. Pour the mixture over the avocado mixture and toss to coat. Taste and add more lime juice and/or salt if necessary.

ITALIAN GREEN BEAN TARTARE

PREP: 15 minutes COOK: 15 minutes

Makes 4 servings

1 pound green beans, cut into 1-inch pieces

3 fresh basil leaves

2 green onions, cut into 1-inch lengths

¾ teaspoon salt or more to taste

½ teaspoon freshly ground black pepper or more to taste

½ cup extra-virgin olive oil (preferably Tuscan)

½ cup finely julienned carrots (pre-packaged is best)

1 garlic clove, crushed through a press

2 tablespoons chopped fresh flat-leaf parsley

½ cup thinly shaved Parmigiano-Reggiano cheese

Toasted rounds of French or Italian bread for serving

1. Cook the green beans in 2 quarts boiling, salted water for 4 minutes; rinse with cold water until cold.

2. Combine the green beans, basil, and green onions in a food processor and pulse until roughly pureed.

Add ½ teaspoon salt and ¼ teaspoon pepper. With the machine running, pour ¼ cup of the olive oil through the feed tube and process until blended. Scrape the mixture into a bowl. Taste and add more salt and pepper if needed.

3. Heat 1 tablespoon of the olive oil in a small skillet over medium-high heat and add the carrots, garlic, and remaining ¼ teaspoon salt and ¼ teaspoon pepper. Sauté until the carrots are bright orange and the garlic is fragrant. Remove from the heat and stir the parsley into the mixture.

4. To serve, spoon a dollop of the bean mixture into the center of 4 flat salad plates. Spread each into a flat-topped cake with the back of a spoon. Arrange pinches of the carrot mixture on each plate around the cake; drizzle the plates and carrots with the remaining 3 tablespoons olive oil. Top each cake with cheese shavings and grind pepper over all. Serve with toasted bread.

RED, BLACK, AND GREEN BEAN SWIRL

PREP: 15 minutes
Makes 6 servings

1 (15-ounce) can refried black beans
½ cup fresh salsa
¼ cup diced pitted black olives
1 (7-ounce) jar roasted red peppers
1 garlic clove, crushed through a press
¾ teaspoon salt or more to taste
½ teaspoon ground cumin
¼ teaspoon cayenne
1 cup queso fresco, crème fraîche, or sour cream
4 green onions, cut into 1-inch lengths
2 limes, zested and juiced, plus more to taste
1 ripe avocado, halved, pitted, and flesh diced
1 jalapeño chile pepper (taste to make sure it is hot), diced (wear gloves when handling)
¼ cup fresh cilantro leaves
Tortilla chips for serving

1. Place the beans, salsa, and olives in a bowl and stir until blended. Spread a thin layer in a large shallow serving bowl or rimmed platter; flatten the top evenly with the back of a spoon.

2. Place the red peppers and any juices, the garlic, ½ teaspoon of the salt, cumin, and cayenne in a food processor or blender and process until smooth. Spoon over the black bean mixture in loose, concentric circles or in a free-form pattern.

3. Combine the queso fresco, green onions, lime zest and juice, avocado, jalapeño, cilantro, and remaining ¼ teaspoon salt in a food processor or blender and process until smooth. Taste and add more lime zest, lime juice, and/or salt if needed. Spoon over the bean dip and red pepper mixtures so that the colors remain separate enough to create a dynamic design. Serve with tortilla chips.

BACON-HORSERADISH DIP WITH DRIED CHERRIES

PREP: 25 minutes
Makes 6 servings

⅓ cup dried cherries
1 cup crème fraîche
3 tablespoons grated fresh horseradish or more to taste
¼ teaspoon white wine vinegar
¼ teaspoon salt
⅛ teaspoon ground white pepper
6 slices lean bacon, cooked until crisp and crumbled
Fried Rice-Paper Wrappers (below)

1. Place the cherries in a small bowl, cover with very warm water, and let soak until softened, about 15 minutes. Drain on paper towels and set aside to dry.

2. Place the crème fraîche in a medium bowl and stir in the horseradish, vinegar, salt, and pepper. Stir in the cherries and bacon. Serve with Fried Rice-Paper Wrappers.

Fried Rice-Paper Wrappers

PREP: 5 minutes   COOK: 2 minutes
Makes 6 servings

Peanut or vegetable oil for frying
6 wedges of Vietnamese rice-paper wrappers
Chinese five-spice powder, curry powder, or ground cinnamon for dusting

Rice-paper wrappers come in several sizes and you can simply break them into irregularly shaped pieces, or buy 12-inch diameter wrappers that have been quartered.

Heat ¼ inch oil in an 8-inch skillet over medium-high heat. Add a wrapper wedge and fry until puffed all the way through, about 20 seconds. Remove with tongs to a paper towel–lined plate and sprinkle with Chinese five-spice powder. Repeat with remaining wrappers.

ROASTED VEGETABLE DIP

PREP: 1 hour 15 minutes COOK: 20 minutes

Makes 8 servings

1 (8-ounce) eggplant, peeled, halved lengthwise,
   and cut crosswise into ½-inch-thick slices

1 tablespoon salt

1 medium onion, cut crosswise into ½-inch-thick rounds

4 ounces mushrooms, halved lengthwise

4 ounces zucchini, cut crosswise into ½-inch-thick rounds

½ cup olive oil

1 head garlic

6 basil leaves, torn

¼ cup sun-dried tomatoes in oil

¼ cup tahini (sesame seed paste)

¼ cup lemon juice

¼ teaspoon freshly ground black pepper

Thin toasted baguette slices for dipping

1. Place the eggplant on a large, heavy baking sheet and
sprinkle with salt. Pat salt into eggplant and place eggplant
in a colander set over the baking sheet to drain for 1 hour.

2. Preheat the oven to 500°F. Pat the eggplant dry with
paper towels, removing as much salt as possible. Line the
baking sheet with foil and arrange the eggplant, onion,
mushrooms, and zucchini in a single layer. (If there is not
enough space, line another baking sheet with foil and divide
the vegetables between the two.) Brush the vegetables on all
sides with all but 1 teaspoon of the olive oil (or drizzle with
the oil, toss to coat, and rearrange in a single layer).

3. Place the garlic on a square of foil large enough to
enclose the head. Drizzle with the remaining 1 teaspoon
olive oil and wrap tightly in the foil. Place on the baking
sheet with the vegetables. Roast the vegetables until fragrant and browned, turning once, about 20 minutes.

4. Transfer the vegetables to a food processor and puree.
Pour into a large bowl. In the same processor, combine the
basil, tomatoes and their marinating oil, the tahini, lemon
juice, and pepper; puree. Scrape the basil puree into the
vegetable puree and stir to mix. Serve with baguette slices.

CREAMY CLAM DIP

PREP: 15 minutes plus chilling

Makes 8 servings

1 (8-ounce) container sour cream
1 (8-ounce) package cream cheese, softened
1 (1-ounce) envelope French-onion soup mix
1 (7½-ounce) can minced clams, drained,
  liquid reserved
¼ cup chopped fresh flat-leaf parsley
2 tablespoons snipped fresh chives
½ teaspoon freshly ground black pepper
¼ teaspoon hot pepper sauce or more to taste
3 cups broccoli and cauliflower florets, blanched
1 cup baby carrots, quartered lengthwise and blanched

1. Combine the sour cream, cream cheese, and soup mix in a medium bowl and whisk until blended. Add the drained clams, parsley, chives, pepper, and hot sauce and stir to mix well. Cover and refrigerate at least 1 hour.

2. Stir enough reserved clam liquid into the dip to make a dipping consistency. Taste and add more hot sauce if needed. Scrape into a shallow serving bowl and serve with the broccoli, cauliflower, and carrots for dipping.

FARM-STAND CAPONATA

PREP: 15 minutes plus draining   **COOK:** 45 minutes

Makes 8 servings (8 cups)

2 (1-pound) eggplants, peeled, cut in half lengthwise,
  seeded, and cut into ½-inch cubes

1 tablespoon kosher salt plus more to taste

¼ to ½ cup olive oil or more if needed

1 medium red onion, chopped

3 celery stalks, cut into ¼-inch dice

Spicy Tomato Sauce (page 437)

1 (2 ounce drained weight) can sliced pitted black olives

⅓ cup green olives with pimiento, quartered

2 tablespoons small capers, packed in salt, rinsed

2 tablespoons toasted pine nuts

2 tablespoons dried currants

3 tablespoons balsamic vinegar

1 teaspoon dried oregano leaves

1. Place the eggplant on a large, heavy baking sheet and sprinkle with salt. Pat salt into eggplant and place in a colander set over the baking sheet to drain for 1 hour.

2. Pat eggplant dry with paper towels, removing as much salt as possible. Heat 3 tablespoons of the olive oil in a large, heavy saucepan over medium-high heat. Add half the eggplant and sauté until browned on all sides; transfer to a large bowl using a slotted spoon. Sauté the remaining eggplant, adding more oil if needed; transfer to the bowl.

3. Drain off all but 2 tablespoons of the oil from the pan or add enough oil to make about 2 tablespoons. Add the onion and sauté over medium-high heat until softened, about 10 minutes. Add the celery and sauté until softened, about 5 minutes. Add the tomato sauce, heat to boiling, and simmer over medium-low heat 10 minutes.

4. Add the sautéed eggplant to the sauce mixture, using a slotted spoon to lift the eggplant from any oil in the bowl. Add the black and green olives, capers, pine nuts, currants, vinegar, and oregano and mix well. Simmer gently without boiling for 10 minutes. Serve at room temperature.

ROASTED MOROCCAN EGGPLANT

PREP: 20 minutes   COOK: 30 minutes

Makes 10 to 12 servings

3 (1-pound) eggplants, heavy for their size

2 tablespoons olive oil

Moroccan Cilantro Sauce (page 440)

Lemon wedges for serving

Warm lavash or pita bread for scooping or serving (optional)

1. Preheat the oven to 500°F. Prick the eggplants on all sides with a fork and place on a large foil-lined baking sheet. Rub all sides with the olive oil. Bake until soft to the point of collapse, about 30 minutes.

2. Cool the eggplants until they can be handled and cut in half. Scrape out the majority of the seeds with a spoon and discard. Remove the flesh from the skin in large pieces. Cut the flesh into bite-size pieces and place in a bowl. Add about 1 cup sauce and toss to coat. Taste and add more sauce as needed to make very saucy.

3. Serve on a plate with lemon for squeezing. Use bread to scoop up the eggplant or eat with a fork.

HOT BEEF-VEGETABLE DIP

½ cup walnut pieces

1 (8-ounce) package cream cheese,
    cut into 1-inch chunks

1 cup sour cream or crème fraîche

4 green onions, cut crosswise into 1-inch lengths

1 small green pepper, cut into 1-inch squares

1 small red pepper, cut into 1-inch squares

1 (4-ounce) package or jar dried beef

¼ teaspoon freshly ground black pepper

⅛ teaspoon cayenne

Crackers for serving

1. Preheat the oven to 350°F. Grease a shallow 1-quart baking dish. Place the nuts in the food processor and pulse to evenly chop. Turn out onto a plate and set aside.

2. Without cleaning the processor bowl, add the cream cheese and sour cream and pulse until blended. Add the green onions, green and red peppers, beef, black pepper, and cayenne and pulse until the beef starts to break up. Scrape down the bowl and pulse until the mixture is evenly textured.

3. Spread the mixture evenly into the prepared baking dish and sprinkle the walnuts on top. Bake until hot and bubbly, about 15 minutes. Serve directly from the dish as a spread for crackers.

SPICY RED LENTIL DIP

PREP: 10 minutes plus chilling   COOK: 15 minutes

Makes about 10 servings

1 cup dried small red lentils

1 bay leaf

¼ cup roughly chopped cashews

1 tablespoon grapeseed or canola oil

½ cup finely chopped shallots

½ cup chopped fresh fennel

2 large garlic cloves, minced

1 teaspoon sea salt

½ teaspoon ground coriander

½ teaspoon ground cumin

¼ teaspoon red pepper flakes

1 large plum tomato, diced

3 tablespoons lemon juice

Pappadams, pita chips, blue corn chips,
   or baked (or fried) vegetable chips for serving

1. Place the lentils and bay leaf in a medium saucepan and cover with enough water to come 2 inches above the lentils. Heat to boiling, cover, and simmer over medium heat until tender, about 8 minutes. Drain well, reserving some of the liquid. Discard the bay leaf.

2. Dry-roast the cashews in a nonstick skillet over medium heat until fragrant and lightly browned. Transfer to a bowl.

3. Heat the oil in the same skillet over medium-high heat and add the shallots, fennel, and garlic. Sauté until softened and fragrant, about 4 minutes. Add the salt, coriander, cumin, and pepper flakes and sauté until fragrant, about 1 minute. Add the tomato and sauté until softened and the liquid has mostly evaporated, about 5 minutes.

4. Remove the skillet from the heat and stir in the lemon juice. Scrape the mixture into a food processor and add the lentils. Process until smooth, adding lentil cooking liquid if needed to make the texture smooth and juicy but not soupy. Scrape the dip into a bowl and sprinkle with the cashews. Serve at room temperature as a dip with pappadams, pita chips, blue corn chips, or vegetable chips.

SEVEN-LAYER TEX-MEX DIP

PREP: 20 minutes
Makes 48 servings (6 cups)

1 (16-ounce) can refried beans
1 tablespoon chili powder or taco-seasoning mix
1 cup sour cream
1 cup salsa
1 cup shredded lettuce
1 cup (4 ounces) shredded yellow cheddar cheese
¼ cup chopped green onions
2 tablespoons sliced ripe pitted olives
Tortilla chips or corn chips for serving

Combine the beans and chili powder in a bowl and mix well. Spread over the bottom of a 9-inch pie plate. Spread the sour cream on top. Cover with the salsa, and sprinkle first with the lettuce, then the cheese, green onions, and olives. Serve with chips for dipping.

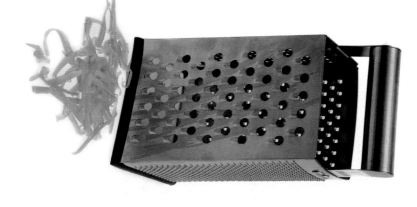

CHILI CON QUESO

PREP: 10 minutes COOK: 25 minutes

Makes 6 servings

¼ cup (½ stick) unsalted butter

1 large onion, chopped

1 garlic clove, crushed through a press

2 tablespoons all-purpose flour

¼ teaspoon cayenne

1 cup heavy cream, heated until steaming

1 (14-ounce) can petite-diced tomatoes

1 (4-ounce) can nacho sliced jalapeños, drained

8 ounces sharp cheddar cheese, shredded

Corn chips or fresh vegetables, such as blanched broccoli and cauliflower florets, and/or blanched zucchini and yellow squash strips, for serving

1. Melt the butter in a 2-quart saucepan over medium-high heat and add the onion. Sauté until softened, about 4 minutes. Add the garlic and sauté until fragrant and sizzling, about 1 minute. Stir in the flour and cayenne and cook until bubbling, about 2 minutes. Gradually stir in the hot cream, stirring constantly, until the mixture is smooth. Simmer, stirring constantly, 2 minutes.

2. Stir in the juice from the tomatoes until blended and bubbly. Add the tomatoes, jalapeños, and a handful of cheese. Cook, stirring, until the mixture is bubbly and cheese has melted. Continue stirring in the cheese, a handful at a time, letting it melt before adding more. When all the cheese has been added and melted, pour the mixture into a warmed fondue pot or chafing dish and set over a heat source. Serve with corn chips or prepared vegetables for dunking.

BAGNA CAUDA

PREP: 15 minutes   COOK: 10 minutes

Makes 6 servings

2 slices white bread, crusts removed

1 cup heavy cream

8 anchovy fillets, chopped

5 garlic cloves

2 teaspoons lemon zest

¼ teaspoon kosher salt or more to taste

⅛ teaspoon freshly ground black pepper or more to taste

½ cup olive oil

¼ cup (½ stick) unsalted butter, cut into pieces

24 trimmed green beans, blanched

12 baby carrots, blanched

12 asparagus spears, steamed

12 strips red bell peppers

12 strips yellow bell peppers

12 trimmed mushrooms, steamed

12 fingers toasted Italian whole-wheat bread

1. Place the bread in a bowl and pour ¼ cup of the cream on top. Turn the bread to soak up the cream evenly; set aside 5 minutes.

2. Squeeze the bread so the liquid goes back into the bowl. Place the bread, anchovies, garlic, lemon zest, salt, and pepper in a food processor and process to a paste. With the machine running, add the olive oil in a thin, steady stream and process until well blended.

3. Melt the butter in a medium saucepan over low heat and gradually add the bread mixture. Whisk over low heat until the mixture is hot. Gradually whisk in the cream from the bread and the remaining ¾ cup cream. Cook until hot but not boiling. Taste and add more salt and pepper if needed.

4. Transfer the bagna cauda to an earthenware pot, fondue pot, or chafing dish set over a heat source. Arrange the vegetables and toasts on a platter in groups with colors and shapes alternating. Serve immediately with forks for dipping the vegetables and bread into the bagna cauda.

TEXAS CAVIAR

PREP: 10 minutes plus standing

Makes 6 servings

1 (14-ounce) can black-eyed peas, rinsed
1 (15-ounce) can white hominy, rinsed
Green Onion Salsa (page 55),
   or 2 cups prepared fresh salsa
Corn chips or tortilla scoops for serving

In a large bowl, combine the peas, hominy, and salsa and mix well. Cover the bowl with plastic wrap and let stand at room temperature 2 hours, stirring occasionally. Serve as a dip with corn chips or tortilla scoops.

EDAMAME HUMMUS

PREP: 20 minutes   COOK: 15 minutes

Makes about 8 servings

½ (16-ounce) package frozen shelled soybeans (edamame)
½ (5-ounce) package frozen baby lima beans
1 garlic clove, thinly sliced
1 teaspoon grated lemon zest
¼ cup lemon juice or more to taste
1 tablespoon tahini (sesame seed paste)
½ teaspoon salt or more to taste
¼ teaspoon Aleppo pepper or black pepper or more to taste
1 teaspoon freshly ground black pepper or ½ teaspoon paprika
½ cup extra-virgin olive oil
1 teaspoon white sesame seeds, toasted
1 teaspoon black sesame seeds (if unavailable, use another teaspoon white sesame seeds)
Pita chips or bagel chips for serving

1. Cook the soybeans in a saucepan as package label directs until tender. While the soybeans cook, cook the lima beans with the garlic in another saucepan as lima bean package label directs. Drain, reserving the cooking liquid, and rinse in a colander under cold running water. Drain well.

2. Place the soybeans, lima beans, and garlic in a food processor and pulse until smooth, adding enough cooking liquid (about 1 cup) to make a stiff but juicy puree. Add the lemon zest, lemon juice, tahini, salt, and black pepper and pulse until thoroughly mixed, adding a little more cooking liquid if necessary to make a spreadable but not wet mixture. Taste and add more lemon juice, salt, and/or pepper if needed. Spoon the hummus into oval patties on serving dishes or spread the whole batch in a shallow bowl, using the back of a spoon to create very shallow trenches.

3. In a measuring cup, stir the Aleppo pepper into the olive oil. Spoon some over the hummus on each plate, making sure some pepper flakes are in each spoonful. Sprinkle each serving with white and black sesame seeds and serve with the pita.

WHITE BEAN AND OLIVE HUMMUS

PREP: 15 minutes   COOK: 15 minutes

Makes 8 servings

1½ cups cooked white beans (cooked from dried)
  or 2 (14-ounce) cans white beans, rinsed and drained

3 garlic cloves, roasted in a 400°F oven for 15 minutes
  and peeled

¼ cup lemon juice

3 tablespoons tahini (sesame seed paste)

1 teaspoon chili powder

¾ cup olive oil or more if needed

½ cup oil-cured black olives, pitted

½ cup large green olives, such as ascolane, pitted

¼ teaspoon salt or more to taste

¼ teaspoon freshly ground black pepper

¼ cup toasted pine nuts

Paprika for dusting

Crusty bread slices or pita wedges for serving

1. Place the beans and garlic in a food processor and process until roughly pureed. Add the lemon juice, tahini, and chili powder and pulse to mix. With the machine running, pour in ½ cup of the olive oil in a thin, steady stream through the feed tube; process until creamy, adding more oil if needed. Add the black and green olives, salt, and pepper and pulse until the olives are very coarsely chopped.

2. Taste the hummus and add more salt if needed. Add the pine nuts and pulse to evenly chop the olives and pine nuts. Spread the hummus in a shallow bowl using the back of a spoon to create very shallow trenches. Drizzle with the remaining ¼ cup olive oil (or more if needed) to cover with a thin layer. Dust with paprika. Serve with bread or pita.

SALSA FRESCA

PREP: 10 minutes

Makes about 1 cup

3 large plum tomatoes, seeded and chopped

1 to 2 jalapeño chile peppers (taste to make sure
   they are hot), minced (wear gloves when handling)

¼ cup finely chopped green pepper

¼ cup finely chopped red onion

2 tablespoons finely chopped fresh cilantro

¼ teaspoon salt or more to taste

Combine the tomatoes, jalapeños, green pepper, onion, cilantro, and salt in a bowl and mix well. Cover with plastic wrap and set aside. Just before serving, taste and add more salt if needed.

SALSA VERDE

PREP: 10 minutes
Makes about 2¼ cups

9 small tomatillos, husked and quartered
1 to 2 jalapeño chile peppers (taste to make sure they
    are hot), chopped (wear gloves when handling)
1 small red onion, quartered
1 cup loosely packed fresh cilantro leaves
2 tablespoons lime juice or more to taste
½ teaspoon salt or more to taste

Combine all the ingredients in a food processor and
pulse to chop. Scrape into a bowl and mix well. Taste
and add more lime juice and/or salt if needed.

LEMON-ONION SALSA

PREP: **10 minutes**

Makes 6 servings

1 store-bought or homemade (below) preserved lemon, peel finely chopped, or 1 tablespoon finely grated lemon peel
¾ cup finely chopped red onion
¼ cup extra-virgin olive oil
2 tablespoons chopped fresh cilantro
2 tablespoons fresh lemon juice
½ teaspoon salt
½ teaspoon paprika
½ teaspoon cayenne

Combine all the ingredients in a bowl and mix well.

Preserved Lemons

PREP: **10 minutes plus chilling**

Makes 16 pieces

4 medium lemons
⅔ cup kosher salt
1 tablespoon black peppercorns
½ cup lemon juice (must be fresh)
Water as needed

1. Wash the lemons well, quarter each lengthwise, and place in a bowl. Add the salt and toss to coat.

2. Place enough of the lemon pieces in a 1½-quart jar to cover the bottom in a single layer. Sprinkle with some peppercorns. Press lightly with a potato masher to release some juices. Repeat with the remaining lemons and peppercorns, pressing on each layer. Add the lemon juice and just enough water to cover the lemons.

3. Cover the top of the jar with plastic wrap and tightly seal with the lid. Refrigerate for 2 to 3 weeks, shaking the jar every day.

4. To use, rinse or scrape the salt off the lemons. Scrape out and discard the pulp. Chop or slice the rind. The lemons will keep about 2 months in the refrigerator.

MANGO-RED PEPPER SALSA

1 ripe mango, pitted, peeled, and diced
1 red bell pepper, diced
2 limes, zested into threads and juiced
1 cup diced peeled jicama
1 teaspoon sambal oelek, or ¼ teaspoon harissa,
    or 1 pinch cayenne
¼ teaspoon salt or more to taste

Combine the mango, pepper, lime zest, lime juice, jicama, sambal oelek, and salt in a medium bowl. Toss to combine. Cover and refrigerate until chilled, about 40 minutes. Remove the salsa from the refrigerator. Stir, taste, and add more salt if needed.

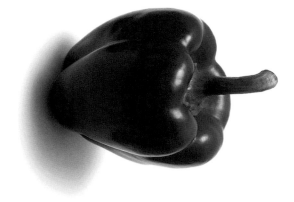

GREEN ONION SALSA

PREP: 10 minutes

Makes 6 servings (1½ cups)

4 green onions, thinly sliced crosswise

2 plum tomatoes, seeded and chopped

1 medium green pepper, finely chopped

2 garlic cloves, crushed through a press

1 jalapeño chile pepper (taste to make sure it is hot),
finely chopped (wear gloves when handling)

¼ cup chopped fresh cilantro

1 tablespoon olive oil

2 teaspoons lime juice

½ teaspoon salt

¼ teaspoon freshly ground black pepper

⅛ teaspoon cayenne

Combine all the ingredients in a large bowl. Let stand at
room temperature until ready to use.

CHAYOTE-MELON SALSA

PREP: 10 minutes

Makes 4 to 6 servings (2 cups)

2 tablespoons chopped fresh mint

2 tablespoons finely chopped red onion

2 tablespoons lemon juice

2 tablespoons lime juice

1 tablespoon grapeseed oil

2 teaspoons grated fresh ginger

½ teaspoon hot red pepper sauce

1 (1-pound) chayote, peeled, seeded, and cut into
   ¼-inch dice

1 cup diced cantaloupe

1 navel orange, peeled, pith removed, sectioned, and diced

Combine the mint, onion, lemon juice, lime juice, oil, ginger, and pepper sauce in a medium bowl and mix well. Add the chayote, cantaloupe, and orange and mix gently to coat.

FRESH PEAR-ORANGE SALSA

PREP: 20 minutes
Makes about 2 cups

2 firm ripe pears
1 navel orange
½ cup thinly sliced green onions
½ cup diced, seeded, peeled cucumber
½ cup diced red pepper
3 tablespoons lime juice
1 tablespoon chopped fresh cilantro
1 tablespoon olive oil
¼ teaspoon salt
⅛ teaspoon freshly ground black pepper

1. Peel, quarter, and core the pears. Cut into ½-inch dice and place in a medium bowl. Grate 1 teaspoon zest from the orange and add to the pears. Place the orange on a cutting board with the stem end up and cut off the peel in lengthwise strips, working your way around the orange. Hold the orange in your hand over the bowl with the pears and remove the sections by cutting to the center of the orange on each side of the section and flicking the sections into the bowl. Squeeze the juice from the remaining part of the orange into the bowl. Quarter each section.

2. Add the green onions, cucumber, red pepper, lime juice, cilantro, olive oil, salt, and black pepper to the pear mixture and stir to mix. Cover and refrigerate until serving.

CRISP CORN SALSA

PREP: 10 minutes plus standing **COOK: 3 minutes**

Makes about 1½ cups

1 cup fresh or thawed frozen corn kernels

3 plum tomatoes, peeled, seeded, and finely chopped

1 jalapeño chile pepper (taste to make sure it is hot), finely chopped (wear gloves when handling)

2 tablespoons chopped red pepper

2 tablespoons finely shredded fresh basil

2 tablespoons snipped fresh chives

2½ tablespoons lime juice

½ teaspoon salt

¼ teaspoon freshly ground black pepper

1. Cook the corn in a small saucepan in ½ cup water over medium-high heat until tender, about 3 minutes for fresh and 1 minute for frozen. Drain in a colander and let cool.

2. Pat the corn dry with paper towels and place in a medium bowl. Add the tomatoes, jalapeño, red pepper, basil, chives, lime juice, salt, and pepper. Mix well. Let stand at least 1 hour before serving.

CHICKEN LIVER PÂTÉ

PREP: 15 minutes plus chilling   COOK: 20 minutes

Makes 12 to 16 servings

6 tablespoons unsalted butter

3 shallots, minced

1 garlic clove, crushed through a press

1 pound chicken livers, rinsed, patted dry, trimmed

3 tablespoons cognac or brandy

1 ½ teaspoons dry mustard

¾ teaspoon salt or more to taste

½ teaspoon freshly ground black pepper

½ teaspoon dried thyme leaves, crushed

⅛ teaspoon freshly grated nutmeg

⅛ teaspoon ground cloves

⅛ teaspoon ground mace (optional)

Crostini (page 166) or crackers for serving

1. Line a terrine or loaf pan with plastic wrap, extending the wrap about 4 inches beyond the sides. Set aside.

2. Melt 3 tablespoons of the butter in a large skillet over medium-high heat. Add the shallots and sauté until soft, about 4 minutes. Add the garlic and sauté until sizzling, about 1 minute. Add half the remaining butter. When the butter melts and the foam subsides, add half the chicken livers. Sauté until browned on the outside and pink on the inside, about 4 minutes. Transfer with a slotted spoon to a food processor. Repeat with the remaining butter and livers.

3. Pour the cognac into the skillet and heat over medium heat, scraping with a wooden spoon to remove any browned bits. Add to the liver mixture in the food processor. Add the mustard, salt, pepper, thyme, nutmeg, cloves, and mace (if using). Process until smooth. Pour the mixture into the prepared terrine and cover with the extended plastic wrap sides. Refrigerate until firm, at least 4 hours.

4. To serve, unfold the plastic wrap from the top and place a serving dish, top side down, on top. Invert the pâté onto the dish and remove the terrine and plastic wrap. Serve with crostini or crackers.

DILLED SALMON PÂTÉ

Unsalted butter, softened, for greasing the pans

1½ pounds skinless salmon fillets

2 egg whites

1 cup cold heavy cream

3 tablespoons snipped fresh dill

1¼ teaspoons salt plus more if needed

⅛ teaspoon cayenne

⅛ teaspoon freshly ground white pepper

1. Preheat the oven to 350°F. Butter 8 ramekins and 8 rounds of parchment the diameter of the ramekins.

2. Cut out eight 1-inch center chunks of salmon and set aside. Cut the remaining salmon into 1-inch chunks and place in a food processor. Add the egg whites and pulse to chop the salmon. With the machine running, pour in the cream through the feed tube. Scrape the mixture into a bowl and stir in the dill, salt, cayenne, and pepper. Poach a

teaspoon of the mixture in a pan of simmering water or cook just until firm in a bowl covered with plastic wrap in the microwave (about 20 seconds on high power).

3. Spoon the salmon mixture into the prepared ramekins and press a chunk of center-cut salmon into the center of each. Top each with a parchment round, buttered side down. Cover tightly with foil.

4. Place the ramekins in a roasting pan and set the pan in the oven. Add enough hot water to the pan to come two-thirds up the sides of the ramekins. Bake until a skewer inserted in the center of a couple ramekins in different parts of the pan comes out coated but not wet, 15 to 20 minutes.

5. Remove the ramekins from the water and place on a kitchen towel. If serving warm, let stand 5 minutes; remove the foil and parchment rounds and unmold each pâté onto warmed plates. If serving cold, let the pâtés stand in the ramekins for 10 minutes before unmolding. Refrigerate to serve later.

FINGER FOODS

PEARL BALLS

PREP: 25 minutes plus standing   COOK: 30 minutes

Makes 6 servings, about 30 balls

¼ cup uncooked glutinous (sticky) rice

4 dried Chinese mushrooms

6 fresh water chestnuts, peeled and finely chopped

2 green onions, finely chopped

1 egg, lightly beaten

1 pound lean ground pork

1 tablespoon soy sauce

2 teaspoons grated fresh ginger

1½ teaspoons salt

½ teaspoon sugar

Lettuce leaves to line steamer baskets

Easy Green Onion Dipping Sauce (page 435)

1. Place the rice in a medium bowl and add 1 cup cold water. Place the mushrooms in a small bowl and add ½ cup hot water. Let stand 2 hours.

2. Drain the rice though a sieve; spread out on a cloth tea towel to dry. Drain the mushrooms, reserving the liquid for another use. Discard the stems and finely chop the caps. Place the caps in a medium bowl. Add the water chestnuts, green onions, egg, pork, soy sauce, ginger, salt, and sugar and mix well.

3. Shape the mixture into 1-inch balls and roll in the soaked rice. Line the bottom of 2 large bamboo steamer baskets with lettuce leaves and arrange the balls on top. Stack the steamer baskets on top of each other and place in a wok set over high heat containing at least 2 inches of boiling water. Cover the top basket with a lid and steam until the balls are cooked through and the rice is tender, about 30 minutes, adding more boiling water to the wok if needed. Serve with the dipping sauce.

ITALIAN RICE BALLS

PREP: 25 minutes plus chilling

COOK: 4 minutes per batch

Makes 24 rice balls

2 cups uncooked rice

½ teaspoon salt

4 eggs, separated

½ cup (2 ounces) grated aged provolone cheese

8 ounces mozzarella cheese, cut into 24 cubes

1 cup Italian-flavored dried bread crumbs

Oil for deep-frying

1. Cook the rice with the salt as package label directs. Place in a large bowl and add the egg yolks and provolone. Mix until the rice is coated with the yolks and the cheese is evenly dispersed. Shape into 24 balls, placing a cube of mozzarella in the center of each; make sure the cheese is completely covered with the rice mixture.

2. Beat the egg whites in a deep pie plate until just

beginning to get frothy. Place the bread crumbs in another pie plate. Gently roll the rice balls in the egg whites until coated and then roll in the crumbs until evenly coated. Place on a rimmed baking sheet and refrigerate until completely firm, at least 1 hour.

3. Preheat the oven to 250°F if serving the rice balls warm. Line a rimmed baking sheet with paper towels. In a large, deep saucepan, add 3 inches of oil (make sure there is at least 2 inches of space between the oil and the top of the pan). Heat the oil over medium-high heat until it registers 375°F on a deep-fat thermometer.

4. Fry the rice balls, about 6 at a time depending on the diameter of the pan (there should be an inch of space between the balls while they are frying), turning once, until the coating is golden brown and crisp, about 4 minutes. Drain on the prepared baking sheet. Keep the fried rice balls warm in the oven while frying the remainder. Serve warm or at room temperature.

SALMON NORI ROLLS

PREP: 1 hour   COOK: 5 minutes

Makes about 12 servings (40 pieces)

1 pound skinless salmon fillet, or 1 (15-ounce)
   can sockeye salmon, drained very well

2 tablespoons roasted garlic teriyaki sauce

1 (8-ounce) package cream cheese, softened

2 tablespoons lemon juice

1 tablespoon grated onion

1 tablespoon creamed horseradish

½ teaspoon salt or more to taste

¼ teaspoon freshly ground black pepper or more to taste

4 large sheets nori (dried seaweed)

1 small red bell pepper, cut lengthwise into thin strips

1 small green bell pepper, cut lengthwise into thin strips

1 cucumber, peeled and cut lengthwise into thin strips

1. If using fresh salmon, place on a foil-lined baking sheet
and brush with the teriyaki sauce. Broil 5 inches from heat
source until barely cooked through, about 5 minutes,
depending on the thickness of the fillet. Let cool to room
temperature. Break into chunks. If using canned salmon,
mix 1 tablespoon of the teriyaki sauce with the salmon.

2. In a food processor, combine the salmon and cream
cheese and pulse to mix. Add the lemon juice, onion,
horseradish, salt, and pepper and process until smooth.

3. Arrange the nori sheets on the work surface so the long
sides are parallel to you. Spread the sheets with the salmon
mixture to within 1 inch of the long sides and ½ inch of
the short sides. Arrange the peppers and the cucumber
strips lengthwise on top of the salmon mixture about ½
inch from the lower edges of the nori sheets. Fold the
lower edges over the vegetables so the nori covers the vegetables and tightly roll up jelly-roll fashion. Place the rolls
on a platter and cover with plastic wrap. Refrigerate until
the salmon mixture sets, about 30 minutes.

5. To serve, transfer the nori rolls to a cutting board and
cut each crosswise with a sharp knife into ½- to ¾-inch-
thick rounds. Arrange cut side up on a serving dish.

PEAR ROLL-UPS

PREP: 15 minutes

Makes 16 roll-ups

2 ripe red-skinned pears

½ lemon

3 ounces goat's milk cheese, crumbled

¼ cup chopped toasted walnuts

4 ounces thinly sliced baked ham, cut into 1-inch-wide strips

1. Halve the pears lengthwise and core. Cut each half lengthwise into 8 wedges. Rub the cut surfaces with the lemon to keep them from browning.

2. Press a nugget of goat cheese into the cored cavity of each piece and sprinkle with a pinch of nuts. Wrap a ham strip around the center of each pear piece and secure with a cocktail pick.

CHICKEN AND HOISIN "EGGROLLS"

PREP: 15 minutes COOK: 8 minutes

Makes 16 rolls

4 eggs, lightly beaten
⅓ cup hoisin sauce
2 cups shredded cooked barbecued chicken
1 cup fresh mint leaves
1 cup fresh cilantro leaves
2 green onions, thinly sliced lengthwise
1 European cucumber,
cut into thin 4-inch strips

1. Heat a medium nonstick skillet or Japanese tamago pan (a narrow rectangular skillet) over high heat. Add ¼ cup of the beaten egg and tilt the pan to swirl the eggs around to coat the bottom, making a thin pancake. Cook until golden, about 30 seconds. Loosen with a heat-safe plastic spatula and turn out onto a plate. Repeat with the remaining eggs to make 8 pancakes.

2. Lay the pancakes on a cutting board, prettiest side down. Spread a little hoisin on the top of each pancake and arrange some chicken, mint, cilantro, green onion, and cucumber across the sauce, with the pieces going the same way. Roll up the mixture in the pancake. Cut the rolls crosswise in half.

PREP: 15 minutes
Makes 48 roll-ups

6 thin slices smoked ham
4 tablespoons garlic-and-herb cheese spread,
   at room temperature
12 leaves Iceberg, butter, or Boston lettuce,
   rinsed well and drained

1. Cut the ham slices in half lengthwise or to about the size of the width of the lettuce leaves. Spread the ham with the cheese spread. Place a slice in the center of each lettuce leaf. Roll up the leaves from the core end, folding in the edges so the ham is encased.

2. Insert 4 evenly spaced thin toothpicks into each roll. Cut in between the rolls to make 4 roll-ups per roll. Transfer the roll-ups (with the toothpicks) to a serving platter and serve immediately.

SOUTHERN SAUSAGE BALLS

PREP: 15 minutes plus overnight chilling

COOK: 10 minutes

Makes about 72 balls

You can prepare the sausage balls ahead of time and freeze for a later use. Bake the frozen uncooked sausage balls for 13 to 15 minutes or until cooked throughout.

1 pound hot bulk pork sausage (uncooked),
at room temperature

3 cups (12 ounces) grated extra-sharp cheddar cheese,
at room temperature

2 cups buttermilk baking mix

2 tablespoons chopped fresh parsley

2 tablespoons grated onion

½ teaspoon freshly ground black pepper

1. Combine the sausage, cheese, baking mix, parsley, onion, and pepper in a large bowl; mix with your hands until there are no dry crumbs. Shape into 1-inch balls and place about ½ inch apart on large rimmed baking sheets. Cover with plastic wrap and refrigerate overnight or refrigerate the number of sausage balls needed immediately and transfer the rest to freezer containers and freeze.

2. Preheat the oven to 400°F. Bake until golden brown and cooked through, 8 to 10 minutes. Drain on paper towels and serve hot.

HOT CHEESE OLIVES

PREP: 45 minutes   COOK: 15 minutes

Makes 50 olives

½ cup (1 stick) unsalted butter, softened

2 cups (8 ounces) grated extra-sharp cheddar cheese

1½ cups unsifted all-purpose flour

¼ teaspoon cayenne

⅛ teaspoon salt

1 large egg beaten with 2 tablespoons cold water

50 small pimiento-stuffed cocktail olives, drained and patted dry

1. Beat the butter until creamy in a large mixing bowl. Add the cheese and mix well. Stir in the flour, cayenne, and salt until smooth. Add the egg mixture and mix just until incorporated. Refrigerate for 30 minutes.

2. Preheat the oven to 350°F. Shape the dough into 1-inch balls. Flatten 1 ball to a thin round. Place an olive on the round and shape the dough around the olive, pinching to repair any breaks. Place on an ungreased baking sheet. Repeat with the remaining balls and olives.

3. Bake until the dough sets, about 15 minutes. Serve hot.

BACON-WRAPPED DATES

16 large Medjool dates
16 blanched whole almonds
3 tablespoons mild blue cheese such
    as Pipo Creme or Bleu de Bresse
8 slices bacon, halved crosswise

Preheat the oven to 400°F. Line a rimmed baking sheet with foil. Make a slit in the side of each date and stuff each with an almond and about ½ teaspoon of the cheese. Press the dates to seal and wrap each with a bacon slice. Arrange seam side down on the prepared baking sheet. Bake until the bacon is crisp, about 20 minutes.

THAI FISH CAKES

PREP: 35 minutes   COOK: 4 minutes per batch

Makes 12 cakes

1 pound skinless catfish fillets, cut into 1-inch chunks
1 stalk lemongrass, white part only, thinly sliced
1 garlic clove, crushed through a press
1 jalapeño chile pepper (taste to make sure it is hot), diced (wear gloves when handling)
2 tablespoons fresh cilantro leaves
2 tablespoons coconut cream
1 tablespoon Thai fish sauce
1 teaspoon grated fresh ginger
¼ cup canola or grapeseed oil
Cucumber-Chili Dipping Sauce (page 434)

1. In a food processor, combine the fish, lemongrass, garlic, jalapeño, cilantro, coconut cream, fish sauce, and ginger; pulse until the fish is cut into small even pieces, but not a paste. Scrape the mixture into a bowl, cover, and refrigerate until firm, about 20 minutes.

2. Shape the mixture into 12 small disks, not flat patties. Line a baking sheet with paper towels.

3. Heat the oil in a large skillet over medium-high heat. In batches, add the cakes and fry, turning once, until crisp, about 4 minutes. Transfer to the prepared baking sheet to drain. Serve with the Cucumber-Chili Dipping Sauce.

BABY SALMON CAKES

PREP: 15 minutes plus chilling

COOK: 3 minutes per batch

Makes 30 cakes

1 egg

1 canned chipotle pepper in adobo sauce, chopped,
    plus 2 teaspoons of the adobo sauce

1 (15½-ounce) can pink salmon, drained

2 green onions, trimmed, finely chopped

2 tablespoons fine bread crumbs

Vegetable oil for frying

Lime Dipping Sauce (page 433)

1. Place the egg, chipotle, and its sauce in a medium bowl and mix until blended. Add the salmon, green onions, and bread crumbs and mix with a fork until blended. Shape into 1½-inch cakes (½-inch-thick) using your hands. Place on a baking sheet. Cover with plastic wrap and refrigerate until firm, about 1 hour.

2. Preheat the oven to 300°F. Line a baking sheet with paper towels. Heat ¼ inch oil in a large, heavy skillet over medium-high heat until hot but not smoking. In batches, add the cakes without crowding the pan and fry, turning once, until lightly browned and hot, about 3 minutes. Transfer to the prepared baking sheet to drain; keep warm in the oven while frying the remaining cakes. Arrange on a warmed platter and serve with wooden picks for dipping into the Lime Dipping Sauce.

MINI CRAB CAKES

PREP: 20 minutes plus chilling

COOK: 1 minute per batch

Makes 24 cakes

8 ounces lump crabmeat, picked over for shells
2 eggs, beaten
2 green onions, finely chopped
1 red pepper, finely chopped
1 cup fresh bread crumbs
½ cup finely chopped celery
1 teaspoon Dijon mustard
½ teaspoon Worcestershire sauce
¼ teaspoon hot pepper sauce
½ cup dry plain bread crumbs plus more if needed
Vegetable oil for frying
Yogurt-Horseradish Sauce (page 439)

1. Combine the crab, eggs, green onions, red pepper, fresh bread crumbs, celery, mustard, Worcestershire sauce, and pepper sauce in a large bowl and mix well. Cover and refrigerate 15 minutes.

2. Shape the mixture into 24 equal-size balls. Place the dry bread crumbs in a bowl and roll each ball in the crumbs to coat. Place the balls on a baking sheet and flatten each to a thick patty. Cover with plastic wrap and refrigerate 1 hour to firm up.

3. Preheat the oven to 275°F. Line a baking sheet with paper towels. Heat 1 inch of oil in a large, deep, heavy skillet over medium heat to 375°F on a deep-fat thermometer. In batches, add the cakes and fry, turning once, until golden brown, 1 to 1½ minutes. Transfer to the prepared baking sheet to drain; keep warm in the oven while frying the remaining cakes. Serve with the Yogurt-Horseradish Sauce for dipping.

STUFFED PEPPER WEDGES

PREP: 20 minutes   COOK: 25 minutes

Makes about 32 wedges

2 large green peppers

2 large red peppers

12 Greek olives, pitted and finely chopped

5 anchovy fillets, rinsed, patted dry and minced

2 garlic cloves, crushed through a press

1 yellow pepper, cut into ¼-inch dice

1 plum tomato, seeded and finely chopped

¼ cup crumbled feta cheese

¼ cup fresh bread crumbs

2 tablespoons capers, packed in salt, rinsed and patted dry

½ teaspoon dried oregano

2 tablespoons olive oil

1. Preheat the oven to 375°F. Halve the green and red peppers lengthwise. Remove the stems, cores, seeds, and ribs. Cut each half into 4 wedges, about 1¼ inches wide at the center.

2. Combine the olives, anchovies, garlic, yellow pepper, tomato, feta, bread crumbs, capers, and oregano in a medium bowl. Toss to mix. Drizzle with the olive oil and toss to coat.

3. Spoon the filling into the pepper wedges, packing it lightly with your fingers. Arrange the pepper wedges, filling side up, on a large baking sheet. Cover with foil and bake 20 minutes. Remove the foil and bake until the peppers are tender but firm enough to hold, about 5 minutes longer. Serve at room temperature.

TOMATOES STUFFED WITH SHRIMP SALAD

PREP: 15 minutes

Makes 20 stuffed tomatoes

1 (3-ounce) package cream cheese, softened

2 tablespoons mayonnaise

1 tablespoon chili sauce

2 teaspoons lemon juice

1 cup chopped cooked shrimp

1 cup finely chopped celery

¼ cup finely chopped parsley

20 cherry tomatoes

1 tablespoon finely snipped fresh chives

1. Combine the cream cheese, mayonnaise, chili sauce, and lemon juice in a medium bowl and mix well. Stir in the shrimp, celery, and parsley. Cover and refrigerate.

2. Meanwhile, cut off a sliver from the blossom end of each tomato so the tomato will stand upright. Cut off the stem end and remove the seeds to make a hollow cup. Fill the tomatoes with the shrimp salad. Top each with a pinch of chives. Arrange on a platter and serve.

BAKED TOMATOES OREGANATA

PREP: 10 minutes   COOK: 20 minutes

Makes 8 tomato halves

4 plum tomatoes

½ cup coarse bread crumbs

¼ cup freshly grated Parmigiano-Reggiano cheese

½ teaspoon dried oregano

⅛ teaspoon salt

⅛ teaspoon freshly ground pepper

2 tablespoons extra-virgin olive oil

1. Preheat the oven to 375°F. Line a baking sheet with foil. Cut the tomatoes in half lengthwise and place cut side up on the prepared baking sheet.

2. Combine the bread crumbs, cheese, oregano, salt, and pepper in a bowl and toss with a fork to blend. Drizzle with the olive oil and toss until the bread crumbs are coated.

3. Spoon the bread-crumb mixture onto the tomato halves. Bake until the tomatoes are heated through, about 20 minutes.

CHEESE-STUFFED ZUCCHINI BITES

PREP: 20 minutes   COOK: 12 minutes

Makes 24 bites

2 (6-inch) green zucchini
2 (6-inch) yellow zucchini
1 egg, lightly beaten
½ cup (2 ounces) crumbled feta cheese
½ teaspoon dried oregano
¼ teaspoon freshly ground black pepper

1. Preheat the oven to 350°F. Line a baking sheet with parchment paper. Trim the ends from the zucchini and cut each crosswise into 6 pieces. Using a small melon-ball scoop or spoon, scoop out the seeds from one end of each piece, without cutting through to the other side, to make small cups. Place, hollowed-out side up, on the prepared baking sheet.

2. In a small bowl, combine the egg, cheese, oregano, and pepper and mix well. Spoon the cheese mixture into the zucchini cups, dividing evenly. Bake until the filling sets and the zucchini is tender, 12 to 15 minutes.

SILVER-DOLLAR CORN CAKES

PREP: 10 minutes COOK: 3 minutes per batch

Makes about 15 cakes

CHILI DIPPING SAUCE

½ cup Thai or Chinese sweet chili sauce

1 tablespoon lime juice

CORN CAKES

2 eggs

½ cup water

⅓ cup milk

1½ cups all-purpose flour

1½ teaspoons baking powder

1 cup fresh or thawed frozen corn kernels, cooked and cooled

½ cup chopped water chestnuts

½ cup frozen peas

¼ cup chopped green onions

¼ cup chopped fresh cilantro

2 tablespoons vegetable oil and more if needed

1. Make the chili dipping sauce: Mix the chili sauce and lime juice in a small bowl and set aside.

2. Make the corn cakes: Combine the eggs, water, and milk in a large bowl and whisk until blended. In a medium bowl, combine the flour and baking powder; whisk into the egg mixture. Add the corn, water chestnuts, peas, green onions, and cilantro and stir until coated and mixed.

3. Preheat the oven to 275°F. Line a baking sheet with parchment paper. Heat the oil in a large nonstick skillet over medium-high heat. In batches, add tablespoons of the batter to the oil and fry, turning once, until deep golden brown and crisp, about 3 minutes. Transfer to the prepared baking sheet and keep warm in the oven while frying the remaining cakes. Serve with the sauce for dipping.

QUICK CHEESE-STUFFED MUSHROOMS

PREP: 5 minutes   COOK: 15 minutes

Makes 24 mushrooms

24 medium mushrooms, stems removed
1 (5-ounce) package garlic-and-herb cheese spread
1 cup canned French-fried onions

Preheat the oven to 400°F. Place the mushrooms, stem-side up, on a baking sheet. Spoon some cheese spread into each. Sprinkle with onions. Bake until the mushrooms are tender, about 15 minutes.

Quick Caponata-Stuffed Mushrooms

Fill the mushroom caps using 2 (4.75-ounce) cans Eggplant Appetizer or 1½ cups Farm-Stand Caponata (page 39) instead of the cheese spread and sprinkle with grated Parmigiano-Reggiano cheese or dry bread crumbs instead of the onions.

Quick Artichoke-Stuffed Mushrooms

Drain a 6½-ounce jar of marinated artichoke hearts (save the marinade to use in a salad dressing). Pulse the artichokes in a food processor with ½ cup fine dry plain bread crumbs and ¼ cup shredded Italian Fontina cheese until the artichokes are evenly chopped. Use to fill the mushroom caps instead of the cheese spread and onions.

Quick Salsa-Stuffed Mushrooms

Mix 1 cup salsa (any kind) with 1 cup (4 ounces) shredded mozzarella, cheddar, or Monterey Jack cheese; use to fill the mushroom caps instead of the cheese spread and onions.

BELGIAN ENDIVE LEAVES WITH SMOKED TURKEY

PREP: 15 minutes

Makes 24 stuffed leaves

3 heads Belgian endive

4 ounces fresh goat's milk cheese, at room temperature

½ cup diced smoked turkey

¼ cup dried cranberries, chopped

¼ cup diced unpeeled Granny Smith apple

1 tablespoon lemon juice

2 teaspoons honey

½ cup chopped toasted pecans

Radish sprouts for garnish

1. Remove 24 perfect leaves from the endives and arrange on a baking sheet. About ½ inch from the base of each leaf, smear a dab of goat cheese about 1 inch long.

2. Combine the turkey, cranberries, apple, lemon juice, and honey in a bowl and mix well. Spoon a dollop of the filling over the cheese on each leaf. Cover with plastic wrap and refrigerate until serving.

3. To serve, unwrap the endive leaves and sprinkle with pecans and then a few radish sprouts. Arrange on a platter and serve immediately.

CELERY FILLED WITH CHICKEN-APPLE SALAD

PREP: 20 minutes plus chilling

Makes 40 pieces

1 bunch celery
½ cup mayonnaise
1 teaspoon lemon juice
½ teaspoon salt
1 cup finely diced cooked chicken
½ cup chopped unpeeled red-skinned apple
2 tablespoons golden raisins, chopped
¼ cup chopped toasted pecans

1. Separate the celery stalks; wash them, pat them dry, and trim the ends, removing any leaves. Chop about ½ of a stalk to make ¼ cup chopped celery.

2. Combine the mayonnaise, lemon juice, and salt in a medium bowl and mix well. Add the chopped celery, chicken, apple, and raisins and toss lightly until coated. Cover and refrigerate at least 2 hours.

3. Cut the remaining celery stalks crosswise to make 40 (2-inch) pieces. Fill each piece with chicken salad and sprinkle with the pecans. Cover and refrigerate until serving.

CURRIED SHRIMP-SALAD CANAPÉS

PREP: 20 minutes

Makes 12 canapés

1 (4¼-ounce) can tiny shrimp,
    rinsed and patted dry

¼ cup shredded carrot

¼ cup mayonnaise

1 tablespoon minced red pepper

1 tablespoon finely chopped toasted
    blanched almonds

1 teaspoon mango chutney

½ teaspoon curry powder

3 (6- by 4-inch) slices challah (egg bread)
    or raisin bread

2 tablespoons unsalted butter, softened

1. Reserve 12 shrimp and chop the remainder. In a bowl,
combine the chopped shrimp, carrot, mayonnaise, pepper, almonds, chutney, and curry powder. Mix well.

2. Place the slices of bread on a cutting board and cut
out 2 (2-inch) squares from the centers of each (there
should be no crusts on them). Cut each square crosswise
to make 2 triangles from each. Spread the butter on the
triangles, dividing evenly, and then the shrimp mixture.
Top each with a reserved shrimp. Place on a baking sheet
and cover with plastic wrap. Refrigerate until serving.

CUCUMBER AND SMOKED-SALMON CANAPÉS

PREP: 20 minutes

Makes 12 canapés

6 to 12 slices whole-wheat bread
2 tablespoons unsalted butter, softened
1 (3-ounce) package cream cheese, softened
¼ cup loosely packed watercress leaves
1 teaspoon grated lemon zest
12 thin slices cut from the center
   of an unpeeled European cucumber
3 ounces sliced smoked salmon,
   cut into 12 equal-size pieces

1. Use a cookie cutter the diameter of the cucumber to cut 12 rounds from the bread slices; place the rounds on a baking sheet. Spread the rounds with the butter, dividing evenly.

2. Mix the cream cheese, watercress, and lemon zest in a bowl until blended. Spread generously over the buttered sides of the rounds. Place a cucumber slice on top. Fold the pieces of salmon to fit the rounds and place on top of the cucumber. Cover with plastic wrap and refrigerate until serving.

POLENTA CANAPÉS WITH TAPENADE

PREP: 15 minutes plus overnight chilling

COOK: 40 minutes

Makes about 18 canapés

2 cups water

1 teaspoon salt

½ cup fine polenta

½ cup freshly grated Parmigiano-Reggiano cheese

½ teaspoon freshly ground black pepper

Tapenade (page 19)

¼ cup chopped red pepper

2 tablespoons finely chopped fresh parsley

1. Line a baking sheet with parchment paper. Heat the water to boiling over high heat in a heavy saucepan. Add the salt and reduce the heat to medium. Gradually add the polenta, whisking constantly; whisk for 5 minutes as the mixture boils. Reduce the heat to low and cook, stirring occasionally, until the mixture begins to come away from the sides of the pan, about 10 minutes. Remove the pan from the heat and stir in the cheese and pepper.

2. Spread the mixture to a ¼-inch thickness on the prepared baking sheet. Cover with plastic wrap and refrigerate until cold, several hours or overnight.

3. Remove the plastic wrap from the polenta, place a cutting board on top of the baking sheet, and invert the polenta onto the cutting board. Cut about 18 rounds with a 1½-inch cookie cutter.

4. Spray a large skillet with nonstick cooking spray and heat over medium-high heat. In batches, add the polenta rounds and cook, turning once, until browned, about 4 minutes. Place the rounds on a platter and dab a small mound of tapenade on top; spread the mound flat with the back of a spoon. Sprinkle with red pepper and parsley and serve warm.

CURRIED CHICKPEA CANAPÉS

PREP: 15 minutes plus chilling   COOK: 50 minutes

Makes about 40 canapés

2⅔ cups cold water

¾ teaspoon fine sea salt

1 cup chickpea flour (besan)

2 tablespoons finely grated unsweetened coconut
(available frozen at Asian grocery stores or use fresh)

2 tablespoons finely chopped salted peanuts

1 tablespoon curry powder

2 tablespoons finely chopped fresh cilantro

1. Line a baking sheet with parchment paper. Heat the water to boiling over high heat in a heavy saucepan. Add the salt and reduce the heat to medium. Gradually add the chickpea flour, whisking constantly; whisk for 5 minutes as the mixture boils. Reduce the heat to medium-low, cover, and simmer, stirring occasionally, 20 minutes.

2. Spread the mixture to a ¼-inch thickness on the prepared baking sheet. Sprinkle evenly with the coconut, peanuts, and curry powder. Refrigerate until firm, about 1 hour.

3. Preheat the oven to 375°F. Place a cutting board on the baking sheet with the chickpea flour mixture. Invert the mixture onto the cutting board. Remove the parchment. Cut into bite-size squares.

4. Line another baking sheet with parchment paper. Place the canapés on the prepared baking sheet. Bake until golden, about 20 minutes. Sprinkle with the cilantro and serve hot.

ROLLED WATERCRESS TEA SANDWICHES

PREP: 20 minutes

Makes about 25 sandwiches

1 large bunch watercress

¾ cup (1½ sticks) unsalted butter, softened

¼ teaspoon salt

1 tablespoon lemon juice

1½ (1-pound) loaves thin-sliced white sandwich bread

1. Wash and dry the watercress. Pick off 50 small center sprigs and reserve.

2. Remove the remaining leaves from the watercress and finely chop. Place in a measuring cup and, if necessary, chop enough of the tender stems to make ½ cup.

3. Beat the butter and salt in a medium bowl until smooth. Gradually beat in the lemon juice. Stir in the chopped watercress.

4. Stack 4 bread slices and trim off the crusts with a serrated knife using a gentle sawing motion; repeat with the remaining bread. Spread each slice with the watercress butter, using about 1½ teaspoons for each slice. Roll up the slices jelly-roll fashion. Insert a watercress sprig into each end. Place the sandwiches in a roasting pan and cover with damp paper towels. Cover the pan tightly with plastic wrap. Refrigerate until serving.

CREAM CHEESE–OLIVE RIBBON SANDWICHES

PREP: 20 minutes

Makes 24 sandwiches

1 (8-ounce) package cream cheese, softened

2 tablespoons mayonnaise

⅓ cup chopped pimiento-stuffed olives

½ cup (1 stick) unsalted butter, softened

12 slices thin-sliced white sandwich bread

12 slices thin-sliced whole-wheat sandwich bread

1. Combine the cream cheese, mayonnaise, and olives in a medium bowl and blend well with a wooden spoon.

2. Lightly butter 4 slices of white bread and 4 slices of whole-wheat bread, then spread with the cream-cheese mixture, using about 2 teaspoons for each slice. Place the white bread slices, cheese side up, on the work surface and top with the whole-wheat slices, cheese side up. Butter 4 more white bread slices and place on top of the sandwiches, buttered side down. Cut off the crusts with a sharp serrated knife using a gentle sawing motion. Cut each sandwich into 3 equal strips. Place the sandwiches in a roasting pan. Cover with damp paper towels.

3. Repeat with the remaining bread, butter, and olive mixture, using the whole-wheat bread for the top and bottom sections of the sandwiches. Cover the pan of sandwiches tightly with plastic wrap. Refrigerate until serving.

TOMATO-CURRY TEA SANDWICHES

PREP: 25 minutes

Makes 24 sandwiches

48 slices thin-sliced white sandwich bread
   or other bread of choice

3 tablespoons unsalted butter, softened

½ teaspoon lemon juice

¼ teaspoon curry powder

¼ teaspoon salt

4 vine tomatoes at least 2 inches in diameter

1. Working in batches, lay out the bread slices on a cutting board and cut out the center of each using a 2-inch scalloped round cutter. Discard the remaining portions of bread. Place 24 of the rounds flat on a baking sheet. Lay out the remaining 24 rounds on the work surface and cut out the centers using a ¾-inch scalloped round cutter; place on another baking sheet and cover with plastic wrap.

2. Combine the butter, lemon juice, curry powder, and salt in a small bowl and mix well. Spread on the uncut rounds.

3. Thinly slice the tomatoes crosswise into rounds; cut out the centers using the same ¾-inch round scalloped cutter. Place a slice on each buttered uncut round. Top each with a cut-out round and press lightly. Place the sandwiches in a roasting pan and cover with damp paper towels. Cover the pan tightly with plastic wrap. Refrigerate until serving.

HAM SALAD TEA SANDWICHES

PREP: 20 minutes
Makes 16 sandwiches

6 ounces baked ham, chopped
3 tablespoons sweet pickle relish
3 tablespoons mayonnaise
⅛ teaspoon freshly ground black pepper
8 slices thin-sliced whole-wheat sandwich bread
2 tablespoons unsalted butter, softened
4 crisp lettuce leaves

Combine the ham, relish, mayonnaise, and pepper in a bowl and mix well. Lay out the bread on a work surface and spread with the butter. Spread the ham mixture evenly on the buttered side of 4 slices and top with a lettuce leaf. Cover each with a remaining slice of bread, buttered side down. Trim off the crusts if desired. Cut each sandwich diagonally both ways to make 4 triangles from each. Place on a plate and cover with plastic wrap. Refrigerate until serving.

OPEN-FACE BEEF TEA SANDWICHES

PREP: 20 minutes

Makes 12 sandwiches

2 tablespoons unsalted butter, softened

1 tablespoon whole-grain Dijon mustard

1 teaspoon prepared horseradish

6 slices marbled rye bread

6 thin slices rare roast beef

4 radishes, thinly sliced

¼ cup mixed sprouts (alfalfa, onion, cilantro)

1. Combine the butter, mustard, and horseradish in a small bowl. Trim the crusts from the bread and cut each slice into 2 squares; cover with plastic wrap. Cut the beef to the size of the bread squares.

2. Lay the bread squares on the work surface and spread with the butter mixture, dividing evenly. Top each with the beef, then the radishes and sprouts, dividing evenly. Place the sandwiches in a single layer in a roasting pan, cover with plastic wrap, and refrigerate until serving.

FRIED PEPPERONI-MOZZARELLA TOASTS

PREP: 30 minutes   COOK: 8 minutes per batch

Makes 16 toasts

2 cups (8 ounces) shredded mozzarella cheese

4 ounces pepperoni, diced

16 slices thin-sliced white or whole-wheat sandwich bread

4 eggs

3 tablespoons milk

1 cup seasoned Italian bread crumbs

⅓ cup canola or grapeseed oil

⅓ cup olive oil

16 fresh sage leaves

1. Preheat the oven to 250°F. Combine the mozzarella and pepperoni in a bowl and toss to mix.

2. Lay out the bread slices on a work surface and mound the mozzarella mixture on one half of each slice, about ¼ inch from the crust edge. Fold the bare side over the filling so the crusts meet; press the crusts so the sandwiches seal (lightly press on the filling towards the last open edge to remove any air pockets). Cut off the crusts and press the edges again to make sure they are sealed.

3. Beat the eggs with the milk in a shallow bowl until blended. Place the bread crumbs in another shallow bowl. Dip a sandwich in the egg to lightly coat both sides, draining off the excess, and then coat lightly and evenly with the crumbs. Place the coated sandwich on a baking sheet. Repeat with the remaining sandwiches.

4. Heat half of each oil and half the sage in a large, heavy skillet over medium-high heat until hot but not smoking. In batches, add the sandwiches and fry, turning once, until golden brown, about 8 minutes, adding more oil and sage as needed. Transfer the toasts to a paper towel–lined baking sheet; keep warm in the oven while frying the remaining sandwiches. Serve hot.

ANCHOVY TOASTS

Makes 18 toasts

1 (2-ounce) can anchovies, drained,
    rinsed and minced
¼ cup (½ stick) unsalted butter, softened
¼ cup extra-virgin olive oil
1 (8-ounce) loaf Italian bread, cut diagonally
    into 18 slices

1. Preheat the broiler. Line a baking sheet with foil.
Combine the anchovies and butter in a bowl and mash
with a fork until blended. Gradually mash in the oil.
Spread over both sides of each slice of the bread.
Place on the prepared baking sheet.
2. Broil the toasts, turning once, until crisp, 1 to 2
minutes on each side.

BAKED HERB-CHEESE WONTONS

PREP: 25 minutes   COOK: 15 minutes

Makes 30 wontons

The wontons can be assembled ahead of time, wrapped well, and frozen. Bake them, frozen, adding a few minutes to the cooking time.

¼ cup hazelnuts, toasted, skins rubbed off,
    nuts finely chopped
1 teaspoon all-purpose flour
2 (5-ounce) packages garlic-and-herb cheese spread,
    at room temperature
30 (3-inch) wonton wrappers
1 large egg white, lightly beaten

1. Preheat the oven to 350°F. Line 2 baking sheets with parchment paper. Place the hazelnuts and flour in a spice or coffee grinder and process until finely ground. Set aside 3 tablespoons of the hazelnut mixture. Combine the remainder with the cheese spread in a medium bowl and mix well.

2. Working with 1 wonton wrapper at a time (cover the remaining wrappers with a damp towel to keep them from drying), spoon about 2 teaspoons of the cheese mixture into the center of a wrapper. Moisten the edges with water; bring 2 opposite corners together, forming a triangle. Press the edges together to seal. Repeat with the remaining wonton wrappers and cheese mixture.

3. Place the wontons on the prepared baking sheets. Brush with the egg white; sprinkle with the reserved hazelnut mixture. Bake the wontons until lightly browned, about 15 minutes. Cool 5 minutes on a wire rack.

VIETNAMESE FRIED SHRIMP ROLLS

PREP: 25 minutes COOK: 10 minutes per batch

Makes 20 rolls

Triangle shaped Vietnamese rice-paper wrappers can be purchased in packages of quartered 12-inch wrappers.

20 medium shrimp without the tails, peeled and deveined
½ teaspoon freshly ground black pepper
1 teaspoon vinegar, mixed with ⅓ cup warm water
20 triangle-shaped Vietnamese rice-paper wrappers
2 large green onions, quartered lengthwise and cut crosswise into 2-inch pieces
1 cup loosely packed fresh cilantro leaves
Vegetable oil for frying
20 Boston or Bibb lettuce leaf cups
20 crosswise slices star fruit (carambola)
20 tender fresh mint sprigs (tops only)
2 Kirby cucumbers, cut lengthwise into thin sticks
1 cup shredded carrots
2 tablespoons Sweet and Sour Dipping Sauce (page 432)

1. Place 1 shrimp on its leg side and hold the head end while lifting up the tail to break the curve. Place in a bowl and repeat with remaining shrimp. Sprinkle with pepper.

2. In batches, lay out wrappers on the work surface with a point facing away from you; brush with the vinegar mixture. Let stand a few minutes. Place 1 shrimp in the center of each wrapper about ½ inch from and parallel to the bottom edge. Top with some green onion and cilantro. Fold up the bottom to cover the shrimp. Fold over the sides and roll the covered shrimp snugly toward the point end to and to seal. Repeat with the remaining shrimp.

3. Heat ½ inch of oil in a deep, heavy skillet over medium heat to 350°F on a deep-fat thermometer. In batches, add the shrimp rolls with space between them; fry, turning once, until golden brown, 10 minutes. Transfer with tongs to a paper towel–lined baking sheet.

4. Serve rolls hot in a lettuce cup with a slice of star fruit, a sprig of mint, a stick of cucumber, and a pinch of carrot. Sprinkle with the sauce.

COCKTAIL SALAMI TURNOVERS

PREP: 25 minutes   COOK: 10 minutes

Makes 16 turnovers

1 (2-ounce) chunk salami (about 6 slices), minced
1 egg yolk plus 1 egg
½ cup shredded mozzarella cheese
2 tablespoons freshly grated Parmigiano-Reggiano cheese
1 tablespoon chopped fresh basil
1 (10-ounce) container refrigerated pizza crust
1 tablespoon water

1. Preheat the oven to 425°F. Line a baking sheet with parchment paper. Combine the salami, egg yolk, mozzarella, Parmigiano-Reggiano, and basil in a small bowl and mix well.

2. Roll out the dough on a floured surface to a 12-inch square. Cut with a pizza cutter into 16 (3-inch) squares. Spoon the salami mixture in the center of each square, dividing evenly. Mix the whole egg with the water in a cup until blended. Brush the mixture over 2 adjoining edges of each dough square; fold the opposite corner over the filling to make a triangle. Lightly press the edges together with a fork to seal.

3. Place the triangles on the prepared baking sheet. Bake until browned, about 10 minutes. Cool briefly before serving.

SAUSAGE THUMBPRINTS

PREP: 15 minutes plus chilling **COOK: 12 minutes**

Makes about 60 thumbprints

½ (1-pound) package frozen puff pastry (1 sheet),
thawed as package label directs, or ½ recipe
Easy Puff Pastry (page 225)
1 pound well-seasoned bulk sausage or sausage
removed from the casing

1. Line baking sheets with parchment paper. Roll out the pastry to a 15½- by 9-inch rectangle. Cut the rectangle lengthwise into 3 (3-inch-wide) strips. Divide the sausage meat into thirds. On a cutting board with wet hands, roll one third into a 15½-inch long snake. Place on one long edge of a rectangle. Wet the opposite edge with water. Starting with the sausage side, roll the sausage up in the pastry; press on the top edge to seal tightly. Repeat with the remaining sausage and pastry. Place the rolls on a prepared baking sheet, cover with plastic wrap, and refrigerate at least 1 hour.

2. Preheat the oven to 400°F. Place the sausage rolls on a cutting board and cut crosswise with a sharp knife into ¾-inch-thick rounds. Place the rolls cut side down on prepared baking sheets. Bake until puffed and golden, about 12 minutes. Drain on paper towels and serve warm.

AVOCADO, MANGO, AND BABY SHRIMP TARTLETS

PREP: 15 minutes
Makes 16 tartlets

1 (3½-ounce) can baby shrimp, drained
½ peeled, pitted ripe avocado, cut into ¼-inch dice
½ peeled, pitted ripe mango, cut into ¼-inch dice
1 tablespoon minced red pepper
2 teaspoons chopped pitted black olives
2 teaspoons chopped jalapeño chile pepper
   (wear gloves when handling)
½ teaspoon finely grated lime zest
1 tablespoon fresh lime juice
1 teaspoon chopped fresh cilantro
½ teaspoon olive oil
⅛ teaspoon salt or more to taste

16 baked Phyllo Tartlet Shells (page 219)
or Tartlet Shells made with shortcrust pastry,
(page 218)

Combine the shrimp, avocado, mango, red pepper, olives, and jalapeño in a medium bowl and mix gently. In a small bowl, combine the lime zest, lime juice, cilantro, oil, and salt and stir until blended. Taste and add more salt if needed. Pour the vinaigrette over the shrimp mixture and toss gently to coat. Spoon into the baked tartlet shells.

TUNA NIÇOISE TARTLETS

PREP: 10 minutes

Makes 16 tartlets

1 (3½-ounce) can albacore tuna, drained

1 small Kirby cucumber, peeled and cut into ¼-inch dice

1 small plum tomato, cored and cut into ¼-inch dice

1 anchovy fillet, rinsed and minced

1 egg, hard-cooked, peeled, and cut into ¼-inch dice

¼ cup finely chopped cooked fresh green beans

1 tablespoon finely chopped pitted oil-cured olives

1 tablespoon olive oil

1 tablespoon red wine vinegar

⅛ teaspoon salt

⅛ teaspoon freshly ground black pepper

16 baked Phyllo Tartlet Shells (page 219)
  or Tartlet Shells made with shortcrust pastry
  (page 218)

2 tablespoons finely snipped fresh chives or slivered basil

Place the tuna in a bowl and flake with a fork. Add the cucumber, tomato, anchovy, egg, green beans, and olives and mix gently with a fork. Drizzle the oil and vinegar on top and sprinkle with the salt and pepper. Toss gently to coat. Spoon into the baked tartlet shells and top each with a pinch of chives.

CURRIED CRAB AND CARROT TARTLETS

PREP: 10 minutes

Makes 16 tartlets

4 to 5 tablespoons whole-milk plain yogurt

½ teaspoon curry powder

1 cup crabmeat, picked over for shells

¼ cup shredded carrots

¼ cup thinly chopped red pepper

2 tablespoons finely sliced green onions

*16 baked Phyllo Tartlet Shells (page 219)
or Tartlet Shells made with shortcrust pastry
(page 218)*

2 tablespoons finely chopped peanuts

Mix 4 tablespoons yogurt with the curry powder in a medium bowl. Add the crab, carrots, red pepper, and green onions and mix until coated, adding more yogurt if needed. Spoon the filling into the baked tartlet shells and sprinkle each with peanuts.

CRAB-ARTICHOKE TARTLETS

PREP: 20 minutes   COOK: 10 minutes

Makes 36 tartlets

1 (9-ounce) box frozen artichoke hearts,
cooked as package label directs, drained,
and cooled

2 tablespoons mayonnaise

1 teaspoon grated lemon zest

1 tablespoon lemon juice

⅛ teaspoon hot pepper sauce

½ cup lump crabmeat, picked over for shells

⅓ cup diced roasted red pepper

1 cup (4 ounces) shredded Emmenthaler
or other Swiss cheese

36 baked Phyllo Cups (page 220) or Tartlet Shells
made with shortcrust pastry (page 218)

1. Preheat the oven to 375°F. Line a baking sheet with
parchment paper. Finely chop the artichoke hearts on
a cutting board or in a food processor and place in a
medium bowl. Add the mayonnaise, lemon zest, lemon
juice, and pepper sauce and mix well. Add the crab,
red pepper, and cheese and mix well.

2. Place the tartlet shells on the prepared baking sheet
and fill each with the artichoke mixture. Bake until the
cheese melts, 10 to 12 minutes.

BACON-CLAM TARTLETS

PREP: 10 minutes   COOK: 20 minutes

Makes 20 tartlets

4 slices bacon, diced

1 small onion, diced

1 small green pepper, diced

1 small garlic clove, crushed through a press

2 (10-ounce) cans whole baby clams, drained, juice reserved

½ cup dried plain bread crumbs

¼ cup chopped fresh flat-leaf parsley

1 teaspoon chopped fresh thyme

½ teaspoon salt

¼ teaspoon freshly ground black pepper

20 baked Phyllo Tartlet Shells (page 219) or Tartlet Shells made with shortcrust pastry (page 218)

1. Preheat the oven to 350°F. Line a baking sheet with parchment paper. Sauté the bacon in a large skillet until crisp. Transfer the bacon to a cup; discard all but 2 tablespoons fat from the skillet. Add the onion and green pepper to the skillet and sauté until softened, about 3 minutes. Add the garlic and sauté 1 minute. Remove the pan from the heat and stir in the bacon, clams, ½ cup clam juice, the bread crumbs, parsley, thyme, salt, and pepper and mix well. Simmer over medium-low heat until most of the liquid has evaporated but the mixture is still really juicy.

2. Arrange the tartlet shells on the prepared baking sheet and fill each with the clam mixture. Bake until hot, 5 to 7 minutes.

BLUE CHEESE CHEESECAKES

Cream Cheese Pastry for Tartlets (page 229)
4 ounces (about ½ cup) crumbled blue cheese of choice
1 (3-ounce) package cream cheese, softened
1 egg
8 seedless green grapes, chopped
¼ cup finely chopped walnuts

1. Preheat the oven to 350°F. Spray 2 (12-cup) mini-muffin pans with nonstick cooking spray. Place a pastry ball into each cup and press evenly to line the bottom and sides of each up to the rim.

2. Combine the blue cheese, cream cheese, and egg in a bowl and stir until blended. Stir in the grapes. Spoon the mixture into the dough-lined muffin cups, dividing evenly. Sprinkle each with walnuts.

3. Bake the tartlets until golden and set, about 20 minutes. Cool slightly before removing from the pans. Serve warm or at room temperature.

LITTLE LEEK QUICHES

PREP: 20 minutes   COOK: 25 minutes

Makes 24 quiches

3 tablespoons unsalted butter

1 pound leeks, white part only, sliced and rinsed

1 small red onion, finely chopped

1 small red pepper, finely chopped

2 eggs, beaten

½ cup heavy cream

⅓ cup shredded Gruyère cheese

¼ teaspoon salt

⅛ teaspoon freshly ground black pepper

24 baked Tartlet Shells (page 218)

1. Preheat the oven to 375°F. Melt the butter in a large skillet over medium heat. Add the leeks, onion, and red pepper and sauté until soft, about 15 minutes. Transfer to a bowl to cool.

2. Add the eggs, cream, cheese, salt, and pepper to the leek mixture and mix well. Place the tartlet shells on a baking sheet. Fill with the leek mixture. Bake until the filling is puffed and set, 7 to 10 minutes. Serve warm or at room temperature.

MUSHROOM-CHEESE MINI QUICHES

PREP: 15 minutes   COOK: 17 minutes

Makes 24 quiches

1 tablespoon unsalted butter

1 green onion, finely sliced

1 cup coarsely chopped mushrooms

2 eggs, beaten

½ cup heavy cream

⅓ cup shredded Swiss cheese

¼ teaspoon minced fresh thyme

¼ teaspoon salt

⅛ teaspoon freshly ground black pepper

24 baked Tartlet Shells (page 218)

1. Preheat the oven to 375°F. Melt the butter in a large skillet over medium heat. Add the green onion and mushrooms and sauté until soft, about 8 minutes. Transfer to a bowl to cool.

2. Add the eggs, cream, cheese, thyme, salt, and pepper to the mushroom mixture and mix well. Place the tartlet shells on a baking sheet and fill with the mushroom mixture. Bake until the filling is puffed and set, 7 to 10 minutes. Serve warm or at room temperature.

TANGY CORN MINI QUICHES

PREP: 15 minutes COOK: 10 minutes

Makes 24 quiches

1 cup fresh or thawed frozen corn kernels

2 eggs, beaten

½ cup heavy cream

⅓ cup shredded cheddar cheese

¼ teaspoon cayenne

¼ teaspoon salt

⅛ teaspoon freshly ground black pepper

24 baked Tartlet Shells (page 218)

1. Preheat the oven to 375°F. Cook the corn in ½ cup water in a small saucepan over medium-high heat until tender, about 3 minutes for fresh and 1 minute for frozen. Drain in a colander and let cool.

2. Combine the corn, eggs, cream, cheese, cayenne, salt, and pepper in a medium bowl and mix well. Place the tartlet shells on a baking sheet and fill with the corn mixture. Bake until the filling is puffed and set, 7 to 10 minutes. Serve warm or at room temperature.

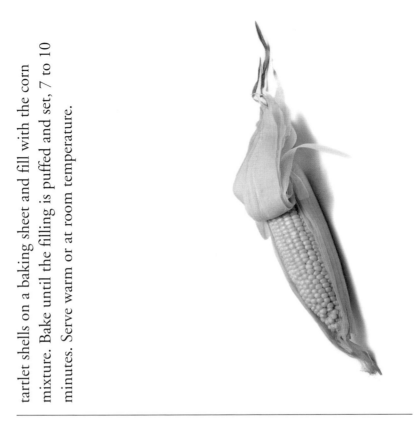

PREP: 10 minutes   COOK: 7 minutes

Makes 24 quiches

½ cup (¼-inch) cubes baked or boiled ham
½ cup (2 ounces) crumbled garlic-and-herb cheese spread
2 eggs, beaten
½ cup heavy cream
¼ teaspoon salt
⅛ teaspoon freshly ground black pepper
⅛ teaspoon cayenne
24 baked Tartlet Shells (page 218)

Preheat the oven to 375°F. Combine the ham, cheese spread, eggs, cream, salt, pepper, and cayenne in a medium bowl and mix well. Place the tartlet shells on a baking sheet. Spoon the ham mixture into the tartlet shells. Bake until the filling is puffed and set, 7 to 10 minutes. Serve warm or at room temperature.

SPICY SAUCY SHRIMP CUPS

PREP: 30 minutes   COOK: 7 minutes

Makes 36 cups

1 teaspoon paprika
1 teaspoon cayenne
1 teaspoon freshly ground black pepper
½ teaspoon red pepper flakes
½ teaspoon dried oregano, crushed
½ teaspoon salt
2 pounds large shrimp, peeled, deveined,
    and cut in half lengthwise
2 teaspoons Worcestershire sauce
1 teaspoon hot pepper sauce
2 tablespoons unsalted butter
4 green onions, trimmed, finely chopped
2 garlic cloves, crushed through a press
½ cup dry white wine
36 Toasted Bread Cups (page 222)

1. Combine the paprika, cayenne, black pepper, pepper flakes, oregano, and salt in a large bowl and stir to mix. Add the shrimp and toss to coat. Cover and refrigerate 15 minutes. Stir in the Worcestershire sauce and the pepper sauce and toss to coat.

2. Melt the butter in a large skillet over high heat. Add the shrimp, green onions, and garlic and sauté 2 minutes. Add the wine and cook until the shrimp are pink and barely cooked through, about 1 minute. Transfer the shrimp to a shallow bowl using a slotted spoon. Boil the mixture in the skillet over high heat until thickened to a few tablespoons, about 1 minute. Pour over the shrimp mixture. Spoon the shrimp and some juice into the bread cups and serve immediately.

SCALLOP CUPS

PREP: 10 minutes   COOK: 13 minutes

Makes 24 cups

24 Toasted Bread Cups (page 222)
Lemon-Watercress Butter Sauce (page 438)
1 pound bay scallops

1. Preheat the oven to 250°F. Place the bread cups on a baking sheet and warm through in the oven about 8 minutes.

2. Heat the sauce in a medium saucepan over medium-high heat until boiling. Add the scallops. Reduce the heat to low and cook until the scallops are cooked through and just opaque throughout, about 2 minutes. Spoon some scallops and sauce into each cup and serve.

SMOKED TROUT CUPS

PREP: 10 minutes

Makes 12 cups

2 smoked trout or whitefish fillets, flaked

½ cup store-bought or homemade (page 462)
   crème fraîche or sour cream

2 tablespoons tartar sauce

2 tablespoons snipped fresh dill plus small sprigs
   for garnish

2 teaspoons lemon juice or more to taste

12 Wonton Cups (page 221)

Combine the trout, crème fraîche, tartar sauce, dill, and
lemon juice in a bowl and mix well. Taste and add more
lemon juice if needed. Spoon the mixture into the wonton cups and garnish each with a dill sprig.

CHEESE PUFFS (GOUGÈRES)

PREP: 20 minutes   COOK: 35 minutes

Makes 40 puffs

1 cup water

½ cup (1 stick) butter, cut into 1-inch chunks

½ teaspoon salt

¼ teaspoon cayenne

1¼ cups sifted all-purpose flour

3 eggs, at room temperature, plus 1 egg beaten with 2 tablespoons water (egg wash)

1½ cups (6 ounces) grated Gruyère cheese, at room temperature, plus 2 tablespoons more for sprinkling

1. Combine the water, butter, salt, and cayenne in a medium saucepan over medium-high heat. Bring to a full boil, stirring constantly with a wooden spoon to quickly melt the butter. Remove the pan from the heat, add the flour all at once, and beat vigorously to combine. Return the pan to medium heat and cook, stirring constantly, until the mixture pulls away from the side of the pan, about 3 minutes.

2. Remove the pan from the heat. Beat in 3 eggs, 1 egg at a time, completely incorporating each one before adding another. Beat in 1½ cups of the cheese. Beat over low heat just until the cheese melts. (The dough can be made ahead of time up to this point, covered, and refrigerated until ready to use; bring to room temperature before shaping and baking.)

3. Preheat the oven to 400°F. Line baking sheets with parchment paper. Spoon or pipe the dough in 1-inch balls onto the prepared baking sheets. Brush with the egg wash and sprinkle with the reserved cheese. Bake until golden brown and crisp, about 20 minutes (do not open the door for the first half of cooking or the puffs will deflate).

4. Insert a thin-bladed knife in the side of each puff near the top to allow the steam to escape. Turn off the oven. Return the puffs on the baking sheet to the oven and let cool with the oven door open. Cut off the tops with a serrated knife and remove any uncooked dough.

GOUGÈRE SQUARES

CHICKEN LIVER AND FONTINA

PREP: 20 minutes   COOK: 65 minutes

Makes 12 squares

1 cup water

½ cup (1 stick) butter, cut into 1-inch chunks

½ teaspoon salt

1¼ cups sifted all-purpose flour

3 eggs, at room temperature

1 cup (4 ounces) grated Italian fontina cheese,
at room temperature

1½ teaspoons grainy mustard

CHICKEN-LIVER TOPPING

2 tablespoons unsalted butter

12 ounces chicken livers, rinsed and patted dry

1 red pepper, cut into ½-inch dice

1 small red onion, finely chopped

1 tablespoon medium-dry sherry

½ cup heavy cream

1 tablespoon Dijon mustard

¼ teaspoon salt or more to taste

⅛ teaspoon freshly ground black pepper

½ cup (2 ounces) grated Italian fontina cheese

1. Combine the water, butter, and salt in a medium
saucepan over medium-high heat. Bring to a full boil, stirring constantly with a wooden spoon to quickly melt the
butter. Remove the pan from the heat, add the flour all at
once, and beat vigorously to combine. Return the pan to
medium heat and cook, stirring constantly, until the mixture pulls away from the side of the pan, about 3 minutes.

2. Remove the pan from the heat. Beat in the eggs, 1 at
a time, completely incorporating each one before adding
another. Beat in the cheese and grainy mustard. Beat
over low heat just until the cheese melts.

3. Butter a shallow 2-quart baking dish. Spread the pastry over the bottom of the baking dish and a little up the sides. Refrigerate while preparing the topping. (The dough can be made to this point, covered, and refrigerated for up to a day; bring to room temperature about 15 minutes before baking.)

4. Preheat the oven to 400°F. Make the topping: Melt the butter in a large skillet over medium-high heat. Add the chicken livers and sauté until browned and firm, about 2 minutes. Transfer to a bowl using a slotted spoon. Add the red pepper and onion to the skillet and sauté until softened, about 3 minutes. Add the sherry and boil until almost all has evaporated. Stir in the cream, Dijon mustard, salt, and pepper and simmer until the liquid has reduced by half. Remove from the heat.

5. Coarsely chop the chicken livers and add to the cream mixture. Spread the mixture over the dough and sprinkle with the cheese. Bake until golden brown and puffed, about 35 minutes. Let cool slightly and cut into squares.

PREP: 10 minutes
Makes 40 servings

40 Cheese Puffs (Gougères) (page 132), made with
Parmigiano-Reggiano cheese instead of Gruyère

Crunchy Chicken Salad Spread (page 30)

Cut the tops off the puffs and set aside. Spoon the salad
inside the gougères and replace the tops.

Crab Gougères

Make the gougères with Monterey Jack cheese instead of
Gruyère. Fill the baked gougères with Chili Crab Salad
(page 31).

Avocado-Mango Gougères

Make the gougères with cheddar cheese instead of
Gruyère. Fill the baked gougères with Green-and-Gold
Avocado-Mango Salad (page 32).

THREE-CHEESE PUFFS

PREP: 10 minutes   COOK: 10 minutes

Makes 12 puffs

¼ cup ricotta cheese

¼ cup (1 ounce) grated Parmigiano-Reggiano cheese

2 tablespoons goat's milk cheese

½ (1-pound) package frozen puff pastry (1 sheet), thawed as package label directs

Tomato Jam (page 17)

1. Preheat the oven to 400°F. Combine the ricotta, Parmesan, and goat cheese in a bowl and mix well.

2. Unroll the pastry sheet on a cutting board. Cut out 12 rounds using a 2-inch cookie cutter. Score the rounds with a fork and press each lightly into a mini-muffin pan cup. Spoon some cheese mixture into each pastry cup, dividing equally.

3. Bake until the pastry is puffed and golden, about 10 minutes. Serve with the Tomato Jam to spread on the puffs.

OPEN-FACE SAMOSAS

PREP: 30 minutes   COOK: 20 minutes

Makes 16 samosas

1½ cups all-purpose flour

1 teaspoon salt

2 tablespoons vegetable oil

2 tablespoons water

8 ounces potatoes, boiled, peeled, and cut into ¼-inch dice

1 small green onion, finely chopped

1 small carrot, peeled and finely chopped

1 small jalapeño chile pepper (taste to make sure it is hot), diced (wear gloves when handling)

1 tablespoon fresh lemon juice

½ teaspoon ground cumin

½ cup fresh raw peas

¼ cup fresh cilantro leaves, chopped

⅓ cup butter, melted, or more if needed for brushing

1. Mix the flour and ½ teaspoon salt in a bowl and make a well in the center. Combine the oil and water in a glass measure and gradually pour into the well, stirring to incorporate the flour. Knead the dough about 5 turns until smooth. (Dough will be oily.) Cover with plastic wrap.

2. Place the potatoes in another medium bowl and mash slightly. Add the green onion, carrot, jalapeño, lemon juice, cumin, and remaining ½ teaspoon salt. Mix well. Stir in the peas and cilantro.

3. Preheat the oven to 400°F. Lightly grease 3 (12-cup) mini-muffin pans. Place pans on baking sheets.

4. Twist the dough with your hands to divide in half. Leave one half in bowl. Break dough from other half into 8 equal pieces; shape each into a ball. Place one ball on lightly floured surface and roll to a 3-inch round. Press into a prepared mini-muffin cup and brush with butter. Repeat with the remaining dough. Fill each dough-lined cup with 1 heaping teaspoon of filling.

5. Lightly brush the samosas with melted butter. Bake on the middle rack until golden brown, about 20 minutes. Cool a few minutes and serve hot or warm.

MARMALADE-GLAZED TURKEY
BISCUIT SANDWICHES

PREP: 10 minutes   COOK: 3 minutes

Makes 36 biscuits

8 slices cooked turkey breast
(leftover or from the deli)

3 tablespoons orange marmalade

¼ teaspoon salt

⅛ teaspoon freshly ground black pepper

36 Pumpkin-Ginger Biscuits (page 188),
warmed

Preheat the broiler. Lay the turkey slices on a foil-lined baking sheet. Place the marmalade in a microwave-safe cup, cover with plastic wrap, and microwave on high power until melted, about 20 seconds. Brush the marmalade over the turkey and sprinkle with the salt and pepper. Broil until hot, about 2 minutes. Slide the foil with the turkey onto a cutting board and cut each slice crosswise into 4 or 5 pieces. Split the biscuits and fill each with a piece of glazed turkey. Serve immediately.

SOUTHERN HAM BISCUITS

PREP: 10 minutes

Makes 12 to 16 biscuits

*Cheesey Buttermilk Biscuits (page 189)
or Tender Cream Biscuits (page 192),
at room temperature*

⅓ cup Honey-Bourbon Mustard Sauce (page 446)

*12 ounces baked ham, trimmed of all fat,
thinly sliced, and cut into pieces the size
of the biscuits*

Split the biscuits in half horizontally and spread about
½ teaspoon sauce on the cut sides of each half. Place
ham on the bottom halves of the biscuits to cover; cover
with the biscuit tops. Arrange on a platter and serve at
room temperature.

PREP: 10 minutes

Makes 12 bread sticks

12 thin Bread Sticks (page 174)

1 tablespoon unsalted butter, softened

12 slices bresaola (Italian air-dried beef),
    about 6 inches long and 1 inch wide

Working with 1 bread stick at a time, with your finger, spread butter about 4 inches from one tip; wrap a piece of bresaola along the smeared part as if wrapping a bandage. Place prepared bread sticks in a heavy, short, wide vase or other clean container and serve.

PIGLETS IN A BLANKET

PREP: 10 minutes　**COOK:** 11 minutes

Makes 8 piglets

1 (4-ounce) can refrigerated crescent rolls (4 rolls)
4 teaspoons shredded cheese of your choice
8 (2-inch) cocktail beef frankfurters
½ cup store-bought or homemade (page 455) mustard (optional)

1. Preheat the oven to 375°F. Line a baking sheet with foil. Unroll the dough, separate the 2 rectangles, and place on a cutting board. Squish the perforations together to seal. Cut each rectangle crosswise into 4 equal-size rectangles. Arrange ½ teaspoon cheese lengthwise down the center of each rectangle, leaving a ½-inch border all around. Place a frankfurter at one end and roll up in the dough, lightly pressing the dough as you roll to seal in the frankfurter and the cheese.

2. Place the piglets on the prepared baking sheet with the seam sides down. Bake until browned, 11 to 13 minutes. Let cool 5 minutes. Serve with mustard for dipping, if you like.

HERBED BUTTER POPCORN

PREP: 5 minutes   COOK: 3 minutes

Makes 4 cups (4 servings)

4 cups freshly popped popcorn

½ teaspoon salt

1 tablespoon unsalted butter

1 tablespoon corn oil or extra-virgin olive oil

½ teaspoon cumin

¼ teaspoon cayenne

1 tablespoon finely chopped fresh cilantro

Place the popcorn in a large bowl and sprinkle with the salt. Toss to coat. Melt the butter in the oil in a small skillet over medium-high heat. Add the cumin and cook, stirring, until fragrant, about 30 seconds. Stir in the cayenne. Pour the mixture over the popcorn. Toss to coat. Add the cilantro and toss to mix.

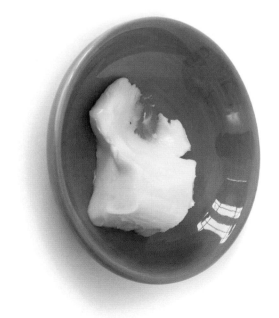

COCKTAIL NUT MIX

PREP: 10 minutes   COOK: 1 hour 10 minutes

Makes 4 cups (16 servings)

The nut mixture can be stored in a covered container for up to 1 month.

1 egg white

1 tablespoon water

2 cups (8 ounces) pecan halves

2 cups (8 ounces) lightly salted cashews

½ cup sugar

1 tablespoon ground cumin

2 teaspoons kosher salt

1¼ teaspoons cayenne

1 teaspoon ground cinnamon

1. Preheat the oven to 250°F. Line a rimmed baking sheet with parchment paper. Whisk the egg white and water until blended in a large bowl. Add the pecans and cashews and toss to coat.

2. Combine the sugar, cumin, salt, cayenne, and cinnamon in a small bowl and mix well. Add the sugar mixture to the nut mixture and toss to coat. Spread on the prepared baking sheet and bake 40 minutes.

3. Stir the nuts with a fork. Reduce the oven temperature to 200°F and bake 30 minutes longer. Stir the nuts again and cool in the pan on a wire rack.

SPICED PECANS

PREP: 10 minutes   COOK: 20 minutes

Makes 4 cups (16 servings)

1 tablespoon canola or grapeseed oil

4 teaspoons Worcestershire sauce

2 teaspoons ground cumin

2 teaspoons ground coriander

1 teaspoon chili powder

1 teaspoon fine sea salt

1/8 teaspoon cayenne

1 pound pecan halves

1. Preheat the oven to 300°F. Line a baking sheet with parchment paper. Combine the oil, Worcestershire sauce, cumin, coriander, chili powder, salt, and cayenne in a medium bowl and mix until blended. Add the pecans and toss well to coat.

2. Spread the pecans on the prepared baking sheet. Bake until crisp and fragrant, about 20 minutes, stirring after 10 minutes. Let cool and store in jars.

FRIED CANDIED NUTS

PREP: 25 minutes plus standing   COOK: 2 minutes

Makes 1½ cups (6 servings)

1½ cups walnut or pecan halves
½ cup sugar
Vegetable oil for frying

1. Place the nuts in a heat-safe bowl and add 3 cups
boiling water. Let cool slightly. Peel off the walnut skins,
keeping the cleaned nuts soaking.

2. Drain the nuts and place in a clean bowl. Add the
sugar and toss to coat. Spread out on a parchment-lined
baking sheet and leave until completely dry, stirring
occasionally, about 8 hours or overnight.

3. Heat about ½ inch oil in a deep, heavy, large skillet
over medium heat until hot but not smoking. Add the
nuts and fry, gently stirring, until the sugar caramelizes,
about 2 minutes (watch carefully and be prepared to
remove the skillet from the heat if the nuts get too hot).
Transfer the nuts to a parchment-lined baking sheet and
let cool, then transfer to a paper towel–lined baking
sheet to drain.

MAPLE-GLAZED MIXED NUTS

PREP: 10 minutes COOK: 1 hour 20 minutes
Makes 2 1/2 cups (10 servings)

¼ cup spiced, dark, or light rum, or bourbon
¼ cup pure maple syrup
3 tablespoons unsalted butter
1 pound salted mixed nuts

1. Preheat the oven to 250°F. Line a baking sheet with parchment paper. Combine the rum, syrup, and butter in a medium saucepan and heat to boiling over high heat, stirring constantly. Reduce heat to medium and simmer, stirring, for 1 minute. Remove the pan from the heat. Stir the nuts into the syrup to coat evenly. Spread out and separate the nuts on the prepared baking sheet using a fork. Drizzle with any remaining glaze.
2. Bake until toasted, 1 hour and 15 minutes, stirring every 20 minutes. Stir the nuts to make sure they are not sticking together. Cool completely. Store in an airtight container for up to 2 weeks.

PROVOLONE-PISTACHIO CRISPS

1 pound aged Provolone cheese, coarsely shredded

½ cup chopped pistachio nuts

Mound 6 tablespoon-size portions of cheese in a large nonstick skillet over medium-high heat; sprinkle each with pistachios. Cook until the cheese melts and sets, about 1 minute. Turn with a flexible spatula and cook until crisp on the other side, about 1 minute. Transfer to a paper towel–lined baking sheet to drain. Wipe out the skillet with a paper towel and repeat with the remaining cheese and pistachios.

TRAIL MIX

PREP: 5 minutes

Makes 9 cups (16 servings)

1 cup dried pineapple chunks
1 cup dried mango chunks
1 cup dried blueberries
1 cup dried cranberries
1 cup salted hulled sunflower seeds
1 cup semisweet chocolate chips or carob chips
1 cup shelled almonds
1 cup salted peanuts
1 cup coconut flakes

Combine all the ingredients in a large bowl and mix well.

BAKED PEPPERONI CHIPS

PREP: 5 minutes COOK: 20 minutes

Makes 12 servings

½ pound pepperoni or other spicy salami, thinly sliced

1. Preheat the oven to 350°F. Line 2 large rimmed baking sheets with parchment; arrange one-fourth of the pepperoni in a single layer on each. Cover with additional sheets of parchment and the remaining pepperoni. Cover with more parchment. Bake until the pepperoni is sizzling and the fat is rendered, about 20 minutes.

2. Transfer the chips to a paper towel–lined rack placed over a baking sheet and cover with paper towels to blot up the grease. Remove the paper towels and allow the pepperoni to cool on the racks until crisp.

TWICE-FRIED PLANTAIN CHIPS

PREP: 10 minutes   COOK: 4 minutes per batch

Makes 2 servings

1 green plantain

2 cups vegetable oil

½ teaspoon salt or more to taste

⅛ teaspoon freshly ground black pepper
or more to taste

1. Peel the plantain and cut crosswise into 1-inch-thick rounds.

2. Heat the oil in a small saucepan until hot but not smoking. Add the plantain rounds 3 or 4 at a time and fry until lightly browned, 2 to 3 minutes. Transfer with tongs to a paper towel–lined baking sheet to drain.

3. When cool enough to handle, working with one at a time with a rolling pin or the heel of your hand, flatten the rounds as much as possible without tearing.

4. Reheat the oil. Add the plantain chips 3 or 4 at a time and fry again until golden brown, about 2 minutes. Transfer the plantains to another paper towel–lined baking sheet and sprinkle with the salt and pepper. Taste and add more salt and pepper if needed. Serve hot or at room temperature.

ZUCCHINI CHIPS WITH FRIED SAGE

PREP: 10 minutes   COOK: 2 minutes per batch

Makes 4 servings

4 cups corn oil

½ cup all-purpose flour

½ cup fine yellow cornmeal

½ teaspoon kosher salt

¼ teaspoon freshly ground black pepper

8 ounces green zucchini, sliced diagonally
   into paper-thin rounds

8 ounces yellow zucchini, sliced diagonally
   into paper-thin rounds

14 large fresh sage leaves

3 tablespoons finely chopped fresh flat-leaf parsley

1 garlic clove, crushed through a press

1 lemon, cut into wedges

1. Heat the corn oil in a large, heavy saucepan over medium heat to 350°F on a deep-fat thermometer. Place a paper towel–lined wire rack over a baking sheet.

2. While the oil is heating, combine the flour, cornmeal, salt, and pepper in a plastic zip-top bag, seal, and shake to mix. Add the zucchini rounds, one-fourth at a time, and coat with flour by shaking in the bag. Shake off excess flour.

3. In batches, add the rounds to the hot oil and fry until deep golden brown and crisp, about 2 minutes. Adjust the heat as necessary so the oil stays at 350°F. Transfer the zucchini to the paper towel–lined rack to drain. Add the sage leaves to the oil and fry until crisp; drain with the zucchini. Mix the parsley and garlic in a cup and sprinkle over the zucchini and sage; toss to mix. Serve with the lemon for squeezing.

SMOKY SWEET POTATO CHIPS

PREP: 10 minutes   COOK: 3 minutes per batch

Makes 16 servings

Vegetable oil for frying

3 (1-pound) sweet potatoes or yams, peeled

1 tablespoon kosher salt

1 teaspoon bittersweet Spanish paprika or other paprika

⅛ teaspoon cayenne

1. Heat 2 inches vegetable oil over medium heat to 365°F on a deep-fat thermometer.

2. While the oil is heating, cut the potatoes crosswise or lengthwise into ¹⁄₁₆-inch thick slices (a mandoline is the best tool for this job).

3. Preheat the oven to 250°F. In batches, add the potato slices to the oil and fry, turning frequently with tongs, until browned, about 3 minutes. Allow the oil to return to temperature between batches. Transfer the fried potatoes to paper towel–lined baking sheets to drain; immediately sprinkle with some salt, paprika, and cayenne. Keep the fried potatoes warm in the oven while frying the remaining potatoes.

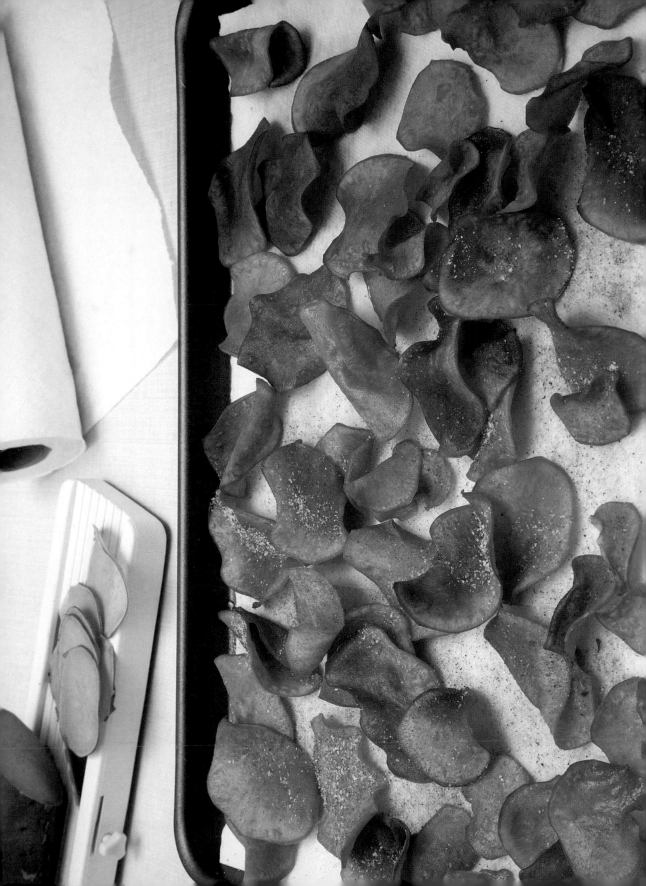

SESAME EDAMAME

PREP: 10 minutes   COOK: 8 minutes

Makes 8 servings

1 (16-ounce) package frozen shelled edamame
  (green soybeans)
1 tablespoon toasted white sesame seeds
1 tablespoon black sesame seeds
1 teaspoon fine sea salt

Cook the edamame as the package label directs. Drain in a colander and rinse until cold under running cold water. Place on a clean kitchen towel and roll up, jelly-roll fashion, to blot the water. Place the edamame in a serving bowl and sprinkle with the white and black sesame seeds and the salt. Toss to coat. Serve immediately with a spoon to scoop them up to be eaten out-of-hand.

Boiled Edamame Pods

Boil 2 pounds edamame in the pods in 2 quarts water salted with 2 tablespoons sea salt until tender, 7 to 10 minutes, depending on how tender you like your edamame. Drain in a colander and rinse until cold under cold running water to set the green color. Sprinkle with kosher salt. To eat, break open the pods with your fingers and pop the soybeans into your mouth.

BREADS, PIZZAS & TARTS

CROSTINI THREE WAYS

*1 loaf crusty Italian bread or 1 French baguette,
sliced into ½-inch-thick slices (about 36 slices)*

¼ cup extra-virgin olive oil, or more if needed

Grill-Pan Crostini

Heat a grill pan over medium-high heat. Arrange the
bread slices on the pan with cut side down and grill until
browned and crisp, about 4 minutes. While bread grills,
brush the tops with the oil. Turn and grill the crostini
until pale golden and crisp, about 5 minutes.

Baked Crostini

Preheat the oven to 400°F. Arrange the bread slices on 2
heavy large baking sheets. Brush the oil on the tops.
Bake until pale golden and crisp, about 15 minutes.

Garlic Crostini

After grilling or baking, rub each crostini with the cut
sides of halved garlic cloves.

LAMB AND ARUGULA CROSTINI

PREP: 10 minutes

Makes 18 crostini

18 slices Crostini (page 166)

Spicy Mixed-Olive Mayonnaise (page 22)

2 cups arugula leaves

1 pound medium-rare roasted lamb, thinly sliced

½ teaspoon kosher salt

¼ teaspoon freshly ground black pepper

Arrange the crostini on a work surface and spread one side with mayonnaise. Top with the arugula and then the lamb. Sprinkle with salt and pepper and serve.

STEAK CROSTINI WITH ONION CONFIT

PREP: 10 minutes

Makes 18 crostini

18 slices Crostini (page 166)
1 pound medium-rare boneless sirloin steak,
   thinly sliced
Onion Confit (below)

Arrange the crostini on a work surface and top with
the steak. Spoon some confit on top and serve.

Onion Confit

PREP: 5 minutes   COOK: 36 minutes

Makes about 1½ cups

2 tablespoons unsalted butter
2 large red onions, halved lengthwise
   and thinly sliced crosswise
2 tablespoons sugar

½ cup golden raisins
1 tablespoon balsamic vinegar
1 teaspoon salt or more to taste
½ teaspoon freshly ground black pepper

Melt the butter in a large skillet over medium heat and
add the onions. Cover and cook, stirring occasionally,
until the onions are softened, about 15 minutes. Add
the sugar and cook, stirring frequently, until soft and
lightly browned, 10 to 15 minutes. Stir in the raisins,
vinegar, salt, and pepper and cook until most of the
liquid has evaporated, about 10 minutes. Taste and add
more salt if needed.

MUSHROOM CROSTINI

PREP: 10 minutes
Makes 36 crostini

Mixed Mushroom Pesto (page 428)
Crostini (page 166)

Spread the mushroom pesto over the crostini. Arrange on a platter and serve.

PANCETTA, BASIL, AND TOMATO JAM CROSTINI

PREP: 10 minutes

Makes 36 crostini

Crostini (page 166)
Tomato Jam (page 17)
4 (¼-inch thick) slices pancetta
 or slab bacon, diced, sautéed until crisp
½ cup finely shredded basil leaves

Spread the crostini generously with the jam and sprinkle with the pancetta and basil.

CHÈVRE AND CARROT CROSTINI

PREP: 10 minutes

Makes 36 crostini

Crostini (page 166)
8 ounces fresh goat's milk cheese (chèvre)
Ginger–Carrot Spread (page 15)
36 whole blanched almonds, toasted

Spread the crostini generously with the cheese and spoon
the carrot mixture on top, leaving a border of the cheese
exposed. Top each with a toasted almond.

PARTY GARLIC-CHEESE LOAF

PREP: 10 minutes COOK: 8 minutes

Makes 16 pieces

1 (10-ounce) loaf Italian bread
¼ cup (½ stick) unsalted butter
3 garlic cloves, crushed through a press
¼ teaspoon red pepper flakes
2 tablespoons chopped flat-leaf parsley
½ teaspoon dried oregano leaves, crushed
8 ounces mozzarella cheese, shredded

1. Preheat the oven to 400°F. Cut the bread lengthwise in half using a serrated knife; place on an aluminum-foil lined baking sheet.

2. Melt the butter in a small skillet over medium-high heat and add the garlic. Sauté until sizzling and fragrant, 1 minute. Add the pepper flakes and cook until sizzling.

3. Remove the pan from the heat and stir in the parsley and oregano. Brush the mixture over the cut sides of the bread and sprinkle with the cheese. Bake the bread on the middle rack until the cheese melts and the bread is hot, 5 to 8 minutes. Transfer to a cutting board and cut crosswise into slices.

BREAD STICKS

PREP: 25 minutes COOK: 20 minutes

Makes 24 bread sticks

1 cup warm water (115°F)

1 envelope quick-acting dry yeast

2 tablespoons honey

1 tablespoon canola oil, plus more for brushing

1 teaspoon table salt

3 to 3½ cups all-purpose flour, plus more if needed

Kosher salt for sprinkling

1. Grease two large baking sheets. Place the water in a large bowl and sprinkle the yeast on top; let stand until bubbly. Stir to dissolve. Add the honey, oil, and table salt and stir until the salt dissolves. Stir in 3 cups flour. Stir in up to ½ cup more flour as needed to make a firm, not sticky, dough.

2. Coat the work surface and your hands with flour. Pinch off 24 equal-size pieces of the dough (about the size of a walnut) and roll each into a cylinder. Roll each cylinder into a thin rope and place on the prepared baking sheets.

3. Place the baking sheet in a cold oven and turn it on to 350°F. Bake 10 minutes. Brush the bread sticks with additional oil and sprinkle with kosher salt. Bake the bread sticks until they are browned and crusty, about 10 minutes longer. Serve warm or at room temperature.

EASY ONION BREAD STICKS

PREP: 10 minutes   COOK: 15 minutes

Makes 8 servings

1 (11-ounce) can refrigerated soft bread sticks
3 tablespoons dehydrated minced onion
1 ½ teaspoons Italian herb seasoning
½ teaspoon lemon pepper
1 egg white, lightly beaten

1. Preheat the oven to 350°F. Line a baking sheet with parchment paper. Unroll the bread stick dough and separate into 8 strips. Twist the strips and place 1 inch apart on the prepared baking sheet. Combine the onion, herb seasoning, and lemon pepper in a cup and mix well. Brush each bread stick with egg white and sprinkle with the onion mixture.

2. Bake until lightly browned, about 15 minutes.

STEAMED CHINESE BUNS

PREP: 50 minutes   COOK: 15 minutes

Makes 15 buns

¼ cup sugar

¾ cup warm water (110°F)

1 envelope quick-rising dry yeast

2 tablespoons vegetable oil or dark sesame oil

2 ½ cups all-purpose flour

1. In a glass measure, dissolve the sugar in the water. Add the yeast, and stir to dissolve. Let mixture stand until bubbly. Stir in the oil.

2. Place the flour in a food processor and, with the motor running, pour the yeast mixture through the feed tube. Process until a dough forms, and allow the ball of dough to bounce around (kneading it) for about 60 seconds.

3. Transfer the dough to a lightly floured work surface and knead a few turns. Form the dough into a long roll and cut crosswise into 14 pieces. Place the pieces cut side down on the work surface and flatten lightly. For each piece, pull the edges underneath so the top is smooth, place on a 2-inch square of waxed paper, and set on a baking sheet. Let rise 30 minutes.

4. Carefully transfer the buns to stackable bamboo steamer baskets. Place the baskets in a wok with 1 inch of boiling water set over high heat. Cover and steam for 15 minutes.

WONTON CRISPS

PREP: 5 minutes   COOK: 1 minute per batch

Makes 12 servings

Vegetable oil for frying
12 small wonton wrappers
1 teaspoon fine sea salt

1. Line 2 baking sheets with paper towels. Heat 1 inch of oil to 370°F in a deep, heavy skillet over medium-high heat.

2. In batches, add the wonton wrappers to the hot oil and fry until crisp and golden brown on both sides, about 1 minute. Transfer to the prepared baking sheets and sprinkle immediately with salt.

CORNMEAL CRISPS

PREP: 15 minutes   COOK: 18 minutes

Makes about 72 crisps

1 cup yellow cornmeal

2 tablespoons unsalted butter

1 tablespoon sugar

½ teaspoon salt

1 cup boiling water

3 green onions, trimmed and minced

1 to 2 jalapeño chile peppers
    (taste to make sure they are hot),
    minced (wear gloves when handling)

¾ cup (3 ounces) shredded cheddar cheese

1 tablespoon chopped fresh red pepper
    or jarred pimiento (optional)

1. Preheat the oven to 425°F. Line baking sheets with parchment paper. Combine the cornmeal, butter, sugar, and salt in a heat-safe bowl. Add the boiling water, stirring until the butter melts and the mixture is smooth. Stir in the green onions, jalapeños, cheese, and red pepper (if using) until well mixed.

2. Drop level teaspoonfuls of the batter 1 inch apart on the prepared baking sheets. With a spatula, flatten each round. Bake until golden and slightly brown around the edges, about 18 minutes.

CHILE-CORNMEAL CRACKERS

PREP: 25 minutes   COOK: 11 minutes

Makes about 32 crackers

1 cup yellow cornmeal

1 teaspoon chili powder

1 teaspoon ground cumin

½ teaspoon baking powder

½ teaspoon table salt

2 tablespoons unsalted butter, softened

1 cup boiling water

1¼ cups all-purpose flour, plus more if needed

Kosher salt for sprinkling

1. Preheat the oven to 425°F. Combine the cornmeal, chili powder, cumin, baking powder, and table salt in a large bowl and mix well. Add the butter and boiling water, stirring with a fork until smooth. Let stand 10 minutes.

2. Stir the flour into the dough using a wooden spoon, adding enough additional flour if needed to make a firm, but not sticky, ball of dough.

3. Divide the dough in half. On a sheet of parchment, roll out one piece of dough to a ⅟₁₆-inch thickness. Trim the edges with a pizza cutter or knife; score the dough into 1½-inch squares or as desired. Sprinkle lightly with kosher salt and transfer the paper and dough to a baking sheet. Repeat with the remaining dough.

4. Bake until lightly browned, about 7 minutes. Turn the crackers with a spatula and bake until lightly browned on top, 4 to 5 minutes longer. Transfer the crackers to wire racks to cool. If crackers are not crisp after cooling, bake a little longer, but not enough to brown them too much.

WALNUT CRACKERS

PREP: 20 minutes   COOK: 11 minutes

Makes about 2 dozen crackers

2 eggs
1 cup all-purpose flour
½ teaspoon baking powder
¼ teaspoon salt
1 cup coarsely ground walnuts

1. Preheat the oven to 350°F. Line a baking sheet with parchment paper. Place the eggs in a medium bowl and whisk until frothy. In another bowl, mix the flour, baking powder, and salt; add to the eggs along with the walnuts. Stir with a wooden spoon until the dough is blended and stiff.

2. On a lightly floured cutting board, roll out the dough to a ¹⁄₁₆-inch thickness. Cut out shapes with a 2-inch cookie cutter. Place on the prepared baking sheet. Press the scraps together, reroll, and cut out more shapes.

3. Bake the crackers until set, 7 minutes. Turn crackers over and bake until lightly browned, 4 to 6 minutes longer. Cool on wire racks.

CREAM CRACKERS

PREP: **20 minutes** COOK: **14 minutes**

Makes about 3½ dozen crackers

2 cups cake flour

1½ teaspoons sugar

1 teaspoon salt

1 teaspoon baking powder

⅔ cup heavy cream, plus more if needed

1. Preheat the oven to 350°F. Line baking sheets with parchment paper. In a large bowl, combine the flour, sugar, salt, and baking powder; stir with a fork to mix. Slowly add the cream, stirring until a dough forms. Stir in 1 to 2 tablespoons additional cream if the dough is crumbly.

2. Turn out the dough onto a lightly floured cutting board; knead 2 to 3 turns to form a ball. Roll the dough to an ⅛-inch thickness. Cut out shapes with a 3-inch round cookie cutter. Prick each round twice with a fork and place on the prepared baking sheets. Press scraps together, reroll, and cut out more shapes. Prick and place on the prepared baking sheets.

3. Bake the crackers for 8 minutes. Turn the crackers over and bake until golden brown on the edges, 6 to 8 minutes longer. Cool crackers on wire racks.

SESAME-RICE CRISPS

Vegetable oil for frying
10 Vietnamese rice spring-roll skins
1 tablespoon Japanese sesame-seed
  chili-pepper seasoning (gomashio)
½ teaspoon fine sea salt

1. Line 2 baking sheets with paper towels. Heat 1 inch of oil to 370°F in a deep, heavy skillet over medium-high heat.

2. Break the spring-roll skins into irregular shapes about 2 inches across. In batches, fry the pieces in the hot oil until evenly puffed, about 20 seconds. Transfer to the prepared baking sheets, and sprinkle immediately with some *gomashio* and salt.

CHEESE WAFERS

1½ cups all-purpose flour

½ cup (2 ounces) freshly grated Parmigiano-Reggiano
cheese

¼ teaspoon salt

½ cup (1 stick) unsalted butter,
cut into small pieces and frozen

1 egg

2 tablespoons milk

½ cup (2 ounces) shredded extra-sharp cheddar cheese

¼ cup chopped walnuts

2 tablespoons chopped fresh flat-leaf parsley

1. Combine the flour, Parmigiano-Reggiano, and salt in a food processor and pulse to mix. Add the butter and pulse until the flour resembles coarse meal. Beat the egg and milk in a cup until blended; pour the egg mixture over the flour mixture. Add the cheddar cheese. Process just until the mixture starts to come away from the side of the bowl.

2. Scrape the dough onto a floured work surface and divide in half. Shape each half into a 5-inch log. Place the walnuts on a sheet of waxed paper and the parsley on another sheet of waxed paper. Roll one log in the walnuts to coat and roll the other log in the parsley to coat. Wrap the logs separately in plastic wrap and refrigerate 2 hours or freeze 1 hour, until the dough is firm.

3. Preheat the oven to 400°F. Line baking sheets with parchment paper. Place the dough logs on a cutting board and cut each log crosswise into ¼-inch-thick rounds. Place the rounds 1 inch apart on the prepared baking sheets.

4. Bake until the edges are browned, about 12 minutes. With a pancake turner, carefully transfer the wafers to a wire rack to cool.

PARMESAN KNOTS AND RINGS

PREP: 15 minutes   COOK: 15 minutes

Makes about 44 knots and rings

For different flavors, add 1 tablespoon caraway, fennel, or sesame seeds to the dough along with the cheese.

1 (16-ounce) package hot-roll mix

1¼ cups hot water

½ cup (2 ounces) grated Parmigiano-Reggiano cheese

3 tablespoons extra-virgin olive oil

1. Preheat the oven to 375°F. Lightly spray 2 large baking sheets with nonstick cooking spray.

2. Prepare the roll mix as the package label directs, adding the hot water, cheese, and olive oil to the dough.

3. Divide the dough in half. On a lightly floured work surface, roll each piece of dough into an 11-inch rope; cut crosswise into ½-inch-thick pieces. Roll each length into a 6-inch rope. Tie half the ropes into knots and shape the other half into rings, pinching the ends together.

4. Place the knots and rings on the prepared baking sheets. Bake until golden brown, about 15 minutes.

PUMPKIN-GINGER BISCUITS

PREP: 25 minutes   COOK: 15 minutes

Makes about 36 biscuits

2½ cups all-purpose flour

1 tablespoon baking powder

1 teaspoon salt

¼ teaspoon Chinese five-spice powder
   or ground allspice

2½ tablespoons brown sugar

½ cup (1 stick) unsalted butter,
   cut into small pieces and frozen

1 (15-ounce) can unsweetened pumpkin puree

2 teaspoons grated orange zest

1 cup finely diced crystallized ginger

2 tablespoons heavy cream

1. Preheat the oven to 400°F. Line a baking sheet with parchment paper. Combine the flour, baking powder, salt, and five-spice powder in a food processor and pulse to mix. Add the brown sugar and pulse to mix. Add the butter and pulse until the flour resembles coarse meal. Add the pumpkin and orange zest and process until smooth (do not overmix). Add the ginger and pulse to mix.

2. Scrape the dough out onto a floured work surface and pat into a ½-inch thickness. Cut out shapes with a 2-inch round cookie cutter and place on the prepared baking sheet. Gather scraps together, reroll, and cut out more shapes. Brush the tops with the cream.

3. Bake the biscuits until the tops are lightly browned, about 15 minutes.

CHEESEY BUTTERMILK BISCUITS

PREP: **20 minutes**   COOK: **10 minutes**

Makes about 16 biscuits

The biscuits can also be made without the cheese.

1¾ cups all-purpose flour

2 teaspoons baking powder

1 teaspoon sugar

½ teaspoon salt

½ teaspoon baking soda

½ cup (1 stick) unsalted butter, cut into pieces and frozen

½ cup (2 ounces) shredded cheddar cheese

¾ cup buttermilk

1. Preheat the oven to 425°F. Line a baking sheet with parchment paper. Combine the flour, baking powder, sugar, salt, and baking soda in a food processor and pulse to combine. Add the butter and process until the mixture resembles coarse meal. Add the cheese and drizzle with the buttermilk. Process just until the mixture forms a dough.

2. Scrape out the dough onto a lightly floured work surface. Knead gently 8 times. Roll out or pat to a ⅓-inch thickness. Cut out shapes with a floured 2-inch round cookie cutter. Press the dough scraps together and cut out more shapes.

3. Place the biscuits on the prepared baking sheet. Bake until golden brown, 10 to 12 minutes.

GREEN ONION FLAT BREAD

3 cups sifted all-purpose flour

1 cup water

1½ teaspoons dark sesame oil, plus more for brushing

10 to 15 green onions, trimmed and finely chopped

1 teaspoon salt

Vegetable oil for frying

1. In a medium bowl, mix the flour, water, and sesame oil to make a stiff dough. Cover the bowl and let stand 30 minutes.

2. Turn out the dough onto a work surface and knead 2 minutes. Twist the dough to divide in half. Roll out one half to a ¼-inch thickness and brush with sesame oil. Sprinkle with half the green onions and ½ teaspoon of the salt. Bring the edges together in the center and pinch to seal, making sure there is no air trapped inside.

Turn the dough over and roll lightly to about a ⅓-inch thickness. Repeat with the remaining dough, green onions, and salt.

3. Heat ¼ inch oil in a large skillet over medium-high heat until hot but not smoking. Place a piece of rolled dough in the oil with the smoother side down. Fry until well browned and crisp on the bottom, about 1½ minutes. Carefully turn over, and fry until browned and crisp on the other side, about 1½ minutes longer. Drain on a paper towel–lined wire rack. Repeat with the remaining bread.

4. Place the flat breads on a cutting board and cut each into 8 wedges.

TENDER CREAM BISCUITS

PREP: 20 minutes   COOK: 10 minutes

Makes about 16 biscuits

2¼ cups all-purpose flour
1 tablespoon baking powder
2¼ teaspoons salt
1¾ cups heavy cream, chilled

1. Preheat the oven to 425°F. Line a baking sheet with parchment paper. Combine the flour, baking powder, and salt in a medium bowl and mix well. Make a well in the center and add the cream. Stir just until a dough forms. Turn out onto a lightly floured work surface. Roll out or pat to a ⅓-inch thickness. Cut out shapes with a floured 2-inch round cookie cutter. Press the dough scraps together and cut out more shapes.

2. Place the biscuits on the prepared baking sheet. Bake until golden brown, 10 to 12 minutes.

MINI POPOVERS

PREP: 10 minutes   COOK: 12 minutes

Makes 30 to 32 popovers

Serve with butter and jam or sprinkle with confectioners' sugar passed through a sieve. Popovers also make a great container for hot and cold fillings.

2 eggs
1 cup milk
1 cup sifted all-purpose flour
1 tablespoon melted unsalted butter
¼ teaspoon salt

1. Preheat the oven to 450°F. Generously grease thirty 5-ounce muffin pan cups.

2. Combine the eggs, milk, flour, butter, and salt in a blender and blend just until combined (do not overmix). Fill the prepared muffin cups one-half full with batter. If there is leftover batter, grease one or two additional muffin cups and fill one-half full with batter.

3. Bake until crisp and browned, about 12 minutes. Turn out the popovers onto a wire rack and make a little slit in the bottom of each to release the steam. Serve immediately.

Cheddar Popovers

Stir ¾ cup (3 ounces) shredded cheddar cheese into the batter before filling the cups.

Parmesan Popovers

Stir ½ cup (2 ounces) grated Parmigiano-Reggiano cheese into the batter before filling the cups.

Bacon–Green Onion Popovers

Stir 4 slices crumbled cooked bacon and 1 minced green onion into the batter before filling the cups.

DOUBLE-TOMATO BRUSCHETTA

PREP: 25 minutes   COOK: 8 minutes

Makes about 36 bruschetta

5 sun-dried tomato halves (not in oil)

½ cup lightly packed basil leaves

½ cup olive oil

6 ripe plum tomatoes, seeded and diced

2½ ounces smoked mozzarella cheese,
    cut into ¼-inch dice

2 tablespoons red wine vinegar

¼ teaspoon salt

1 (1-pound) loaf Italian bread,
    cut diagonally into ½-inch-thick slices

1. Preheat the oven to 350°F. To make the tomato-basil
oil: Place the dried tomatoes in a heat-safe bowl and add
½ cup boiling water. Let soak 5 minutes. Drain, pat dry,
and mince. Mince half the basil leaves. In a small bowl,
combine the minced basil and minced dried tomatoes.
Add ¼ cup of the olive oil and mix well. Set aside.

2. Stack the remaining basil leaves and thinly slice crosswise into shreds. Place in a medium bowl and add the
remaining ¼ cup olive oil, the fresh tomatoes, cheese,
vinegar, and salt. Mix well.

3. Brush the bread slices on both sides with the tomato-
basil oil. Arrange the bread on a baking sheet. Bake until
golden and crisp, 8 to 10 minutes. Top with the fresh-
tomato mixture and serve immediately.

SAGE-CREAMED CORN BRUSCHETTA

PREP: 10 minutes   COOK: 25 minutes

Makes about 36 bruschetta

1 cup heavy cream

6 fresh sage leaves

2 garlic cloves, crushed through a press

2 teaspoons olive oil

2 green onions, thinly sliced

2 cups fresh corn

1 red pepper, diced

½ teaspoon salt

¼ teaspoon freshly ground pepper

1 (1-pound) loaf Italian bread,
cut diagonally into ½-inch-thick slices

1. Preheat the oven to 350°F. Combine the cream, sage, and garlic in a small saucepan and heat to simmering over medium heat. Simmer until the cream is reduced by half; set aside.

2. Heat the olive oil in a medium skillet over medium-high heat. Add the green onions and sauté 1 minute. Add the corn and red pepper and sauté until tender, about 5 minutes. Strain the cream mixture through a sieve into the corn. Stir in the salt and pepper and simmer until only a little liquid remains.

3. While the mixture cooks, arrange the bread on a baking sheet. Bake until golden and crisp, 8 to 10 minutes.

4. Spoon the corn mixture over the toasts and serve immediately.

CELERY AND ROASTED PEPPER BRUSCHETTA

PREP: 10 minutes   COOK: 8 minutes

Makes 36 bruschetta

1 (1-pound) loaf Italian bread,
   cut diagonally into ½-inch-thick slices
1 large garlic clove, cut in half
Roasted-Pepper Parmigiano-Reggiano Spread (page 16)
Extra-virgin olive oil for drizzling
½ cup celery leaves and innermost stalks
   and heart, finely chopped

1. Preheat the oven to 350°F. Arrange the bread on a baking sheet. Bake until golden and crisp, 8 to 10 minutes. Rub the cut side of garlic over one side of each toast.

2. Coat the garlic side of the breads with the pepper-cheese spread and drizzle with olive oil. Garnish with the celery and serve.

BRUSSELS SPROUTS AND BACON BRUSCHETTA

1 (1-pound) loaf Italian bread,
    cut diagonally into ½-inch-thick slices

1 large garlic clove, cut in half

4 slices bacon, cooked until crisp and crumbled

2 cups shredded cooked Brussels sprouts

1 cup (4 ounces) shredded Gouda cheese

1. Preheat the oven to 350°F. Arrange the bread on a baking sheet. Bake until golden and crisp on both sides, 8 to 10 minutes. Rub the cut side of the garlic over one side of each toast.

2. Combine the bacon and sprouts in a bowl and mix well. Sprinkle the mixture over the garlic toasts, dividing evenly, and sprinkle with the cheese.

3. Return to the oven and bake until very hot, about 5 minutes. Serve on plates or with thick napkins.

EASY OLIVE FOCACCIA

PREP: 10 minutes   COOK: 16 minutes

Makes 6 servings

Cornmeal for sprinkling
1 (10-ounce) package refrigerated pizza dough
1 tablespoon olive oil
1 large red onion, sliced
¼ cup Kalamata olives, pitted and slivered
1 tablespoon finely chopped fresh rosemary leaves
¼ teaspoon kosher salt
¼ teaspoon freshly ground black pepper

1. Grease a baking sheet with nonstick cooking spray and sprinkle with cornmeal. Unroll the pizza dough and, following the package directions for thin crust, spread to the edges of the prepared pan.

2. Heat the oil in a small skillet over medium heat. Add the onion and sauté until softened, 6 to 8 minutes.

Stir in the olives and rosemary. Spread the mixture over the pizza dough and sprinkle with the salt and pepper.

3. Bake until golden, 10 to 12 minutes.

4. Slide the focaccia onto a cutting board and cut into irregular-size pieces with a pizza cutter or kitchen shears.

Bacon-Spinach Focaccia

Thaw 1 (10-ounce) package chopped spinach and squeeze dry. Sprinkle the spinach and 1 cup chopped Canadian bacon over the pizza dough instead of the olives and rosemary. Sprinkle with ¼ teaspoon garlic salt instead of the kosher salt and then the pepper. Continue as recipe directs.

RED ONION FLAT BREAD

PREP: 15 minutes plus dough rising

COOK: 45 minutes

Makes 30 slices

4⅓ cups bread flour

2 tablespoons plus 1 teaspoon sugar

1 teaspoon salt

¼ cup lukewarm water (115°F)

1 envelope quick-acting dry yeast

1 egg, slightly beaten

1 cup lukewarm milk (about 115°F)

½ cup mayonnaise

4 tablespoons (½ stick) unsalted butter

1¼ cups thinly sliced red onions

2 tablespoons sesame seeds

½ teaspoon garlic salt

½ teaspoon paprika

1. Combine 2 cups of the flour, 2 tablespoons of the sugar, and the salt in a small bowl and mix well; set aside. Combine the water and the remaining 1 teaspoon sugar in a large bowl and sprinkle the yeast on top. Stir until the sugar and yeast dissolve; let stand in a warm place until the yeast is bubbly, about 5 minutes.

2. In another small bowl, whisk the egg, milk, and mayonnaise until blended. Stir into the yeast mixture. Stir in the flour mixture with a wooden spoon until smooth. Stir in just enough remaining flour to form a smooth, not sticky, dough. Turn out the dough onto a floured surface and knead until elastic and satiny, about 2 minutes.

3. Grease a 15- by 10-inch baking sheet and large bowl with 1 tablespoon of the butter. Add the dough to the bowl and turn over so the greased side is up. Cover with plastic wrap and let the dough rise until doubled in bulk, 45 to 60 minutes.

4. While the dough rises, melt the remaining 3 tablespoons butter in a large skillet over medium heat.

Transfer 1 tablespoon to a cup and set aside. Add the onions to the skillet and cook, stirring, until soft and translucent, about 9 minutes. Set aside to cool.

5. Preheat the oven to 375°F. Punch down the dough. Add ½ cup of the onions and knead in the bowl to mix. Turn out the dough onto a work surface and form into a ball. Roll out to a 15- by-10-inch rectangle and place on the prepared baking sheet. Brush the reserved 1 tablespoon melted butter over the dough, top with the remaining onions, and sprinkle with the sesame seeds, garlic salt, and paprika.

6. Bake until well browned, about 35 minutes. Slide bread onto a cutting board. With a pizza cutter or knife, cut the bread in half lengthwise and then crosswise into 1-inch-thick slices. Serve warm or cool.

POLENTA AND ASPARAGUS TART

PREP: 10 minutes   COOK: 10 minutes

Makes 12 servings

This recipe calls for thin asparagus, but you can use thicker asparagus if you prefer. For thicker asparagus be sure to blanch the tips in boiling water for 1 minute before using in the recipe. Rinse until cool and pat dry.

Baked Pastry Case (page 226)
2 cups milk
⅓ cup instant polenta
½ cup (2 ounces) shredded Italian fontina cheese
1 teaspoon minced fresh thyme
½ teaspoon salt
¼ teaspoon freshly ground black pepper
12 pencil-thin asparagus spears, top 2 inches only

1. Preheat the oven to 475°F. Place the baked pastry crust on a baking sheet.

2. Heat the milk to boiling in a medium saucepan over medium heat. Whisk in the polenta until smooth. Cook, whisking, until thickened, about 5 minutes. Whisk in the cheese, thyme, salt, and pepper. Spread the polenta in the pastry crust. Arrange the asparagus spears neatly in the polenta.

3. Bake the tart until the top is lightly browned, about 5 minutes. Slide the tart onto a cutting board. With a pizza cutter, cut into 12 pieces with an asparagus spear in each piece.

SUMMER BLT TART

Tart-Shell Shortcrust Pastry (page 228)

2 pounds firm, ripe plum tomatoes, each cut into 8 wedges

1 teaspoon salt

4 ounces pancetta, cut into ½-inch dice

2 shallots, finely chopped

1 cup fresh bread crumbs

½ cup (2 ounces) shredded Monterey Jack cheese with jalapeños

2 teaspoons dried oregano

4 outer leaves romaine lettuce or escarole, split in half lengthwise and cut crosswise into ½-inch strips

2 tablespoons extra-virgin olive oil

1. Line a large baking sheet with parchment paper. On a lightly floured surface, roll out the pastry to a ¼-inch-thick, 13- by 16-inch rectangle. Fold the pastry in half, and then in half again. Transfer to the prepared baking sheet. Unfold the pastry. Fold in 1 inch on all sides. Refrigerate the pastry until firm, at least 15 minutes.

2. Meanwhile, place tomatoes in a colander placed over a bowl and sprinkle with salt. Let drain 15 minutes.

3. Preheat the oven to 425°F. Sauté the pancetta in a large skillet over medium-high heat until the fat starts to render, about 6 minutes. Add the shallots and sauté until the pancetta is browned and crisp and the shallots are tender, about 6 minutes. Drain off all but 3 tablespoons drippings from pan. Add the bread crumbs and sauté until browned, about 3 minutes. Scrape the mixture into a bowl.

4. Dry the tomatoes with paper towels. Sprinkle half the bread crumb mixture over the bottom of the pastry shell; arrange the tomatoes on top with the skin sides down. Sprinkle with the remaining bread crumb mixture, then the cheese and oregano. Sprinkle with the lettuce and drizzle with the olive oil.

5. Bake until the pastry is cooked through, about 20 minutes.

BALSAMIC ONION AND OLIVE TART

3 large sweet onions, cut crosswise into ½-inch-thick rings

3 tablespoons olive oil

1 medium red pepper, thinly sliced

1 medium yellow pepper, thinly sliced

2 tablespoons balsamic vinegar

1 tablespoon brown sugar

1 (1-pound) package frozen puff pastry (2 sheets), thawed as package label directs

1 cup (4 ounces) shredded Italian fontina cheese

10 marinated sun-dried tomatoes, slivered

¼ cup oil-cured black olives, pitted and halved

¼ cup green olives, such as picholine, pitted and halved

2 tablespoons fresh oregano leaves or 2 teaspoons dried leaves

1. Preheat the oven to 400°F. Line 2 large, heavy baking sheets with parchment paper.

2. Combine the onions and oil in a large, heavy skillet over medium heat and cook, stirring, until the onions are softened, about 10 minutes. Add the red and yellow peppers and sauté until they are tender and the onions are golden, 5 to 10 minutes. Add the balsamic vinegar and brown sugar; cook, stirring, until sizzling, about 2 minutes. Scrape the vegetables onto a platter and let cool.

3. Roll out one pastry sheet on a lightly floured work surface to an ⅛-inch thickness. Transfer to a prepared baking sheet. Repeat with the second pastry sheet. Score the pastry sheets all over with a fork. Sprinkle each pastry sheet with half the cheese. Sprinkle the onion mixture evenly on top. Top with the tomatoes and black and green olives and then the oregano.

4. Bake until the pastry is cooked through and puffed, 20 to 25 minutes. Using the parchment, slide the tarts onto a cutting board. Slice into bite-size squares with a pizza cutter.

THREE-CHEESE BROCCOLI PIZZA

PREP: 10 minutes   COOK: 15 minutes

Makes 8 servings

Cornmeal for sprinkling

12 ounces store-bought pizza dough
   or Pizzetta/Pizza Dough (page 223)

½ cup ricotta cheese

¼ cup (2 ounces) grated Parmigiano-Reggiano cheese

1½ cups blanched fresh broccoli florets,
   or thawed frozen broccoli florets, dried

2 tablespoons sliced pitted black olives

1 cup (4 ounces) shredded Italian fontina cheese

1 teaspoon dried Italian-herb seasoning, crushed

1. Preheat the oven to 450°F. Spray a 12-inch pizza pan with nonstick cooking spray and sprinkle with cornmeal.

2. On a floured surface, roll out the pizza dough to a 13-inch round. Place in the prepared pan, fold the edge in ½ inch, and crimp. Spread the ricotta evenly on the dough. Sprinkle with half the Parmigiano-Reggiano and all the broccoli, olives, and fontina. Sprinkle with the remaining Parmigiano-Reggiano and the Italian seasoning.

3. Bake the pizza until crisp, about 15 minutes.

EASY EGGPLANT PIZZA

PREP: 25 minutes   COOK: 15 minutes

Makes 8 servings

1 small green zucchini, trimmed and shredded
   on the diagonal
1 small yellow zucchini, trimmed and shredded
   on the diagonal
1 teaspoon salt
Cornmeal for sprinkling
12 ounces store-bought pizza dough or Pizzetta/Pizza
   Dough (page 223)
¾ cup store-bought caponata or Farm-Stand
   Caponata (page 39)
1 cup (4 ounces) shredded mozzarella cheese

1. Preheat the oven to 450°F. Place the green and yellow zucchini in a bowl, sprinkle with the salt, and toss to coat. Let stand at least 10 minutes to sweat.

2. Meanwhile, spray a 12-inch pizza pan with nonstick cooking spray and sprinkle with cornmeal. On a floured surface, roll out the pizza dough to a 13-inch round. Place in the prepared pan, fold the edge in ½ inch, and crimp.

3. Rinse the salt off the zucchini and pat dry with paper towels. Spread the caponata evenly on the dough. Sprinkle evenly with the zucchini and then the mozzarella.

4. Bake the pizza until crisp, about 15 minutes.

HAM AND MUSHROOM PIZZA

PREP: 15 minutes   COOK: 15 minutes

Makes 8 servings

Cornmeal for sprinkling

12 ounces store-bought pizza dough or Pizzetta/Pizza
   Dough (page 223)

1 tablespoon extra-virgin olive oil

1 cup (4 ounces) shredded Emmenthaler
   or other Swiss cheese

1 cup sliced mushrooms

½ cup shredded baked ham

1 shallot, very thinly sliced crosswise into rings

1 tablespoon chopped fresh parsley

1. Preheat the oven to 450°F. Spray a 12-inch pizza pan
   with nonstick cooking spray and sprinkle with cornmeal.

2. On a floured surface, roll out the pizza dough to a
   13-inch round. Place in the prepared pan, fold the edge
   in ½ inch, and crimp. Brush the pizza with the oil and
   sprinkle with half the cheese. Sprinkle with the mushrooms, then the ham. Sprinkle with the remaining
   cheese, then the shallot and parsley.

3. Bake the pizza until crisp, about 15 minutes.

CHICKEN AND GORGONZOLA PIZZA

PREP: 15 minutes COOK: 15 minutes

Makes 8 servings

Cornmeal for sprinkling

12 ounces store-bought pizza dough or Pizzetta/Pizza
  Dough (page 223)

¼ cup marinated sun-dried tomatoes, drained
  and chopped, plus 1 tablespoon marinating oil

1 cooked chicken breast, shredded

¾ cup store-bought Alfredo pasta sauce

½ cup (2 ounces) crumbled Gorgonzola cheese

1. Preheat the oven to 450°F. Spray a 12-inch pizza pan with nonstick cooking spray and sprinkle with cornmeal.

2. On a floured surface, roll out the pizza dough to a 13-inch round. Place in the prepared pan, fold the edge in ½ inch, and crimp. Brush the pizza with the marinating oil. Combine the sun-dried tomatoes, chicken, and Alfredo sauce in a small bowl. Spread over the pizza dough. Sprinkle with the Gorgonzola.

3. Bake the pizza until crisp, about 15 minutes.

BBQ CHICKEN PIZZA

PREP: 20 minutes   COOK: 20 minutes

Makes 8 servings

Cornmeal for sprinkling

12 ounces store-bought pizza dough or Pizzetta/Pizza
   Dough (page 223)

Extra-virgin olive oil for brushing

2 cups shredded barbecued chicken

½ cup store-bought barbecue sauce
   or Kentucky Barbecue Sauce (page 451)

2 cups (8 ounces) shredded mozzarella cheese

1 large zucchini, halved lengthwise and thinly sliced

6 green onions, sliced into ½-inch pieces

1 teaspoon dried oregano

½ teaspoon salt

½ teaspoon freshly ground black pepper

1. Preheat the oven to 450°F. Spray a baking sheet with nonstick cooking spray. Sprinkle a work surface with cornmeal. Roll out the pizza dough to a 15- by 10-inch oval; slide onto the prepared baking sheet. Brush the dough with olive oil.

2. Combine the chicken and barbecue sauce in a bowl and toss to coat. Sprinkle the chicken on top of the dough and top with the cheese. Scatter the zucchini on top and then the green onions. Crumble the oregano over the pizza and sprinkle with the salt and pepper.

3. Bake the pizza until the crust is golden and the cheese is melted, about 20 minutes.

MELTING-POT PIZZA

PREP: 10 minutes   COOK: 15 minutes

Makes 15 servings

1 (10-ounce) container refrigerated pizza dough

1 cup store-bought or homemade marinara sauce

⅓ cup store-bought pesto or Classic Basil Pesto (page 427)

2 cups (8 ounces) shredded Monterey Jack cheese

¼ cup sliced canned ripe olives

1 (4-ounce) can nacho sliced jalapeños

¼ cup sliced green onions

1. Preheat the oven to 450°F. Spray a 15- by 10-inch jelly-roll pan with nonstick cooking spray. Roll out the pizza dough onto the prepared baking sheet as package label directs, pressing the dough to the sides of the pan. Bake the crust until golden brown, 10 to 12 minutes.

2. Spread half the crust with the marinara sauce and the other half with the pesto. Sprinkle the cheese on top, and then the olives, jalapeños, and green onions.

3. Bake the pizza until the cheese melts, 5 to 10 minutes.

QUICK AND THIN ROASTED
RED PEPPER MINI-PIZZAS

PREP: 25 minutes   COOK: 8 minutes

Makes 8 servings

Cornmeal for sprinkling

1 (16-ounce) package hot-roll mix

2 tablespoons olive oil

1 (6.5-ounce) jar marinated artichoke hearts, drained and marinade reserved

2 garlic cloves, crushed through a press

1 teaspoon dried oregano

1 (10-ounce) jar roasted red and yellow peppers or all roasted red peppers, drained and patted dry

½ cup (2 ounces) grana padano or Pecorino Romano cheese

1 teaspoon freshly ground black pepper

1. Preheat the oven to 450°F. Spray 2 large baking sheets with nonstick cooking spray and sprinkle with cornmeal.

2. Prepare the roll mix as package label directs for pizza dough, using the olive oil. Divide the pizza dough into 8 equal pieces and, on a well-floured work surface, roll each to a 6-inch round. Arrange 4 rounds on each baking sheet.

3. In a small bowl, combine the artichoke marinade, garlic, and oregano. Brush the mixture over the pizza-dough rounds.

4. Cut the artichoke hearts lengthwise into thirds. Cut the peppers into ¼-inch slices. Sprinkle half the cheese and the black pepper over the pizzas. Arrange the peppers and artichoke hearts over the pizzas and sprinkle with the remaining cheese.

5. Bake the pizzas until crisp, about 8 minutes.

RICOTTA PIZZETTAS WITH ARUGULA AND TOMATOES

PREP: 10 minutes   COOK: 8 minutes

Makes 8 servings

12 ounces store-bought pizza dough or Pizzetta/Pizza
Dough (page 223)
Cornmeal for sprinkling
Extra-virgin olive oil for brushing and drizzling
½ cup Classic Basil Pesto (page 427)
1 cup whole-milk ricotta cheese
1 cup torn arugula leaves
½ cup mixed red and yellow grape tomato halves
¼ cup (1 ounce) freshly grated Parmigiano-Reggiano
cheese
1 teaspoon salt
½ teaspoon freshly ground black pepper

1. Divide the pizza dough into 8 equal portions. Sprinkle a work surface with cornmeal. Roll out each piece of dough to an ⅛-inch-thick round. Lightly brush both sides of each with oil. Heat a grill pan over medium-high heat or prepare an outdoor grill. Grill the rounds until browned and crisp, 3 to 5 minutes.

2. Turn over the pizzas; quickly spread each with 1 tablespoon pesto, and dot with about 2 tablespoons ricotta cheese. Continue grilling until the crust is browned and crisp on the bottom and the cheese starts to melt.

3. Transfer the pizzas to a serving platter and sprinkle with the arugula, tomatoes, Parmigiano-Reggiano, salt, and pepper. Drizzle each with a little olive oil and serve immediately.

PIZZETTAS WITH OLIVE TAPENADE AND PECORINO CHEESE

PREP: 10 minutes   COOK: 15 minutes

Makes 8 servings

12 ounces store-bought pizza dough
  or Pizzetta/Pizza Dough (page 223)
Cornmeal for sprinkling
Extra-virgin olive oil for brushing
½ cup Tapenade (page 19)
4 ounces Pecorino Romano cheese,
  shaved with a vegetable peeler
2 tablespoons finely snipped chives
½ teaspoon freshly ground black pepper

1. Preheat the oven to 400°F. Divide the pizza dough into 8 equal portions. Sprinkle a work surface with cornmeal. Roll out each piece of dough to an ⅛-inch-thick round. Lightly brush one side of each with oil. Place, oiled-side down, on large baking sheets. Spread the tapenade on the pizzas and cover with the cheese shavings. **2.** Bake the pizzas 15 minutes or until the crust is browned and crisp and the cheese starts to melt. Cool about 5 minutes. Sprinkle with the chives and pepper and serve immediately.

PIZZETTAS WITH RED ONIONS, GOAT CHEESE, AND PROSCIUTTO

PREP: 15 minutes   COOK: 30 minutes

Makes 8 servings

5 large red onions, halved lengthwise
  and cut into thin wedges through
  the root (about 3 cups)

3 tablespoons olive oil plus more for brushing

12 ounces store-bought pizza dough or Pizzetta/Pizza
  Dough (page 223)

Cornmeal for sprinkling

4 ounces fresh goat's milk cheese

4 thin slices prosciutto di Parma, cut into quarters

½ cup alfalfa sprouts

1. Combine the onions and oil in a large, heavy skillet over medium heat and cook, stirring, until the onions are softened, 15 to 20 minutes.

2. Preheat the oven to 400°F. Line 2 large, heavy baking sheets with parchment paper.

3. Divide the pizza dough into 8 equal portions. Sprinkle a work surface with cornmeal. Roll out each piece of dough to an ⅛-inch-thick round. Lightly brush one side of each with oil. Place, oiled-side down, on the prepared baking sheets. Spread the onions on the pizzas and dollop with the cheese.

4. Bake the pizzas 15 minutes or until the crust is browned and crisp and the cheese starts to melt. Top each pizza with two loosely piled pieces of prosciutto and sprinkle with some sprouts.

CHOCOLATE-CHIP MINI MUFFINS

PREP: 10 minutes   COOK: 10 minutes

Makes 36 muffins

2 cups all-purpose flour

½ cup plus 2 tablespoons granulated sugar

1 tablespoon baking powder

½ teaspoon salt

½ cup mini semisweet chocolate pieces

1 egg, lightly beaten

¾ cup milk

¼ cup vegetable oil

2 tablespoons brown sugar

1. Preheat the oven to 400°F. Spray 36 mini-muffin cups with cooking spray. Combine the flour, ½ cup granulated sugar, baking powder, salt, and chocolate in a large bowl and mix well. In a medium bowl, whisk the egg, milk, and oil. Pour the egg mixture into the flour mixture and stir just until the dry ingredients are moistened (the batter should be lumpy).

2. Spoon the batter into the prepared cups to fill three-fourths full. Combine 2 tablespoons granulated sugar and the brown sugar in a cup and mix well. Sprinkle over the muffins.

3. Bake until golden brown, 10 to 15 minutes. Immediately run a knife around the sides of the muffins to loosen from the pan and transfer to wire racks. Serve warm.

Mini Fruit Muffins

Use 1 cup blueberries or chopped fresh strawberries, raspberries, or peaches instead of the chocolate pieces and increase the oil to ⅓ cup.

TARTLET SHELLS

PREP: 25 minutes   COOK: 15 minutes

Makes 18 to 24 (1½- to 1¾-inch wide) tartlet shells

Shortcrust Pastry (page 230), Sweet Pie Crust Pastry (page 231), or Shortbread Pastry (page 232)

1. Roll out the pastry to an ⅛-inch thick round on a lightly floured work surface. Cut out shapes with a round cookie cutter about ¼- to ¾-inch wider than the width of the bottom of the tartlet mold so each round will come up the side (measure the height of the mold to be sure). Press the pastry scraps together, reroll, and cut out as many rounds as you can (only reroll once or the pastry will get tough).

2. Flour your fingers and press a dough round into each tartlet mold, pressing lightly first against the bottom and then up the sides so the pastry extends to the top of the mold. Trim any excess so the top edge is cleanly cut.

3. For baked, unfilled shells: Prick the shells thoroughly with a fork and lightly spray each with nonstick cooking spray. Pack aluminum foil into disks the size of the molds and place in each to hold the sides open while baking. Refrigerate until baking.

4. To bake the unfilled tartlet shells: Preheat the oven to 400°F. Place the molds on a baking sheet (if you are using mini muffin pans you can skip this). Bake the tartlet shells until the pastry has set, about 10 minutes. Remove the foil and bake until the pastry is golden brown, 5 to 10 minutes longer.

5. Remove the pastry shells from the oven and let cool briefly on a wire rack. Carefully nudge the shells out of the molds with the tip of a paring knife. Let cool completely.

PHYLLO TARTLET SHELLS

PREP: 20 minutes   COOK: 8 minutes

Makes 18 to 24 (1½- to 1¾-inch wide) tartlet shells

*20 sheets phyllo dough, thawed overnight
   in the refrigerator if frozen*

6 to 8 tablespoons unsalted butter, melted

1. Place the phyllo on a baking sheet and cover with plastic wrap and then a damp kitchen towel. Lightly butter 18 to 24 (1½- to 1¾-inch) tartlet molds.

2. Place one sheet of phyllo on a cutting board (keep the remainder covered) and brush lightly with butter (about 1½ teaspoons per sheet) starting at the edges. Repeat with 4 more phyllo sheets, making a 5-layer stack. Cut out as many rounds as possible from the stack with a round cookie cutter ¼- to ¾-inch wider than the width of the bottom of the tartlet mold so each round will come up the side (measure the height of the mold to be sure). Fit each round into a mold, patting the dough onto the bottom and side. Refrigerate until baking.

3. To bake the unfilled shells: Preheat the oven to 350°F. Bake the tartlet shells until golden brown, 8 to 10 minutes. Transfer pans to a wire rack and cool 5 minutes. Remove shells from the pans.

PHYLLO CUPS

PREP: 15 minutes　COOK: 8 minutes

Makes about 12 phyllo cups

10 sheets phyllo dough, thawed overnight in the refrigerator if frozen

3 to 4 tablespoons unsalted butter, melted

1. Place the phyllo on a baking sheet and cover with plastic wrap and then a damp kitchen towel. Lightly butter 12 mini-muffin cups.

2. Place one sheet of phyllo on a cutting board (keep the remainder covered) and brush lightly with butter (about 1½ teaspoons per sheet) starting at the edges. Repeat with 4 more phyllo sheets, making a 5-layer stack. Cut out as many 3-inch squares as possible. Fit each square into a muffin cup, patting the square onto the bottom and side of the mold, with the corners pointing up. Refrigerate until baking.

3. To bake the unfilled shells: Preheat the oven to 350°F. Bake the phyllo cups until golden brown, 8 to 10 minutes. Transfer pans to a wire rack and cool 5 minutes. Remove cups from the pans.

WONTON CUPS

PREP: 15 minutes   COOK: 8 minutes

Makes 12 cups

12 (3-inch round) wonton wrappers

1. Preheat the oven to 350°F. Spray 12 mini-muffin pan cups with cooking spray. Line each cup with a wonton wrapper, crimping along the sides to fit, with the corners of the wrappers pointing up out of the cups.
2. Bake until golden brown and crisp, about 8 minutes. Pull the cups out of the pan gently and cool on a wire rack.

TOASTED BREAD CUPS

PREP: 20 minutes   COOK: 15 minutes

Makes 24 cups

24 slices bread (any unsweetened will do),
about ⅜ inch thick

1 egg

½ teaspoon water

6 tablespoons unsalted butter, melted

1. Preheat the oven to 300°F. Line a baking sheet with parchment paper. With a 2-inch round cookie cutter, cut out 2 rounds from each slice of bread. Arrange half of the rounds on the prepared baking sheet. With a 1½-inch round cookie cutter, cut out a hole in the remaining rounds. (Discard the smaller rounds, or toast and use for canapés.)

2. Beat the egg with the water in a cup. Brush a little of the egg mixture onto one side of a round with the hole in the middle and place, egg side down, on one

of the rounds on the baking sheet to form a cup. Repeat with the remaining rounds. Brush the cups lightly with melted butter.

3. Bake the cups until golden, about 15 minutes.

PIZZETTA/PIZZA DOUGH

PREP: 15 minutes plus dough rising

Makes about 12 ounces dough,

enough for one 12-inch pizza or 8 pizzettes

To bake the dough, preheat the oven to 450°F. Spray a 12-inch pizza pan with nonstick cooking spray and sprinkle with cornmeal. After rising, shape dough over pan, top as desired, and bake until crisp, about 15 minutes.

2 cups all-purpose flour

1 envelope quick-rising dry yeast

1 teaspoon salt

½ teaspoon sugar

⅔ cup very warm water (120°F to 130°F)

2 tablespoons olive oil

1. Combine 1 cup of the flour, the yeast, salt, and sugar in a large bowl of an electric mixer. With the mixer at low speed, add the water and oil. Beat at medium speed 3 minutes, scraping down the side of the bowl with a rubber spatula. With a wooden spoon, gradually stir in the remaining 1 cup flour; stir until the dough leaves the sides of the bowl. Scrape out the dough onto a work surface and knead until smooth and elastic, about 5 minutes.

2. Grease a large bowl. Add the dough and turn so the greased side is up. Cover with plastic wrap and let rise in a warm place until doubled in bulk, about 45 minutes. Shape, top, and bake as desired.

CHOUX PASTRY

PREP: 10 minutes   COOK: 6 minutes

Makes about 48 small puffs or 36 small éclairs

or 12 large puffs or éclairs

This special pastry (pronounced "shoo") is used to make cream puffs, éclairs, and savory cocktail hors d'oeuvre.

1 cup water

½ cup (1 stick) butter, cut into 1-inch chunks

1 teaspoon sugar (if making sweet puffs)

½ teaspoon salt

1 cup all-purpose flour

4 eggs, at room temperature

1. Combine the water, butter, sugar (if using), and salt in a medium saucepan over medium-high heat. Bring to a full boil, stirring constantly with a wooden spoon to quickly melt the butter. Remove the pan from the heat, add the flour all at once, and beat vigorously to combine. Return the pan to medium heat and cook, stirring constantly, until the mixture pulls away from the side of the pan, about 3 minutes. Turn out the dough onto a plate and let cool.

2. Place the dough in a bowl or in the bowl of an electric mixer fitted with a paddle attachment. Beat in the eggs, one at a time, completely incorporating each egg before adding another one. The dough can be made ahead of time, covered, and refrigerated until ready to use; bring to room temperature before shaping and baking.

Chocolate Pâte à Choux

Substitute cocoa powder for ½ cup of the flour and increase the amount of sugar by 3 tablespoons.

EASY PUFF PASTRY

PREP: 25 minutes plus chilling

Makes 2 (2- by 10-inch) tarts or 36 canapé bases
or 36 (1¹/₂- to 1³/₄-inch wide) tartlet shells

You can use 2½ cups all-purpose flour instead of the all-purpose and cake flour combination if it is more convenient. This pastry can be used to make Baked Pastry Case (page 226).

2 cups all-purpose flour
½ cup plain cake flour
¾ teaspoon salt
1½ cups (3 sticks) plus 1 tablespoon chilled
  unsalted butter, cut into ½-inch dice
6 tablespoons ice water

1. Combine the all-purpose flour, cake flour, and salt in a medium bowl and mix well. Add the butter. Working quickly so the butter doesn't soften, mix the dough with your hands, pressing the butter into 1-inch flakes. Drizzle 6 tablespoons of the water over all and quickly stir to make a dough that sticks together but is not sticky.

2. Turn out the dough onto a lightly floured work surface and press with a rolling pin into a 12- by 14-inch rectangle, with a short side facing you. Lightly flour the top. With a dough scraper or flat cookie sheet, fold the bottom third over the middle third. Fold the top third over all. Turn the dough so the furthest edge faces to the right. Lightly press the top, bottom, and right side edges together with the rolling pin to seal. Lightly press the rolling pin across the dough rectangle about every 2 inches. If the dough is not too "tense" and resistant to rolling, repeat rolling and folding. If dough is tense, wrap the dough in a zip-top plastic bag and let rest in the refrigerator 30 minutes to 1 hour.

3. Repeat two more times the process of twice rolling and folding, for a total of 6 rolls. Allow the finished dough to rest for 2 hours.

BAKED PASTRY CASE

PREP: 10 minutes plus chilling   COOK: 15 minutes

Makes 1 pastry case

Easy Puff Pastry (page 225)

1. Roll out the pastry on a floured surface to a ¼-inch thick, 4¼ by 12¼-inch rectangle. Slide the pastry onto a cutting board. Trim the edges to make a 4- by 12-inch rectangle (cutting the edges will ensure that the pastry rises evenly). Trim ½-inch strips from all the sides of the pastry. Brush the edges of the main pastry sheet with a little water, and place the trimmed pieces on top to form a border. Prick the bottom of the tart shell all over with a fork. Slide a sheet of parchment under the tart shell and lift onto a baking sheet. Refrigerate the pastry case 1 hour.

2. Preheat the oven to 425°F. Bake the pastry case until nicely browned and crisp, 15 to 20 minutes. Slide the pastry case onto a wire rack to cool.

QUICK FLAKY PASTRY

PREP: 10 minutes plus chilling

Makes about 1¹/₂ pounds pastry, enough

for 2 (4- by 8-inch) tart shells or 36 canapé bases

or 36 (1¹/₂- to 1³/₄-inch wide) tartlet shells

1 cup (2 sticks) unsalted butter

2 cups all-purpose flour

¹/₂ cup sour cream

1. In a large bowl, cut the butter into the flour using a pastry blender or two knives used scissors fashion, until the mixture resembles coarse crumbs. Add the sour cream and stir with a fork until blended.

2. Turn out the dough onto a lightly floured work surface and knead briefly until smooth. Divide the pastry in half and pat into two ¹/₂-inch-thick squares. Wrap each in plastic wrap and refrigerate at least 2 hours before using.

TART-SHELL SHORTCRUST PASTRY

PREP: 10 minutes plus chilling

Makes 1 (12- by 15-inch) tart shell

2 cups all-purpose flour

¼ teaspoon salt

½ cup (1 stick) unsalted butter,
cut into ½-inch chunks and frozen

2 eggs, beaten

1. Combine the flour and salt in a food processor bowl and pulse to blend. Add the butter and pulse 3 or 4 times to coat with flour. With the machine running, add the eggs through the feed tube and stop the machine. Scrape down the side of the work bowl. Pulse until the dough looks like wet sand.

2. Scrape the dough out onto a work surface, shape into a ½-inch-thick disk, and wrap with plastic wrap. Let rest in the refrigerator at least 1 hour or up to overnight before rolling out. (Pastry can also be wrapped and frozen for up to 2 weeks.)

CREAM CHEESE PASTRY FOR TARTLETS

PREP: 10 minutes plus chilling

Makes 24 (1¹/₂- to 1³/₄-inch) tartlet shells

½ cup (1 stick) unsalted butter, softened
1 (3-ounce) package cream cheese, softened
1 cup all-purpose flour

1. Combine the butter and cream cheese in a large bowl and mix until blended. Stir in the flour just until blended (do not overmix).

2. Divide the pastry into 24 equal parts; roll each into a ball. Place on a baking sheet, cover with plastic wrap, and refrigerate 20 minutes.

SHORTCRUST PASTRY

PREP: 10 minutes plus chilling

Makes 1 (9-inch) pie or tart crust or about 24
(1¹/₂- to 1³/₄-inch wide) tartlet shells

1½ cups all-purpose flour

½ teaspoon salt

½ cup (1 stick) unsalted butter,
cut into ½-inch chunks and frozen

4 to 5 tablespoons ice water

1. Combine the flour and salt in a food processor bowl
and pulse to blend. Add the butter and pulse 3 or 4
times to coat with flour. Drizzle 4 tablespoons ice water
over the mixture and pulse 3 or 4 times. Scrape the bowl
side with a plastic spatula. If the dough is dry, sprinkle
with the remaining 1 tablespoon ice water and pulse 2
to 3 times more to form 1½-inch clumps of dough.

2. Scrape the dough out onto a work surface, shape into
a ½-inch high disk, and wrap with plastic wrap. Let rest
in the refrigerator at least 1 hour before rolling out.

SWEET PIE CRUST PASTRY

PREP: 10 minutes plus chilling

Makes 1 (10-inch) pie or tart shell or about 18 (1½- to 1¾-inch) tartlet shells

1¼ cups all-purpose flour

½ cup confectioners' sugar

¼ teaspoon salt

½ cup (1 stick) unsalted butter,
cut into ½-inch chunks and frozen

2 large egg yolks

1½ to 3 teaspoons ice water

1. Combine the flour, sugar, and salt in a food processor bowl and pulse to blend. Add the butter and pulse 3 or 4 times to coat with flour. Mix the egg yolks with 1½ teaspoons of the water until blended. Drizzle over the flour mixture and pulse until the dough sticks together, pulsing in up to 1½ teaspoons more ice water if needed.

2. Scrape the dough out onto a work surface, shape into a ½-inch-thick disk, and wrap with plastic wrap. Let rest in the refrigerator at least 1 hour before rolling out.

SHORTBREAD PASTRY

PREP: 10 minutes plus chilling

Makes 1 (9½-inch) tart shell or 24
(1½- to 1¾-inch) tartlet shells

1 egg yolk

1 teaspoon vanilla extract

¾ cup all-purpose flour

⅓ cup confectioners' sugar

¼ cup blanched almonds

⅛ teaspoon salt

5 tablespoons unsalted butter, cut into pieces and frozen

1. Mix the egg yolk and vanilla in a cup until blended. Combine the flour, sugar, almonds, and salt in a food processor and process until the nuts are finely ground. Add the butter and pulse until the mixture resembles coarse meal. Drizzle the egg-yolk mixture over the flour mixture and pulse until the dough starts to clump together.

2. Turn out the dough onto a sheet of plastic wrap. Press the dough into the pan mold or molds as desired. Refrigerate 30 minutes before baking.

CRÊPES

PREP: 40 minutes COOK: 4 minutes per crêpe

Makes 24 to 30 crepes

1½ cups milk

1 cup all-purpose flour, sifted

1 egg

1 egg yolk

1 tablespoon canola oil plus more for cooking

¼ teaspoon salt

1. In a blender, combine the milk, flour, egg, egg yolk, oil, and salt. Blend until perfectly smooth. Pour the batter into a bowl, cover, and let stand at least 30 minutes. (The batter can be made a day ahead and stored in the refrigerator.)

2. Heat a crêpe pan or small nonstick skillet over high heat. Rub the bottom with a paper towel dipped in a little oil.

3. When the pan is hot but not smoking, remove it from the heat and pour in ¼ cup batter. Immediately swirl the batter in the pan to coat it completely. Pour off excess batter if necessary so the crêpe will have an even thickness.

4. Set the pan back on the heat and cook until the edges curl up and the crêpe is evenly dark golden brown, about 2 minutes. Pick it up with your fingers and turn it over. Cook on the other side until it looks dry and is firm to the touch, about 2 minutes (but do not over-cook, it will only get browned in speckled parts).

5. Turn out the crêpe onto a plate and repeat with remaining batter and additional oil if needed.

SMALL PLATES

ARTICHOKE FRITTATA

PREP: 10 minutes   COOK: 18 minutes

Makes 16 pieces

3 tablespoons unsalted butter

1 large onion, halved lengthwise and thinly
   sliced crosswise

1 (9-ounce) package frozen artichoke hearts,
   thawed and squeezed dry

1 (7½-ounce) jar roasted red peppers,
   patted dry and diced

1 teaspoon dried oregano, crushed

¾ teaspoon salt

¾ teaspoon freshly ground black pepper

8 large eggs

4 ounces mozzarella cheese, diced

3 tablespoons freshly grated
   Parmigiano-Reggiano cheese

1. Preheat the broiler. Melt the butter over medium-high
heat in a large nonstick skillet with an oven proof handle. Add the onion and sauté until soft, about 4 minutes.
Add the artichoke hearts, red peppers, oregano, ¼ teaspoon salt, and ¼ teaspoon pepper; sauté 3 minutes.

2. Combine the eggs and remaining ½ teaspoon salt
and ½ teaspoon pepper in a large bowl and whisk until
blended. Pour the mixture over the vegetables in the
skillet; sprinkle with the mozzarella. Cook over medium
heat until the edges set, 5 minutes, lifting the eggs with
a spatula and tilting the pan so the uncooked eggs run
under the cooked portion and shaking the pan frequently
to keep the eggs from sticking. Sprinkle with the
Parmigiano-Reggiano.

3. Broil 4 inches from the heat until the cheese browns
slightly and the top sets, about 4 minutes. Slide the frittata onto a cutting board and cut crosswise into 4 rows
each way to make 16 pieces. Serve warm or at room
temperature.

SPINACH AND FETA FRITTATA

PREP: 10 minutes   COOK: 14 minutes

Makes 16 pieces

2 tablespoons olive oil

4 green onions, sliced

1 zucchini, thinly sliced

1 garlic clove, crushed through a press

1 (10-ounce) package frozen chopped spinach,
    thawed and squeezed dry

¼ cup canned sliced ripe olives

¼ cup chopped marinated sun-dried tomatoes

12 large eggs

½ teaspoon salt

½ teaspoon freshly ground black pepper

½ cup crumbled feta cheese

1. Preheat the broiler. Heat the oil over medium-high heat in a large nonstick skillet with an oven proof handle. Add the green onions and zucchini and sauté until softened, 2 to 3 minutes. Add the garlic and sauté 1 minute. Add the spinach, olives, and sun-dried tomatoes and mix well.

2. Combine the eggs, salt, and pepper in a large bowl and whisk until blended. Pour the mixture over the vegetables in the skillet and sprinkle with the feta. Cook over medium heat until the edges set, 5 minutes, lifting the eggs with a spatula and tilting the pan so the uncooked eggs run under the cooked portion and shaking the pan frequently to keep the eggs from sticking.

3. Broil 4 inches from the heat until the cheese browns slightly and the top sets, about 4 minutes. Slide the frittata onto a cutting board and cut crosswise into 4 rows each way to make 16 pieces. Serve warm or at room temperature.

MOSAIC VEGETABLE TERRINE

PREP: 30 minutes   COOK: 1 hour 45 minutes

Makes about 24 slices

12 tablespoons (1½ sticks) unsalted butter

1 pound carrots, peeled and cut into ¼-inch rounds

1 pound parsnips, peeled and cut into ¼-inch rounds

½ teaspoon dried oregano, crushed

1 teaspoon salt

1 teaspoon freshly ground black pepper

4 ounces mushrooms, sliced

1½ pounds Swiss chard, stems discarded, leaves washed well and cut into 1-inch pieces

6 eggs

1 cup (4 ounces) grated Swiss cheese

1. Line an 8½- by 4½- by 2½-inch loaf pan with foil. Butter the foil with 2 tablespoons of the butter. Arrange the oven racks so the top rack is in the middle.

2. Melt 4 tablespoons of the butter in a large skillet over medium heat. Add the carrots and parsnips and sauté slowly until tender, about 20 minutes. Place in a food processor and chop coarsely. Scrape into a large shallow bowl, sprinkle with the oregano, ½ teaspoon salt, and ½ teaspoon pepper; stir to mix. Set aside to cool.

3. In the same (unwashed) skillet, melt 2 tablespoons of the butter over high heat. Add the mushrooms and sauté until tender, about 2 minutes. Chop coarsely in the unwashed processor and add to the carrot mixture.

4. In the same (unwashed) skillet, melt the remaining 4 tablespoons of the butter over medium-high heat. Add the chard and sauté until tender, about 5 minutes.

Serve slices of the hot terrine on salad plates at a sit-down dinner or cut the slices into halves or thirds and arrange on a warmed platter for a buffet. For a cold terrine, cool in the pan, cover with plastic wrap, and refrigerate until set, about 4 hours. Invert and remove the foil, wrap in plastic wrap, and refrigerate. Remove from the refrigerator about 30 minutes before serving.

Scrape the chard onto a large plate and pull it apart with a fork (so it will cool quickly); set aside to cool.

5. Preheat the oven to 400°F. Whisk 2 eggs in a bowl until blended. Add the cooled chard and the remaining ½ teaspoon salt and ½ teaspoon pepper; mix thoroughly. Whisk the remaining 4 eggs in a large bowl until blended. Add the carrot mixture and the cheese and mix well.

6. Spread half the carrot mixture evenly in the prepared pan, cover with all the chard mixture, and then top with the remaining carrot mixture. Place the loaf pan in a roasting pan and set the pan in the oven. Add enough boiling water to the roasting pan to come two-thirds up the sides of the loaf pan. Bake the terrine until the blade of a thin knife inserted in center comes out clean, about 1 hour and 15 minutes.

7. Remove the terrine from the water and place on a kitchen towel. Pat the sides of the pan dry. Place a flat serving platter over the terrine and, with a pot holder pressing the terrine onto the platter with one hand and holding the bottom of the platter with the other, carefully invert the terrine and platter in one quick motion. Remove the pan and then the foil. To serve, cut the terrine into ⅓-inch-thick slices with a thin-bladed knife.

FRESH MUSHROOMS WITH PARMESAN

PREP: 10 minutes

Makes 6 to 8 servings

1 pound trimmed, sliced mixed mushrooms (hen of the woods, porcini, cremini, shiitake, white button, chanterelle, etc.)

⅓ cup coarsely chopped fresh flat-leaf parsley

¼ cup extra-virgin olive oil

2 tablespoons lemon juice

½ cup shavings Parmigiano-Reggiano, shaved with a vegetable peeler

Combine the mushrooms and parsley on a serving platter and toss to mix. Drizzle the oil and lemon juice on top and toss to coat. Sprinkle with the cheese shavings.

MUSHROOM-CHÈVRE TERRINE

PREP: 10 minutes   COOK: 1 hour

Makes 8 servings

2 tablespoons unsalted butter

2 medium onions, finely chopped

1 green pepper, finely chopped

1 (4 ounce) portobello mushroom cap, finely chopped

3 eggs

7 ounces fresh goat's milk cheese (chèvre)

2 tablespoons finely chopped fresh parsley

1 teaspoon finely chopped fresh thyme

1 teaspoon sea salt

½ teaspoon freshly ground black pepper

1 cup fine dried bread crumbs

1. Preheat the oven to 375°F. Grease a 4-cup terrine or loaf pan with nonstick cooking spray.

2. Melt the butter in a large skillet over medium heat. Add the onions and sauté until softened, about 7 minutes. Add the green pepper and mushroom and sauté until tender, about 5 minutes.

3. Beat the eggs until blended in a large bowl. Add the cheese, parsley, thyme, salt, and pepper and mix well. Scrape the onion mixture into the cheese mixture, add the bread crumbs, and mix well. Spread evenly in the prepared pan and cover with foil. Bake until a thin-bladed knife inserted in the center comes out clean, about 45 minutes. Invert onto a serving platter and cut into slices.

BABY SCALLOP-GINGER MOUSSES

PREP: 30 minutes plus chilling   COOK: 15 minutes

Makes 12 servings

1 pound sea scallops, tough membranes removed

Unsalted butter, softened for greasing the molds

1 cup heavy cream

3 egg whites

1 (2-inch) piece ginger, peeled and grated

½ teaspoon fine sea salt or more to taste

¼ teaspoon freshly ground white pepper or more to taste

Tomato-Pepper Sauce (page 426) or Frozen Fresh-Tomato Cocktail (page 247)

1. Puree the scallops in a food processor; transfer to a stainless-steel mixing bowl. Set the bowl in a larger bowl of ice and water to chill the scallops thoroughly, about 15 minutes.

2. While waiting for the scallops to chill, butter the insides of 12 dariole molds (1-inch straight-sided cylinders) or

heat-safe shot glasses or small, tall juice glasses. Freeze the molds until the butter hardens. Butter again. Cut out 12 rounds of parchment paper the diameter of the molds.

3. Beat the cream in a bowl or glass measure until soft peaks form when the beaters are raised. Add one-third of the whipped cream and 1 egg white to the scallops and whisk (over the ice and water) until mixed evenly. Let the mixture chill 15 minutes in the ice bath, adding more ice and removing some of the water if necessary. Repeat 2 times, each time with another third of the cream and another egg white.

4. Arrange the oven racks so the top rack is in the middle. Preheat the oven to 350°F. Put the ginger in a double thickness of cheesecloth and squeeze the juice into the mousse. Discard the ginger solids. Whisk the salt and pepper into the mousse. Poach a teaspoon of the mousse in a small pan of simmering water or cook just until firm in a small bowl covered with plastic wrap in the microwave (about 20 seconds on high power).

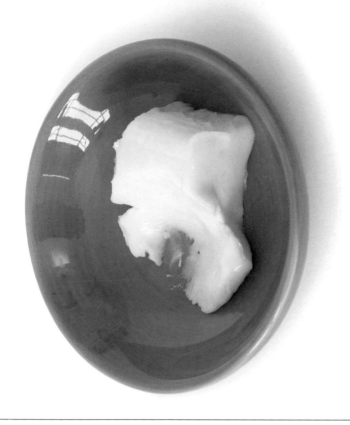

Taste and add more salt and pepper if needed. If the mousses will be served cold, add a little more seasoning.

5. Fill the molds three-fourths full with the mousse mixture and lightly press a parchment round on the top of each. Place in a roasting pan and set the pan in the oven. Add enough hot (but not boiling) water to come two-thirds up the sides of the molds. Bake the molds until a skewer inserted in the center of a couple mousses in different parts of the pan comes out coated but not wet, 15 to 20 minutes.

6. Remove the molds from the water and place on a kitchen towel. Let stand 5 minutes. Remove the parchment rounds. If serving warm, unmold each mousse onto a small plate and transfer to a warmed serving platter. If serving cold, cool in the molds 15 minutes, unmold, transfer to a storage container, and refrigerate for later use. Serve the warm mousses with Tomato-Pepper Sauce and the cold mousses with Frozen Fresh-Tomato Cocktail.

VIETNAMESE GRILLED SHRIMP ON SUGAR CANE

PREP: 25 minutes   COOK: 11 minutes

Makes 10 servings

These appetizers are traditionally eaten by removing the shrimp portion from the cane and wrapping it in a tender lettuce leaf—Boston or Bibb lettuce is nice—with some mint leaves and cucumber slices that have been sprinkled with fish sauce. For a cocktail party, it may be easier to serve the savory shrimp on the sugar canes and splash with the sweet and sour sauce.

1 ounce fresh white pork fat (from trimmings of a loin of pork), finely diced or 2 tablespoons melted butter
1 pound shrimp, peeled and deveined
1 egg white, lightly beaten
1 large green onion, white part only, minced
½ teaspoon sea salt
½ teaspoon freshly ground black pepper
10 (6-inch) pieces split (quartered lengthwise) fresh sugar cane or 10 (3-inch) pieces canned sugar cane in syrup, drained and patted dry
Sweet and Sour Dipping Sauce (page 432)

1. If using pork fat, boil it in an inch of water in a small saucepan until translucent, about 2 minutes. Drain, cool, and cut into fine dice. Place in a medium bowl. If using butter, place in a medium bowl.

2. Lay the shrimp out in a single layer on a parchment paper–lined baking sheet and freeze until firm, about 10 minutes. Place on a cutting board and chop finely, leaving some pieces larger so there is an interesting texture. Scrape into a bowl with the pork fat or butter and add the egg white, green onion, salt, and pepper. Stir until blended and smooth.

3. With oiled hands, press about 3 tablespoons of the shrimp mixture in a ½-inch thickness around one end of each 6-inch piece of sugar cane, about 1 inch from the top. If using the short pieces of sugar cane, press the shrimp mixture around the cane, leaving about ½ inch of each end exposed.

4. Place the shrimp sticks in oiled bamboo steamer baskets. Place the baskets in a wok with 1 inch of boiling water set over high heat. Cover and steam until the shrimp is almost cooked through, about 3 minutes. (The sticks can be prepared ahead up to this point and refrigerated. Bring to room temperature before finishing.)

5. Place the sticks on an oiled baking sheet and preheat the broiler, or preheat a grill. Brush the sticks lightly with oil and broil or grill until deep brown on all sides and hot, turning frequently, 6 to 8 minutes. Serve with the Sweet and Sour Dipping Sauce.

FROZEN FRESH-TOMATO COCKTAIL

PREP: 15 minutes plus freezing

Makes 8 servings

3 pounds ripe plum tomatoes, peeled and seeded

2 cups mascarpone cheese or sour cream
plus more for garnish

4 teaspoons grated lemon zest

½ cup lemon juice

2 teaspoons Spanish bittersweet (smoked) paprika
or 1 pinch cayenne plus more for garnish

2 teaspoons salt or more to taste

1 teaspoon freshly ground black pepper or more to taste

16 fresh chive sprigs for garnish

1. Puree the tomatoes in a food processor or blender. Add the mascarpone, lemon zest, lemon juice, paprika, salt, and pepper and process until blended. Taste and add more salt and pepper if needed.

2. Pour the mixture into a shallow freezer-safe container and freeze at least 3 hours or overnight, stirring the mixture with a fork to break it up every 30 minutes for the first 1½ hours.

3. If the mixture is hard-frozen, allow it to stand at room temperature for 30 minutes, break it up into chunks, and pulse it in the food processor until it is a thick slush. To serve, spoon into glasses. Garnish each serving with a small dollop of mascarpone, a dusting of paprika, and chives cut to extend a few inches above the height of the glasses. Serve immediately.

SKEWERED BEEF STRIPS

PREP: 15 minutes plus marinating

COOK: 5 minutes

Makes 16 skewers

1 cup fresh or canned pineapple juice

½ cup finely chopped onion

1 garlic clove, crushed through a press

1 pound flank steak, cut across the grain
   into paper-thin strips and cut crosswise in half

1 cup Chunky Pineapple-Peanut Sauce (page 443)

1. Combine the pineapple juice, onion, and garlic in a shallow glass bowl and mix well. Add the steak strips and toss to coat. Cover and marinate in the refrigerator at least 1 hour.

2. Soak 16 (6-inch) bamboo skewers in water for 30 minutes.

3. Preheat the broiler or prepare a grill for barbecue. Thread the meat in ribbons onto the skewers. Place on a foil-lined baking sheet. Broil the skewers on the baking sheet or grill on an oiled grill 6 inches from the heat, turning once, until the meat is sizzling, 5 to 6 minutes. Serve with the Chunky Pineapple-Peanut Sauce for dipping.

LEMON CHICKEN SKEWERS

PREP: 15 minutes   COOK: 1 minute

Makes 25 skewers

1 pound chicken cutlets (about 3 cutlets)
½ cup store-bought or homemade (page 53)
preserved lemon (about 3 quarters), flesh discarded,
peel finely chopped
2 tablespoons olive oil
1 garlic clove, crushed through a press
1 teaspoon red pepper flakes
1 teaspoon dried oregano, crushed
½ teaspoon salt
½ teaspoon freshly ground black pepper

1. Soak 25 (6-inch) bamboo skewers in water for 30 minutes.

2. Place the chicken breasts between sheets of waxed paper on a cutting board and pound with a rolling pin or meat mallet until barely ¼-inch thick. Cut the pieces into 1-inch-wide strips.

3. Combine the preserved lemon, oil, garlic, pepper flakes, oregano, salt, and pepper in a bowl and mix well. Add the chicken and toss to coat.

4. Preheat the broiler. Line a baking sheet with foil. Thread the chicken strips onto the skewers. Place the skewers on the prepared baking sheet and broil until cooked through, 1 to 2 minutes.

CURRIED CHICKEN SATÉ

PREP: 15 minutes plus marinating   COOK: 6 minutes

Makes 12 satés

1 cup plain yogurt

2/3 cup unsweetened coconut milk

1½ teaspoons kecap manis (sweet soy sauce)

1 cup plain yogurt — *or regular soy sauce*

¾ teaspoon curry powder

¼ teaspoon ground coriander

1 teaspoon cornstarch

12 ounces chicken cutlets, cut into 12 strips about ½-inch wide (about 2 cutlets)

½ cup Indonesian Peanut Sauce (page 441)

1. Combine the yogurt, coconut milk, kecap manis, curry powder, coriander, and cornstarch in a medium bowl and mix well. Add the chicken and toss to coat. Cover and refrigerate at least 1 hour or overnight.

2. Soak 12 (6- to 8-inch) bamboo skewers in water for 30 minutes.

3. Preheat the broiler or prepare a grill for barbecue. Thread the chicken pieces onto the skewers and place on a foil-lined baking sheet. Broil the skewers on the baking sheet or grill on an oiled grill, turning once, until cooked through, about 6 minutes. Serve with the Indonesian Peanut Sauce for dipping.

SPICY SHRIMP SATÉ

PREP: 15 minutes plus marinating COOK: 6 minutes

Makes 24 satés

4 shallots, peeled and quartered

4 garlic cloves, peeled and halved

1 (2-inch) piece ginger, peeled and thinly sliced

1 tablespoon sambal oelek

1 tablespoon dark sesame oil

1 teaspoon ground coriander,
   sautéed in a skillet until fragrant

24 large shrimp with tails, peeled, deveined,
   and butterflied through the inner curve
   so the shrimp open flat

1 cup Indonesian Peanut Sauce (page 441)

1. Place the shallots, garlic, ginger, sambal oelek, sesame oil, and coriander in a food processor and process until a paste forms. Scrape the paste into a bowl and add the shrimp. Toss to coat, cover, and refrigerate at least 4 hours or overnight.

2. Soak 48 (6- to 8-inch) bamboo skewers in water for 30 minutes.

3. Preheat the broiler or prepare a grill for barbecue. Thread a skewer through one side of the shrimp parallel to the tail. Thread another skewer through the other side of the shrimp parallel to the tail. Place the satés on a foil-lined baking sheet and repeat with the remaining shrimp. Broil the satés on the baking sheet or grill on an oiled grill, turning once, until cooked through, about 6 minutes. Serve with the Indonesian Peanut Sauce for dipping.

ORANGE-ANCHO PORK SKEWERS

PREP: 15 minutes plus marinating COOK: 6 minutes

Makes 8 skewers

2¼ cups sour orange juice or 2 cups orange juice
mixed with ¼ cup freshly squeezed lime juice

2 tablespoons ancho chili powder

2 garlic cloves, coarsely chopped

1¼ pounds trimmed pork tenderloin,
cut into ¾-inch cubes

¾ teaspoon kosher salt

Bibb or Boston lettuce leaves, for serving

Easy Green Onion Dipping Sauce (page 435)

8 sprigs mint (tender tips only)

1. Combine the orange juice, chili powder, and garlic in a large nonreactive baking dish. Add the pork cubes and turn to coat. Cover and refrigerate for 4 to 6 hours or overnight.

2. Soak 8 (6-inch) bamboo skewers in water at least 30 minutes.

3. Preheat the broiler or prepare a grill for barbecue. Thread the pork onto the skewers and sprinkle with the salt. Place on a foil-lined baking sheet. Broil the skewers on the baking sheet or grill on an oiled grill, turning once, until cooked through completely, about 6 minutes. Place each skewer in a Bibb lettuce leaf, drizzle with the dipping sauce, and garnish with mint.

GRILLED LAMB ON ROSEMARY SKEWERS

PREP: 25 minutes   COOK: 10 minutes

Makes 24 skewers

24 fresh rosemary sprigs

1½ pounds boneless lean lamb,
    cut into ¾-inch cubes

½ cup mint jelly

1 garlic clove, crushed through a press

3 tablespoons olive oil

1 tablespoon Dijon mustard

1 teaspoon salt

½ teaspoon freshly ground pepper

1. Preheat the broiler or prepare a grill for barbecue. Remove the leaves from the bottom two-thirds of each rosemary sprig and discard. Through the cleared end, thread 3 or 4 pieces of lamb onto the rosemary; place on a foil-lined baking sheet.

2. Combine the mint jelly, garlic, oil, and mustard in a small saucepan and heat over medium heat until melted. Brush the mint sauce over the lamb and sprinkle with the salt and pepper. Broil the skewers on the baking sheet or grill on an oiled grill 4 inches from the heat, turning once, about 6 minutes for medium.

AROMATIC CHICKEN SKEWERS

PREP: 15 minutes plus overnight marinating

COOK: 6 minutes

Makes 16 skewers

1 tablespoon whole cumin seeds

1 tablespoon whole coriander seeds

2 teaspoons whole black peppercorns

3 tablespoons vegetable oil

2 tablespoons soy sauce

1½ teaspoons turmeric

¾ teaspoon ground cinnamon

1½ pounds chicken cutlets, cut crosswise into ½-inch-wide strips (about 5 cutlets)

1. Combine the cumin and coriander seeds in a small dry skillet over medium heat and toast until fragrant, about 2 minutes. Cool completely and place in a zip-top plastic bag. Add the peppercorns and seal the bag. Crush until coarse with a rolling pin or the bottom of a heavy pan. Pour into a shallow baking dish and add the oil, soy sauce, turmeric, and cinnamon. Mix well. Add the chicken and toss to coat. Cover and marinate in the refrigerator overnight.

2. Remove the chicken from the refrigerator and let stand 1 hour before cooking. Soak 16 (6-inch) bamboo skewers in water for 30 minutes.

3. Preheat the broiler or prepare a grill for barbecue. Thread the chicken in ribbons onto the skewers. Place on a foil-lined baking sheet. Broil the skewers on the baking sheet or grill on an oiled grill 4 inches from the heat, turning once, until the chicken is cooked through, 6 to 8 minutes.

CAJUN-FRIED CHICKEN STRIPS

PREP: 15 minutes   COOK: 4 minutes per batch

Makes about 32 pieces, 8 servings

Instead of the Cajun seasoning, you can mix together 1 teaspoon paprika, ½ teaspoon garlic powder, ½ teaspoon onion powder, ¼ teaspoon salt, ¼ teaspoon dried thyme, and ⅛ teaspoon freshly ground black pepper.

Vegetable oil for frying
1 cup all-purpose flour
1 tablespoon Cajun seasoning
1 teaspoon salt
1 egg, beaten
¼ cup milk
2 tablespoons hot pepper sauce
1¼ pounds chicken cutlets, cut crosswise into ½-inch thick strips (about 4 cutlets)

1. Heat ½ inch oil in a large skillet over medium heat to 400°F on a deep-fat thermometer. Preheat the oven to 200°F.

2. While the oil heats, combine the flour, Cajun seasoning, and salt in a large zip-top plastic bag. Seal and shake to mix. Place the egg, milk, and pepper sauce in another zip-top bag and add the chicken. Seal and shake to coat. In batches, drain the chicken and add to the flour mixture. Seal and shake to coat.

3. In batches, add the chicken to the hot oil and fry, turning once, until browned and cooked through, about 4 minutes. Transfer to paper towel–lined baking sheets to drain. Keep warm in the oven while frying remaining chicken.

FRIED COCONUT SHRIMP

PREP: 25 minutes   COOK: 2 minutes per batch

Makes 10 servings

½ cup sweetened coconut cream

1 egg

⅓ cup milk

½ cup all-purpose flour

1 tablespoon curry powder

2 cups (6 ounces) unsweetened shredded coconut

2 pounds large shrimp with tails, peeled and deveined

1 teaspoon salt

1 teaspoon freshly ground black pepper

¼ teaspoon cayenne

Vegetable oil for deep-frying

Napa cabbage leaves or frisée for lining serving platter

Pineapple Chutney (page 444) for dipping

1. Combine the coconut cream, egg, and milk in a large bowl and whisk until blended. Add the flour and curry powder and whisk until blended. Spread the coconut on a baking sheet. Holding a shrimp by the tail, dip it into the batter to coat. Drain off the excess. Dredge the shrimp in the coconut to coat and place on a wire rack over a baking sheet. Repeat with the remaining shrimp. Let the shrimp stand until the batter sets, about 5 minutes.

2. Preheat the oven to 250°F. Combine the salt, pepper, and cayenne in a cup and mix well. Heat 1 inch of oil in a deep, large skillet over medium-high heat to 350°F on a deep-fat thermometer. Reduce the heat to medium to keep the temperature constant. In batches, add the shrimp to the oil (do not crowd the pan) and fry, turning once, until browned and just cooked through, about 2 minutes. Transfer to a paper towel–lined baking sheet to drain and immediately sprinkle with some of the salt mixture. Keep warm in the oven while frying the remaining shrimp. Allow the oil to return to 350°F between batches.

3. When the last batch is prepared, arrange the shrimp on a cabbage-lined platter with a wooden pick inserted in each. Serve with the Pineapple Chutney.

CRUNCHY COCKTAIL MEATBALLS

PREP: 15 minutes COOK: 15 minutes

Makes about 50 meatballs

12 ounces ground pork

6 ounces ground sirloin

2 green onions, finely chopped

½ cup chopped pineapple

½ cup chopped red pepper

¼ cup chopped macadamia nuts

¼ cup chopped water chestnuts

1 tablespoon soy sauce

¼ teaspoon salt

¼ teaspoon freshly ground black pepper

2 cups store-bought or homemade (page 432)
sweet and sour dipping sauce (optional)

1. Preheat the oven to 400°F. Spray a large rimmed baking sheet with nonstick cooking spray. Combine all the ingredients in a bowl and mix well. Shape into 1-inch balls using your hands or a melon-ball scoop. Place on the prepared baking sheet with about ½ inch of space between the meatballs.

2. Bake the meatballs until cooked through, about 15 minutes. Serve with sweet and sour dipping sauce, if you like.

BEEF AND CHEESE COCKTAIL MEATBALLS

PREP: 15 minutes   COOK: 15 minutes

Makes about 40 meatballs

1 egg

1 pound lean ground beef

2 garlic cloves, crushed through a press

¼ cup freshly grated Parmigiano-Reggiano cheese

¼ cup finely chopped fresh flat-leaf parsley

1 tablespoon dry Italian-seasoned bread crumbs

¼ teaspoon salt

¼ teaspoon freshly ground black pepper

2 cups store-bought or homemade (page 432) sweet and sour dipping sauce (optional)

1. Preheat the oven to 400°F. Spray a large rimmed baking sheet with nonstick cooking spray. Combine all the ingredients in a bowl and mix well. Shape into 1-inch balls using your hands or a melon-ball scoop. Place on the prepared baking sheet with about ½ inch of space between the meatballs.

2. Bake the meatballs until cooked through, about 15 minutes. Serve with sweet and sour dipping sauce, if you like.

LAMB AND FETA MEATBALLS

PREP: 15 minutes   COOK: 15 minutes

Makes about 40 meatballs

1½ pounds ground lean lamb

1 (12-ounce) eggplant, finely chopped

1 small onion, finely chopped

1 egg

¾ cup (3 ounces) crumbled feta cheese

½ cup fine dry plain bread crumbs

2 tablespoons finely chopped fresh flat-leaf parsley

1 teaspoon minced fresh rosemary

½ teaspoon salt

¼ teaspoon freshly ground black pepper

2 cups Yogurt–Horseradish Sauce (optional, page 439)

1. Preheat the oven to 400°F. Spray a large rimmed baking sheet with nonstick cooking spray. Combine all the ingredients in a bowl and mix well. Shape into 1-inch balls using your hands or a melon-ball scoop. Place on the prepared baking sheet with about ½ inch of space between the meatballs.

2. Bake the meatballs until cooked through, about 15 minutes. Serve with Yogurt–Horseradish Sauce, if you like.

ONION-STUFFED MEATBALLS

PREP: 20 minutes   COOK: 15 minutes

Makes about 40 meatballs

1 pound ground beef

¾ cup soft bread crumbs

1 egg

2 tablespoons store-bought steak sauce

28 cocktail onions

1 (18-ounce) jar grape jelly

⅓ cup prepared yellow mustard

1. Preheat the oven to 400°F. Spray a large rimmed baking sheet with nonstick cooking spray. Combine the beef, bread crumbs, egg, and steak sauce in a medium bowl and mix well. For each meatball, shape 1 tablespoon of the meat mixture around a cocktail onion.

2. Place the meatballs on the prepared baking sheet with about ½ inch of space between the meatballs. Bake until cooked through, about 15 minutes.

3. While the meatballs cook, make the sauce: Mix the jelly and mustard in a large microwave-safe bowl and cover with plastic wrap. Microwave on high power until the jelly is melted and the mixture is smooth, 1 to 3 minutes, stirring every 1 minute.

4. Drain the meatballs, add to the sauce, and stir to coat. Serve the meatballs in the sauce.

CLASSIC BUFFALO CHICKEN WINGS

PREP: 20 minutes   COOK: 9 minutes per batch

Makes 32 pieces

2½ pounds chicken wings (about 16)
Vegetable oil for frying
½ cup all-purpose flour
¾ teaspoon cayenne
½ teaspoon salt
2 tablespoons hot pepper sauce
2 tablespoons red wine vinegar
Blue Cheese Dipping Sauce (page 447)
Celery sticks

1. Cut the wing tips off the wings and discard. Cut the remaining wings in half at the joint.

2. Preheat the oven to 300°F. Heat ¾ inch of oil in a deep, heavy, large skillet to 400°F on a deep-fat thermometer. Combine the flour, cayenne, and salt in a large zip-top plastic bag, seal, and shake to mix. Add the wing pieces and shake to coat.

3. In batches, add the wing pieces to the hot oil without crowding the pan and fry, turning once, until crisp and cooked through, about 9 minutes. Use long tongs to transfer to paper towel–lined baking sheets to drain. Keep warm in the oven while frying the remaining chicken.

4. Combine the pepper sauce and vinegar in a large bowl and mix well. Add the wings and toss to coat. Serve with the Blue Cheese Dipping Sauce and celery sticks.

GARLIC-CAYENNE CHICKEN WINGS

1½ pounds chicken wings (about 9)
1¼ teaspoons garlic salt
½ teaspoon freshly ground black pepper
½ teaspoon cayenne
Herbed Tomato Dipping Sauce (page 448)

1. Preheat the broiler. Line a baking sheet with foil. Cut the wing tips off the wings and discard. Cut the remaining wings in half at the joint. Place the wing pieces on the prepared baking sheet.

2. Mix the garlic salt, pepper, and cayenne in a cup. Sprinkle the mixture over the wings and toss to coat. Broil 4 inches from the heat, turning once, until cooked through and crisp, 10 to 12 minutes. Serve with the dipping sauce.

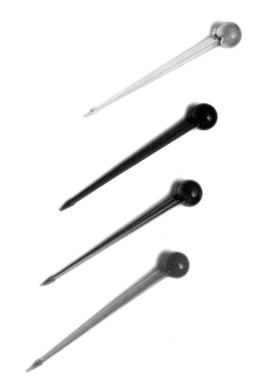

LEMON CRUNCH WINGS

PREP: 20 minutes COOK: 35 minutes

Makes about 36 pieces

Try this wonderful coating and sauce with chicken drumsticks.

3 pounds chicken wings (about 18)
⅓ cup soy sauce or more if needed
½ cup coarsely ground blanched almonds
¼ cup fine dried bread crumbs
½ teaspoon garlic powder
½ teaspoon paprika
½ teaspoon cayenne
½ teaspoon salt
Lemony Green Onion Dipping Sauce
   (page 449)

1. Preheat the oven to 400°F. Line 2 baking sheets with parchment paper. Cut the wing tips off the wings and discard. Cut the remaining wings in half at the joint. Place in a large bowl and add the soy sauce. Toss to coat, adding a little more soy sauce if needed.

2. Combine the almonds, crumbs, garlic powder, paprika, cayenne, and salt in a zip-top plastic bag; seal and shake to combine. In batches, add the chicken wings, seal the bag, and shake to coat the chicken.

3. Place the coated wings on the prepared baking sheets with space in between the pieces. Bake until golden brown and fork-tender, about 35 minutes. Serve with the dipping sauce.

TANGERINE WINGS

PREP: 25 minutes plus marinating   COOK: 50 minutes

Makes about 36 pieces

3 pounds chicken wings (about 18)

3 tangerines or oranges

2 garlic cloves, crushed through a press

2 tablespoons soy sauce

2 tablespoons honey

½ teaspoon freshly ground black pepper

1. Cut the wing tips off the wings and discard. Cut the remaining wings in half at the joint.

2. Grate 1 tablespoon zest from the tangerines and place in a large shallow baking dish. Squeeze the juice from the tangerines into the dish with the zest and add the garlic, soy sauce, honey, and pepper. Mix well with a fork. Add the chicken and toss to coat. Cover with plastic wrap and marinate in the refrigerator at least 2 hours, turning occasionally.

3. Preheat the oven to 400°F. Line 2 baking sheets with foil. Lift the chicken pieces from the marinade, gently shake over the baking dish, and place 1 inch apart on the prepared baking sheets. Strain the marinade into a small saucepan. Heat to boiling over medium-high heat. Boil until reduced by half, about 10 minutes.

4. Bake the wings until cooked through, about 40 minutes, basting every 10 minutes with the reduced marinade.

HERB-CRUSTED WINGS

PREP: **20 minutes** COOK: **40 minutes**

Makes about 36 pieces

3 pounds chicken wings (about 18)

1½ cups fine fresh bread crumbs

¾ cup freshly grated Asiago or kasseri cheese

1 tablespoon chopped fresh thyme (no stems)

1 tablespoon finely chopped fresh rosemary

1 teaspoon dried oregano, crushed

1 teaspoon salt

1 teaspoon freshly ground black pepper

1½ cups buttermilk

1. Preheat the oven to 425°F. Line 2 baking sheets with foil. Cut the wing tips off the wings and discard. Cut the remaining wings in half at the joint.

2. Combine the bread crumbs, cheese, thyme, rosemary, oregano, salt, and pepper in a large zip-top plastic bag. Seal and shake to mix. Place the buttermilk in another zip-top bag and add the chicken. Seal and shake to coat. Drain the chicken and, in batches, add to the crumb mixture. Seal and shake to coat. Place the wings about 1 inch apart on the prepared baking sheet.

3. Bake the wings until cooked through, about 40 minutes.

STICKY-GLAZE WINGS

PREP: 20 minutes plus marinating   COOK: 40 minutes

Makes about 36 pieces

3 pounds chicken wings (about 18)

½ cup roasted-garlic teriyaki sauce

½ cup cocktail sauce

¼ cup honey

¼ teaspoon cayenne

1. Line 2 rimmed baking sheets with parchment paper. Cut the wing tips off the wings and discard. Cut the remaining wings in half at the joint.

2. Combine the teriyaki sauce, cocktail sauce, honey, and cayenne in a large roasting pan and mix well. Add the wing pieces and toss to coat. Place the wings about 1 inch apart on the prepared baking sheets, cover with plastic wrap, and marinate in the refrigerator for at least 1 hour.

3. Preheat the oven to 400°F. Bake the wings, turning every 10 minutes, until cooked through, about 40 minutes.

CRISPY OREGANO WINGS

PREP: 25 minutes plus marinating   COOK: 40 minutes

Makes about 36 pieces

3 pounds chicken wings (about 18)
2 garlic cloves, crushed through a press
¼ cup olive oil
1 teaspoon salt
1 teaspoon dried oregano, crushed
½ teaspoon freshly ground black pepper
¼ teaspoon cayenne
1 cup Wondra flour, rice flour, or fine cornmeal
1 teaspoon paprika

1. Cut the wing tips off the wings and discard. Cut the remaining wings in half at the joint.

2. Combine the garlic, oil, salt, oregano, pepper, and cayenne in a large roasting pan and mix well. Add the wing pieces and toss to coat. Cover with plastic wrap and marinate in the refrigerator at least 2 hours, turning occasionally.

3. Preheat the oven to 425°F. Line 2 baking sheets with foil. Combine the flour and paprika in a small bowl and mix well. Lift the chicken pieces from the marinade, gently shake over the baking dish, and place 1 inch apart on the prepared baking sheets. Sprinkle the chicken liberally on one side with the flour mixture, turn the chicken over, and sprinkle on the other side.

4. Bake the wings until cooked through, about 40 minutes.

CIDER-GLAZED SPARERIBS

PREP: 20 minutes COOK: 1 hour 48 minutes

Makes 16 servings

5 pounds pork spareribs, in slabs
1¾ teaspoons salt
1¼ teaspoons freshly ground black pepper
Cider-Honey Barbecue Sauce (page 450)

1. Preheat the oven to 350°F. Line a large roasting pan with a double thickness of aluminum foil, extending the ends far enough to fold over and seal in the center. Place the ribs in the pan, sprinkle on both sides with the salt and pepper, and fold the foil over the ribs so the ends meet, then fold the ends over each other a couple of times. Fold the foil at the sides of the pan together and seal. Bake the ribs until cooked through and tender, 1½ hours. Let cool in the foil package.

2. Prepare a grill for barbecue or preheat the broiler. Line a baking sheet with foil. Unwrap the ribs and place on the prepared baking sheet. Grill or broil 6 inches from the heat, for 18 to 20 minutes, turning every 5 minutes with tongs. In the last 10 minutes, baste on both sides with the Cider-Honey Barbecue Sauce.

3. Cut the ribs in between the bones and serve with the remaining sauce.

KENTUCKY-STYLE COUNTRY RIBS

PREP: **15 minutes**   COOK: **3 hours 18 minutes**

Makes 16 servings

5 pounds country-style pork ribs
   (about 16 pieces)
1 teaspoon salt
½ teaspoon pepper
2 cups Kentucky Barbecue Sauce
   (page 451)

1. Preheat the oven to 250°F. Line a large roasting pan with a double thickness of aluminum foil, extending the ends far enough to fold over and seal in the center. Place the ribs in the pan, sprinkle on both sides with the salt and pepper, and fold the foil over the ribs so the ends meet, then fold the ends over each other a couple of times, then fold the foil at the sides of the pan together and seal. Bake until cooked through and tender, 3 hours. Let cool in the foil package.

2. Prepare a grill for barbecue or preheat the broiler. Line a baking sheet with foil. Unwrap the ribs and place on the prepared baking sheet. Brush on both sides with about half the Kentucky Barbecue Sauce. Grill or broil 6 inches from the heat, for 18 to 20 minutes, turning every 5 minutes with tongs. In the last 10 minutes, baste on both sides with sauce.

MUSTARD-GLAZED SPARERIBS

PREP: 20 minutes   COOK: 1 hour

Makes 16 servings

3 pounds pork spareribs, cut lengthwise through
the slabs to make 2-inch-wide strips of ribs
(ask the butcher to do this)

1 cup cider vinegar

1 cup boiling water

GLAZE

1 (12-ounce) jar currant jelly

1 cup store-bought or homemade (page 432)
sweet and sour dipping sauce

¼ cup Dijon mustard

¼ cup prepared horseradish

1. Preheat the oven to 500°F. Line a large roasting pan
with a double thickness of aluminum foil, extending the
ends far enough to fold over and seal in the center. Place
the ribs in the pan, pour the vinegar and boiling water

on top, and fold the foil over the ribs so the ends meet.
Fold the ends over each other a couple of times, then
fold the foil at the sides of the pan together and seal.
Bake 30 minutes.

2. Meanwhile, make the glaze: Combine all the glaze
ingredients in a medium saucepan and heat to boiling
over medium-high heat, stirring to dissolve the jelly.
Reduce the heat to low and simmer 10 minutes, stirring
occasionally.

3. Line a baking sheet with foil. Remove the roasting pan
from the oven. Reduce the oven temperature to 375°F.
Carefully unfold the foil to avoid getting blasted by the
steam. Transfer the ribs to the prepared baking sheet using
tongs. Discard the vinegar cooking liquid. Return the ribs
to the pan and brush the ribs on both sides with half the
glaze. Bake, uncovered, 15 minutes. Turn the ribs over,
baste with glaze, and bake 15 minutes longer.

4. Place the ribs on a cutting board and cut through the
ribs leaving meat equally spaced on the bones.

EAST-MEETS-WEST SPARERIBS

PREP: 20 minutes   COOK: 1 hour 5 minutes
Makes 12 to 15 servings

3 pounds pork spareribs, baby backs, full-size slabs,
  or country-style
1 teaspoon salt
½ teaspoon pepper
Balsamic-Soy Barbecue Sauce (page 452)

1. Preheat the oven to 375°F. Line a large roasting pan with a double thickness of aluminum foil, extending the ends far enough to fold over and seal in the center. Place the ribs in the pan, sprinkle on both sides with the salt and pepper, and fold the foil over the ribs so the ends meet. Fold the ends over each other a couple of times, then fold the foil at the sides of the pan together and seal. Bake 45 minutes.

2. Line a baking sheet with foil. Unwrap the ribs and place on the prepared baking sheet. Brush the ribs on both sides with half the Balsamic-Soy Barbecue Sauce. Bake 20 minutes. Brush the ribs with the remaining sauce and bake 20 minutes longer, basting with pan juices every 5 to 7 minutes. Cut through the ribs (unless you're using country ribs) and serve.

HOISIN RIBS

PREP: 20 minutes **COOK: 1 hour 33 minutes**

Makes 16 servings

2 (1- to 1½-pound) slabs baby-back pork ribs

1 teaspoon salt

½ teaspoon freshly ground black pepper

¼ cup dry mustard

Water as needed

¼ cup toasted sesame seeds

½ cup hoisin sauce

1. Preheat the oven to 400°F. Line a large roasting pan with a double thickness of aluminum foil, extending the ends far enough to fold over and seal in the center. Place the ribs in the pan, sprinkle on both sides with the salt and pepper, and fold the foil over the ribs so the ends meet. Fold the ends over each other a couple of times, then fold the foil at the sides of the pan together and seal. Bake until the meat is fork-tender, about 1½ hours.

2. Meanwhile, make the mustard sauce: Place the mustard in a small bowl and thin to a dipping consistency with water. Stir in the sesame seeds. Set aside.

3. Prepare a grill for barbecue or preheat the broiler. Line a baking sheet with foil. Unwrap the ribs and place on the prepared baking sheet. Combine the hoisin sauce with enough water to thin to a thick glazing consistency; brush on both sides of the ribs. Grill or broil 6 inches from the heat until nicely browned, 3 to 4 minutes. Cut through the ribs and serve with the mustard sauce for dipping.

SCALLOP SEVICHE AND MANGO NACHOS

PREP: 10 minutes plus marinating   COOK: 3 minutes

Makes 16 nachos

½ cup lime juice
1 teaspoon Tabasco sauce
8 ounces bay scallops
16 blue corn chips
4 ounces fresh goat's milk cheese (chèvre), crumbled
1 cup Mango–Red Pepper Salsa (page 54)

1. In a medium bowl, combine the lime juice and Tabasco. Add the scallops and toss to coat. Cover and marinate in the refrigerator 2 hours.

2. Preheat the broiler. Drain the scallops. Spread out the corn chips on a baking sheet and sprinkle with the cheese. Broil until the cheese melts, about 3 minutes. Sprinkle the nachos with the salsa and top with the scallops.

BEEF AND AVOCADO NACHOS

PREP: 15 minutes   COOK: 15 minutes

Makes 48 nachos

1 teaspoon vegetable oil

1 garlic clove, crushed through a press

8 ounces lean ground beef

1½ teaspoons chili powder

¼ teaspoon ground cumin

¼ teaspoon salt

1 avocado

1 tablespoon lemon juice

12 corn tortillas

1 (16-ounce) can bean dip, stirred to soften

1 (4-ounce) can nacho sliced jalapeños, drained

1½ cups (6 ounces) shredded Monterey Jack cheese

Salsa Fresca (page 51)

Sour cream or queso fresco

¼ cup thinly sliced green onions

1. Preheat the oven to 400°F. Heat the oil in a large skillet over medium heat. Add the garlic and beef and sauté until the beef is browned, about 5 minutes, stirring with a wooden spoon to break up the beef. Stir in the chili powder, cumin, and salt and cook 2 minutes. Remove from the heat.

2. Peel and pit the avocado, place in a bowl, and mash with a fork. Sprinkle with the lemon juice but do not mix it in. Cover with plastic wrap and set aside.

3. Cut the tortillas crosswise into fourths. Spread out the wedges on 2 baking sheets. Spoon a little beef mixture, bean dip, and jalapeños on each and sprinkle with cheese. Bake until the cheese melts, about 7 minutes.

4. Place the nachos on a serving platter. Mix the avocado with the lemon juice and spoon a dollop on each nacho. Top each with some salsa, sour cream, and green onions and serve.

BLACK BEAN AND HOMINY NACHOS

PREP: 10 minutes   COOK: 3 minutes

Makes 16 nachos

16 large yellow corn chips

1½ cups (6 ounces) shredded cheddar cheese

1 cup Texas Caviar (page 47)

Preheat the broiler. Spread out the corn chips on a baking sheet. Sprinkle with the cheese and top with the Texas Caviar. Broil until the cheese melts, about 3 minutes.

HAM AND CHAYOTE NACHOS

PREP: 10 minutes   COOK: 3 minutes

Makes 16 nachos

16 large white corn chips
1½ cups (6 ounces) shredded Jarlsberg
    or other Swiss cheese
4 thin slices smoked ham, cut into ½-inch dice
1 cup Chayote-Melon Salsa (page 56)

Preheat the broiler. Spread out the corn chips on a baking sheet and sprinkle with the cheese. Broil until the
cheese melts, about 3 minutes. Sprinkle with the ham
and top with some salsa.

CHICKEN AND PINTO BEAN MINI TOSTADAS

PREP: 10 minutes

Makes 36 tostadas

1 cup cooked pinto beans (drained and rinsed if canned or cooked if from dried)

1 cup shredded cooked chicken

2 tablespoons chopped fresh cilantro

2 tablespoons lime juice

¼ teaspoon salt

¼ teaspoon freshly ground black pepper

36 round, flat tortilla chips

½ cup sour cream or more if needed

2 cups shredded romaine lettuce

1 cup (4 ounces) shredded Monterey Jack cheese with jalapeños

1 firm ripe avocado, pitted, peeled, thinly sliced, and cut into 1-inch pieces

1. Combine the beans, chicken, cilantro, lime juice, salt, and pepper in a bowl and mix well.

2. Spread one side of each tortilla chip with some sour cream and sprinkle with some lettuce. Top with the bean mixture to cover but not enough to fall off when the tortilla chip is picked up. Sprinkle with a thin layer of cheese and top with a piece of avocado.

GRILLED BLACK BEAN AND PEAR-SALSA QUESADILLAS

PREP: 15 minutes   COOK: 2 minutes

Makes 30 wedges

1 (10-ounce) package flour tortillas
2 cups (8 ounces) shredded Monterey jack cheese
*   with jalapeños*
1 cup fresh cilantro leaves
1 cup cooked black beans (drained and rinsed if canned
*   or cooked if from dried)*
½ cup Fresh Pear–Orange Salsa (page 57)

1. Prepare a grill for barbecue or preheat the broiler. Line a baking sheet with foil. Spread 5 tortillas out on the prepared baking sheet and sprinkle each with cheese, cilantro, beans, and salsa, dividing evenly. Top each with a remaining tortilla.

2. Carefully transfer each quesadilla to a hot grill or oven rack and grill or broil about 4 inches from the heat until the cheese starts to melt, 1 to 2 minutes. Turn and grill or broil until browned on the other side, 1 to 2 minutes. Place the quesadillas on a cutting board and cut each into 6 wedges using a pizza cutter. Serve hot.

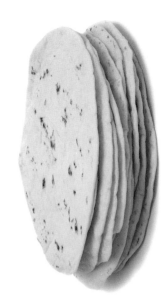

RICE AND BEAN QUESADILLAS

PREP: 10 minutes   COOK: 8 minutes

Makes 24 wedges

6 (10-inch) flour tortillas
1 (16-ounce) can refried beans
1 cup Salsa Fresca (page 51)
1 cup cooked rice
1 cup (4 ounces) shredded Monterey Jack cheese
Sour cream

1. Preheat the oven to 400°F. Lay 3 tortillas on the work surface and spread each with one-third of the beans. Cover the beans with salsa and sprinkle with the rice and then the cheese. Cover each with a remaining tortilla. Place the quesadillas on 2 baking sheets. Bake until the cheese melts, about 8 minutes.

2. Let the quesadillas stand 4 minutes. Slide them onto a cutting board and cut each into 8 wedges using a pizza cutter. Serve immediately with sour cream.

PULL-APART THREE-CHEESE QUESADILLAS

PREP: 15 minutes COOK: 10 minutes

Makes 8 wedges

4 (7-inch) corn tortillas

½ cup ricotta cheese

1⅓ cups (about 5 ounces) shredded mozzarella

¼ cup crumbled feta cheese

12 fresh basil leaves

1. Preheat the oven to 400°F. Line a baking sheet with parchment paper. Place 2 tortillas on the prepared baking sheet and spread each with half the ricotta. Sprinkle with the mozzarella and the feta, dividing evenly. Stack the basil leaves on a cutting board and cut crosswise into fine shreds. Sprinkle onto the cheese-topped tortillas. Cover each with a remaining tortilla and press lightly.

2. Bake the quesadillas 5 minutes. Carefully turn the quesadillas over. Bake until golden and the cheeses have melted, about 5 minutes longer. Slide the parchment and the quesadillas onto a cutting board and cut each into 4 wedges using a pizza cutter. Serve the quesadillas intact so the pieces can be pulled apart from each other.

BARBECUED CHICKEN QUESADILLA GRANDE

PREP: 10 minutes   COOK: 6 minutes

Makes 5 pieces

2 (14-inch) flour sandwich wraps
1 (4-ounce) can chopped mild green chiles
2 cups shredded cooked barbecued chicken
2 cups (8 ounces) shredded cheddar cheese
½ cup Salsa Verde (page 52)

1. Preheat the oven to 425°F. Place 1 wrap on a large baking sheet and sprinkle with the chiles, chicken, cheese, and salsa. Top with the remaining wrap and press lightly. Bake until the cheese starts to melt, about 3 minutes.

2. Place another baking sheet on top of the quesadilla and invert so the quesadilla sits on the second baking sheet. Bake until the cheese is really melted, about 3 minutes.

3. Slide the quesadilla onto a cutting board and use a pizza cutter to cut into slices. Slide the cookie sheet under the quesadillas and use it to transfer the pieces to a serving platter. Serve immediately.

COCKTAIL-SIZE BURRITOS

PREP: 20 minutes   COOK: 18 minutes

Makes 24 burritos

6 (7- to 8-inch) flour tortillas
8 ounces lean ground beef
2 teaspoons chili powder
¼ teaspoon salt
1 cup Crisp Corn Salsa (page 58)
½ cup (2 ounces) shredded Monterey Jack cheese
    with jalapeños
1 bunch fresh chives

1. Preheat the oven to 400°F. Cut out 4 rounds from each tortilla using a 3-inch cookie cutter. Cover the rounds with plastic wrap and set aside.

2. In a large skillet over high heat, combine the beef with the chili powder and salt and sauté until browned. Remove the pan from the heat and stir in the salsa and cheese.

3. Working in batches, lay out the rounds on the work surface and spread 1 heaping tablespoon of the beef mixture across the center of each. Fold the sides over the filling so the filling is exposed on the two ends of the burrito; tie a chive around it to hold the burrito together.

4. Place the burritos on a baking sheet. Bake until hot, about 10 minutes.

DESSERTS

CUT-YOUR-OWN BROWNIE SLAB

PREP: 10 minutes   COOK: 40 minutes

Makes 24 pieces

8 ounces bittersweet chocolate

1 cup (2 sticks) unsalted butter, cut into 1-inch pieces

1½ cups superfine or granulated sugar

3 eggs

2 cups all-purpose flour

½ teaspoon baking powder

½ cup Chocolate Ganache (page 461)
   or ½ cup Chocolate Glaze (page 463) (optional)

Place a knife alongside the brownie so guests can cut at will. Instead of the ganache or glaze, you can dust with sifted confectioners' sugar and/or cocoa powder.

1. Preheat the oven to 350°F. Grease a 9-inch square cake pan with butter. Line the bottom with parchment and grease the parchment.

2. Place the chocolate in a food processor and process until finely chopped. Place in a large, wide saucepan and add the butter. Heat over low heat, stirring occasionally, until melted and smooth. Pour into a large bowl.

3. If using granulated sugar, while the chocolate and butter melt, place the sugar in the same (unwashed) food processor and process until as fine as plain salt.

4. Combine the sugar and eggs in another large bowl and beat with an electric mixer at high speed until light and thick. Fold the egg mixture into the chocolate mixture. Mix the flour with the baking powder and fold into the chocolate mixture until no white streaks remain. Pour into the prepared pan and spread evenly.

5. Bake until set but not dry, about 30 minutes (a wooden pick inserted in the center should come out with moist crumbs on it). Cool completely on a wire rack.

6. Invert the brownie onto a cookie sheet and remove the pan and paper. Place another cookie sheet on the brownie and flip the sheets and brownie over in one motion. Slide onto a cutting board. If you like, spread the brownie with Chocolate Ganache or Chocolate Glaze.

FRIED PUMPKIN RAVIOLI

PREP: 20 minutes plus standing

COOK: 2 minutes per batch

Makes 12 ravioli

½ cup ricotta cheese

2 Italian amaretti cookies or gingersnaps, crushed

½ cup pumpkin puree

¼ cup sugar

2 tablespoons finely chopped candied ginger

1 teaspoon grated lemon zest

1 teaspoon amaretto liqueur or ¼ teaspoon vanilla extract

⅛ teaspoon salt

24 (3-inch) wonton or gyoza wrappers

Vegetable oil for deep-frying

Confectioners' sugar for dusting

1. Place the ricotta in a sieve lined with a double thickness of cheesecloth and set over a bowl; let stand 4 hours or overnight in the refrigerator to drain.

2. Combine the drained ricotta, cookies, pumpkin puree, sugar, ginger, lemon zest, liqueur, and salt in a bowl and mix well.

3. Lay out 4 wrappers on a work surface. Draw lines in the pumpkin filling with a spoon to estimate 3 portions. Spoon one-fourth of one portion onto the center of each wrapper. Brush the outside edges of the wrapper with water and cover with another wrapper, making sure not to trap any air inside the ravioli. Press the edges together to seal. Place the ravioli on a baking sheet and cover with a damp kitchen towel. Repeat with remaining wrappers and filling.

4. Heat 2 inches of oil in a wide, heavy saucepan or deep skillet over medium-high heat to 375°F. A few at a time, fry the ravioli until crisp, about 2 minutes, leaving space between them in the pan so they will brown evenly and turning them with long-handled tongs (do not use tongs with spiked ends or they may puncture the ravioli). Drain on a paper towel–lined baking sheet. Dust with confectioners' sugar while hot. Repeat with remaining ravioli.

MOCHA POTS DE CRÈME

1 cup semisweet chocolate chips

½ cup sugar

1 tablespoon espresso-coffee powder

3 cups half-and-half

6 egg yolks

1 teaspoon vanilla extract

Chantilly Cream (page 456)

Plain or chocolate-covered coffee beans

1. Preheat the oven to 325°F. Combine the chocolate, sugar, coffee powder, and 1 cup half-and-half in a medium saucepan. Cook over low heat, stirring occasionally, until the chocolate melts and mixture is smooth. Combine the egg yolks and vanilla in a large bowl and stir until blended. Gradually whisk in the warm chocolate mixture until blended and smooth. Whisk in the remaining 2 cups half-and-half until blended.

2. Pour the mixture into 8 (6-ounce) pots de crème cups or 16 (3-ounce) ramekins or heat-safe glass cups. Place in a shallow roasting pan. Place the pan on the oven rack and add enough hot water to the pan to come halfway up the sides of the dishes. Bake until the edges are set, the centers are trembling, and a thin-bladed knife inserted in the centers come out clean, 40 to 45 minutes for the pots de crème cups, or 20 minutes for the ramekins. (The mixture will firm up upon cooling and chilling.)

3. Remove the pots de crème from the roasting pan and cool on a wire rack. Place on a baking sheet, cover with a flat paper towel and then plastic wrap, and refrigerate overnight.

4. To serve, pipe a Chantilly Cream rosette onto each serving and garnish with a coffee bean.

CLASSIC CHOCOLATE MOUSSE

PREP: 20 minutes COOK: 5 minutes

Makes 4 or 8 servings

¼ cup granulated sugar

¼ cup water

3 egg yolks

6 ounces bittersweet chocolate, chopped and melted

1 teaspoon vanilla extract

¾ cup heavy cream, chilled and whipped until stiff, plus optional additional whipped cream for serving

1. Combine the sugar and water in a small saucepan and stir to dissolve the sugar. Heat to boiling over high heat; boil 3 minutes.

2. Whisk the egg yolks in a heat-safe medium bowl until thick and pale. Gradually whisk in the hot syrup until blended and the egg yolks are cooked; whisk until cool, about 5 minutes. Add the chocolate and whisk until blended. Whisk in the vanilla. Fold in one-third of the whipped cream using a rubber spatula. Fold in the remaining whipped cream until no white streaks remain.

3. Spoon the mousse into 4 glass compote dishes or 8 martini glasses. Refrigerate until serving. If you like, garnish with piped rosettes or dollops of extra whipped cream just before serving.

FRUIT FOOL SHOTS

½ pint blueberries

¼ cup sugar

2 tablespoons crème de cassis

1 tablespoon water

1 cup crème fraîche

½ cup heavy cream

Red currants, raspberries, or a few
reserved blueberries for garnish

1. Place the blueberries in a small saucepan. Add the sugar, crème de cassis, and water. Cover and cook over medium heat until the berries start to pop, about 10 minutes. Stir to dissolve the sugar and cook 5 minutes longer. Pour the mixture into a food processor and puree. Strain through a sieve into a bowl.

2. Combine the crème fraîche and cream in a large, shallow bowl and whisk until blended and smooth. Drizzle the blueberry puree over the cream. Briefly stir the puree into the crème fraîche mixture to make swirls without blending completely. Spoon the fool into shot glasses or small glass cups. Refrigerate until firm. Garnish with a few fresh berries.

For a layered look, you can start with a base of the crème fraîche, add the puree, and then repeat. Top with the cream mixture.

Foolish Tarts

Instead of serving the fool in glasses, spoon it into Chocolate Cups (page 366), Honey-Sesame Cups (page 367), or baked Tartlet Shells (page 218) just before serving.

PERSIMMON MOUSSE IN CHOCOLATE CUPS

PREP: 20 minutes plus chilling

Makes 12 servings

3 ripe Japanese persimmons

¼ cup sugar

1 tablespoon lemon juice

¼ teaspoon salt

¼ cup finely diced candied orange peel

¼ cup finely diced candied pineapple

½ cup heavy cream

12 small Chocolate Cups (page 366)

1. Cut the persimmons in half, discard the seeds, and scoop the pulp into a food processor. Add the sugar, lemon juice, and salt and process until smooth. Scrape the mixture into a medium bowl and stir in the orange peel and pineapple.

2. Beat the cream in a bowl or glass measure until soft peaks form when the beaters are raised. Fold the cream into the persimmon mixture until no white streaks remain. Spoon or pipe the persimmon mousse mixture into the chocolate cups. Transfer to a freezer container, cover, and freeze until firm, about 2 hours. Remove the cups from the freezer about 10 minutes before serving.

CREAM PUFFS

PREP: 20 minutes COOK: 40 minutes

Makes 12 cream puffs

Choux Pastry (page 224)
1 egg beaten with 2 tablespoons water (egg wash)
Chantilly Cream (page 456) or Pastry Cream (page 457)
Sliced fresh strawberries, peaches, plums,
    or blueberries or a mix of fruits (optional)
Confectioners' sugar for dusting

1. Preheat the oven to 425°F. Line a baking sheet with parchment paper. Spoon the pastry into 2-inch-wide balls 3 inches apart on the prepared baking sheet. Brush the tops of the balls with the egg wash, smoothing them with your finger as you brush.
2. Bake the pastry for 20 minutes. Reduce the oven temperature to 350°F and bake until the puffs are golden brown and crisp, about 20 minutes longer. (Do not open the door for the first half of baking or the puffs will deflate.) Carefully cut off the tops with a serrated knife (hot steam will come out) and remove any uncooked dough. Turn off the oven. Return the puffs and tops on the baking sheet to the oven and let cool with the oven door open.
3. Just before serving, pipe or spoon a generous amount of Chantilly Cream or Pastry Cream into the puffs, spoon or arrange fruit on top, and replace the tops. Dust with confectioners' sugar placed in a sieve and serve.

Mini Cream Puffs

Pipe or spoon 2-teaspoon amounts of the dough into balls spaced 1½ inches apart. Bake at 425°F until golden and crisp, about 17 minutes. Prepare, fill, and garnish as for regular Cream Puffs. Makes about 48 mini puffs.

PROFITEROLES

Choux Pastry (page 224)

1 egg beaten with 2 tablespoons water (egg wash)

Pastry Cream (page 457) or 1 quart vanilla ice cream

Caramel Sauce (page 471)

Mocha Rum Sauce (page 472)

1. Preheat the oven to 425°F. Line 2 baking sheets with parchment paper. Spoon or pipe the pastry into 1½-inch balls onto the prepared baking sheets. (You will need only 18 balls but you can pipe and bake a whole batch and use the puffs for something else, or freeze the remaining dough for later.) Brush the tops of the balls with the egg wash, smoothing them with your finger as you brush.

2. Bake the pastry for 20 minutes. Reduce the oven temperature to 350°F and bake until the puffs are golden brown and crisp, about 10 minutes longer. (Do not open the door for the first half of cooking or the puffs will deflate.) Carefully cut off the tops with a serrated knife (hot steam will come out) and remove any uncooked dough. Turn off the oven. Return the puffs and tops on the baking sheet to the oven and let cool with the oven door open.

3. Just before serving, fill the bottoms with Pastry Cream and cover with the pastry tops. Place 3 on each serving plate and drizzle the profiteroles and the plates with the caramel and mocha sauces.

CHOCOLATE ÉCLAIRS

PREP: 20 minutes COOK: 40 minutes

Makes 12 éclairs

Choux Pastry (page 224)
1 egg beaten with 2 tablespoons water (egg wash)
Pastry Cream (page 457)
Chocolate Glaze (page 463)

1. Preheat the oven to 425°F. Line a baking sheet with parchment paper. Place the pastry in a pastry bag fitted with a ¾-inch plain tip (a spoon doesn't work as well). Pipe into 12 (4-inch-long, 1½-inch-wide) strips 3 inches apart on the prepared baking sheet. Brush the tops of the strips with the egg wash.

2. Bake the pastry for 20 minutes. Reduce the oven temperature to 350°F and bake until the puffs are golden brown and crisp, about 20 minutes longer. (Do not open the door for the first half of cooking or the puffs will deflate.) Carefully cut off the tops with a serrated knife (hot steam will come out) and remove any uncooked dough. Turn off the oven. Return the puffs and tops on the baking sheet to the oven and let cool with the oven door open.

3. Just before serving, pipe or spoon a generous amount of Pastry Cream into the éclairs and replace the tops. Spread Chocolate Glaze on the top of each éclair and serve.

Mini Chocolate Éclairs

Pipe or spoon 1 tablespoon-amounts of the dough into 36 (2-inch-long, ½-inch-wide) strips spaced 1½ inches apart. Bake at 425°F until golden and crisp, about 17 minutes. Cool, split, and clean out uncooked dough as for regular éclairs. Pipe Pastry Cream into the bottoms, replace the tops, and coat the tops with Chocolate Glaze. Makes 36 mini éclairs.

CRÊPE TORTE WEDGES

PREP: 15 minutes   COOK: 20 minutes

Makes 12 servings

2 (10-ounce) boxes frozen raspberries
or strawberries, thawed

1 tablespoon cornstarch

Crêpes (page 233), made as thinly as possible
(dilute the batter with 2 to 3 tablespoons water
and add more as needed as batter thickens
as it stands)

2 tablespoons brandy or heavy cream

1. Puree the berries in a food processor and strain
through a sieve into a small saucepan. Combine the
cornstarch with 2 tablespoons puree in a cup and stir
until blended. Whisk the mixture into the remaining
puree and heat just to boiling, whisking until thickened
and clear.

2. Preheat the oven to 300°F. Place 1 crêpe on a large
round heat-safe serving platter with the nicest looking
side up and spread a thin layer of puree on top. Repeat
with enough of the remaining crêpes to make a stack
about 2 inches high. Bake until heated through, about
10 minutes.

3. Stir the brandy into the remaining puree and add
enough hot water to thin it to a thin sauce consistency.
Heat until simmering.

4. Cut the torte into wedges and pour the sauce on the
platter around the torte or cut the torte into wedges,
place on dessert plates, and pour a little sauce around
each.

HAZELNUT-CREAM CRÊPE CIGARS

PREP: 10 minutes

Makes 24 pieces

12 Crêpes (page 233)
¾ cup hazelnut-chocolate spread
6 tablespoons store-bought or homemade (page 462)
   crème fraîche
Confectioners' sugar for dusting

Working with one crêpe at a time, place the crêpe with the nicer side down on the work surface. Spread with 1 tablespoon hazelnut-chocolate spread and a thin layer of about 1½ teaspoons crème fraîche. Roll up into a cigar shape and cut in half. Dust with confectioners' sugar.

PUMPKIN-GINGER CHEESECAKE

PREP: 25 minutes plus cooling   COOK: 1 hour 12 minutes

Makes 20 servings

1½ cups gingersnap cookie crumbs

5 tablespoons unsalted butter, melted

½ cup finely chopped toasted pecans

4 (8-ounce) packages cream cheese, softened

1 cup sugar

1½ teaspoons vanilla extract

4 eggs

¼ cup grated peeled fresh ginger and its juice

1 (1-pound) can pumpkin puree

1 tablespoon ground cinnamon

½ teaspoon ground allspice

½ teaspoon freshly grated nutmeg

1. Preheat the oven to 350°F. Combine the crumbs, butter, and pecans in a bowl and mix well. Press over the bottom of a 9-inch springform pan. Bake until the edges are brown, about 12 minutes. Set aside to cool.

2. Combine the cream cheese and sugar in a bowl of an electric mixer and beat at high speed until fluffy and smooth. Beat in the vanilla. Beat in the eggs, one at a time, beating well after each addition. Transfer 1 cup of the mixture to a bowl and add the ginger. Mix well. Add the pumpkin, cinnamon, allspice, and nutmeg to the cheese mixture in the mixer bowl and beat until blended.

3. Pour half the pumpkin mixture over the crumb crust and dot with half the ginger mixture. Swirl the mixtures with a knife to make swirls without blending. Top with the remaining pumpkin mixture and repeat with remaining ginger mixture.

4. Bake the cheesecake 1 hour. Turn off the oven and let cheesecake sit in the oven for 1 hour. Cool on a wire rack, cover with plastic wrap, and refrigerate overnight.

5. Remove the plastic wrap and the sides of the springform pan. Slide the cheesecake onto a serving platter. Slice with a hot, thin-bladed knife, wiping off the knife with a hot, wet cloth with each cut if necessary.

BITTERSWEET CHOCOLATE TART

PREP: 20 minutes plus chilling   COOK: 30 minutes

Makes 10 to 12 servings

Shortbread Pastry (page 232)

FILLING
¾ cup heavy cream
¼ cup whole milk
8 ounces bittersweet chocolate, grated
1 egg, beaten

TOPPING
1 cup confectioners' sugar
1 tablespoon milk or more if needed
2 teaspoons anise-flavored liqueur or Limoncello
(Italian lemon-flavored liqueur)

1. Grease a 9½-inch tart pan with a removable bottom and press the dough evenly into the pan to line the bottom and side. Refrigerate 30 minutes.

2. Preheat the oven to 350°F. Bake the tart shell until golden and baked through, 14 to 16 minutes. Cool completely.

3. Make the filling: Combine the cream and milk in a small saucepan and heat to simmering over medium heat. Remove the pan from the heat and add the chocolate. Whisk until the chocolate melts and the mixture is smooth. Set aside to cool.

4. Preheat the oven to 375°F. Add the egg to the filling and beat until blended. Pour the filling into the prepared tart shell. Bake on the center rack until the filling is firm around the edges but still trembling in the center, 12 to 15 minutes. Cool on a wire rack. Remove the pan side and slide the tart onto a serving platter.

5. To make the topping: Combine the confectioners' sugar, milk, and liqueur in a bowl and stir until smooth, adding more milk if needed to make a thin sauce. Drizzle the sauce over the tart to make a frenzied, energetic design. Serve the tart warm or at room temperature.

CHOCOLATE-PECAN TART

PREP: 45 minutes   **COOK:** 35 minutes

Makes 16 to 24 servings

Sweet Pie Crust Pastry (page 231)

1½ cups sugar

½ cup water

1 cup heavy cream

4 cups pecan halves

¼ teaspoon salt

2 eggs, beaten

2 (1-ounce) squares semisweet chocolate, chopped

1. Line a baking sheet with parchment paper. Roll out the pastry to a 12½-inch square and place on the prepared baking sheet. Fold the edges up and over to make a ½-inch-wide rim. Prick the surface of the center of the tart with a fork. Freeze 15 minutes.

2. Preheat the oven to 350°F. Bake the pastry until set, 15 to 18 minutes.

3. Combine the sugar and water in a large saucepan and stir until the sugar dissolves. Heat to boiling over high heat. Simmer over medium heat until the syrup is golden brown, 10 to 12 minutes. Remove the pan from the heat and carefully pour in the cream (the mixture will sputter). Return the pan to the heat and cook over medium heat, stirring, until the caramel melts and the mixture is smooth, about 1 minute. Pour the filling into a heat-safe bowl and cool, stirring frequently, 20 minutes.

4. Add the pecans and salt to the filling and mix well. Add the eggs and mix well. Pour into the pastry shell. Bake until set, 20 to 25 minutes.

5. Place the chocolate in a small saucepan and heat over low heat, stirring, until melted. Pour the chocolate over the tart and set aside to set. Cut into 1-inch squares and serve.

FRESH FRUIT CHEESECAKE TART

PREP: 15 minutes   COOK: 1 minute

Makes 12 servings

1 Baked Pastry Case (page 226)
1 (8-ounce) package cream cheese, softened
½ cup confectioners' sugar
2 tablespoons heavy cream
2 tablespoons brandy (optional)
3 peaches or nectarines, pitted and each cut
*   into 6 wedges*
1 cup red seedless grapes, halved
1 cup green seedless grapes, halved
½ cup Apricot Glaze (page 465) or ½ cup apple jelly
*   or more if needed*

1. Place the pastry case on a flat serving dish. Combine the cream cheese, sugar, cream, and brandy (if using) in a medium bowl and beat until light and fluffy. Spread the mixture evenly in the pastry case. Top with the peaches and red and green grapes, arranged cut side down in a lively design.

2. Heat the glaze in a small saucepan until melted and boiling (or place in a heat-safe cup, cover, and microwave on high power about 20 seconds). Brush over the fruit.

Fresh Fruit Cheesecake Tartlets

Spread the cream-cheese mixture over the bottoms of 24 baked shallow Phyllo Tartlet Shells (page 219) and top with small blueberries, strawberries, raspberries, fresh currants, and/or Champagne grapes. Brush with the hot Apricot Glaze and garnish with the tips of mint sprigs or herb flowers. Makes 24 tartlets.

FRUIT TART STRIPS

PREP: 25 minutes   COOK: 30 minutes

Makes 12 servings

½ (1-pound) package frozen puff pastry (1 sheet), thawed as package label directs

1 egg, lightly beaten

¼ cup ground almonds

3 tablespoons brown sugar

3 plums (1 black, 1 red, 1 green), quartered lengthwise and pitted

1 tablespoon granulated sugar

½ teaspoon ground cinnamon

½ cup blueberries

1. Preheat the oven to 400°F. Arrange the pastry on a cutting board. Trim a ½ inch strip from each side of the pastry. Brush the top edges of the pastry sheet with a little egg and place the trimmed pieces on top to form a border. Prick the bottom of the tart shell all over with a fork. Slide a sheet of parchment under the tart shell and lift it onto a baking sheet.

2. Mix the almonds and 1 tablespoon brown sugar together in a cup and sprinkle over the bottom of the tart shell. Arrange the plum slices cut side up, alternating colors and spacing them equally from each other, in two rows along the length of the tart shell (the slices should be parallel to the short sides).

3. Mix the remaining 2 tablespoons brown sugar with the granulated sugar and cinnamon in a cup. Sprinkle the blueberries around the plums and then sprinkle with the cinnamon sugar. Brush the top of the pastry border with egg. Bake until the pastry is puffed, golden brown, and crisp and the plums are tender, about 30 minutes.

4. Slide the paper with the tart onto a cutting board and cut in half lengthwise between the rows of plums. Cut crosswise so each slice contains a wedge of plum. Slide the tart, with the arrangement of the slices intact, onto a flat serving plate.

CREAMY STRAWBERRY TART

PREP: 10 minutes   COOK: 1 minute

Makes 12 servings

1 Baked Pastry Case (page 226)

Pastry Cream (page 457) or Easy Lemon Curd
(page 458)

1 pint strawberries, hulled, halved lengthwise

2 kiwifruit, peeled, cut crosswise into
¼-inch-thick slices, and quartered

½ cup Apricot Glaze (page 465) or ½ cup apple jelly
or more if needed

1. Place the pastry case on a flat serving dish. Spread
the pastry cream evenly in the pastry case. Top with the
strawberries, arranged cut side down in rows. Arrange
a kiwifruit quarter at the stem end of each berry.

2. Heat the glaze or jelly in a small saucepan until
melted and boiling (or place in a heat-safe cup, cover,
and microwave on high power about 20 seconds).
Brush over the fruit.

Blueberry, Blackberry, Dark Grape,
or Plum Tart

Use dark berries, grapes, or plum slices instead of the
strawberries and glaze with hot Red Currant Glaze
(page 466) instead of the Apricot Glaze.

LEMON MERINGUE TART

PREP: 10 minutes COOK: 15 minutes
Makes 12 servings

1 Baked Pastry Case (page 226)
Easy Lemon Curd (page 458)
4 egg whites, at room temperature
⅛ teaspoon salt
⅛ teaspoon cream of tartar
¼ cup sugar

1. Preheat the oven to 350°F. Place the pastry case on a baking sheet. Spread the lemon curd evenly in the pastry case.

2. Combine the egg whites, salt, and cream of tartar in a large bowl of an electric mixer and beat at high speed until they hold a soft peak when the beaters are raised. Gradually beat in the sugar, 1 tablespoon at a time. Beat until the meringue holds a stiff peak.

3. Spread the meringue over the lemon curd to seal the curd under the meringue. Bake until the meringue is set, about 15 minutes. If the meringue is not lightly browned, set the tart on a low oven rack and broil carefully to brown it.

EASY MINCEMEAT TART

PREP: 10 minutes   COOK: 15 minutes

Makes 12 servings

1 Baked Pastry Case (page 226)
3 cups prepared mincemeat
Brandied Hard Sauce (page 470)

1. Preheat the oven to 350°F. Place the pastry case on a baking sheet. Spread the mincemeat evenly in the pastry case.

2. Bake the tart until the mincemeat is bubbling, about 15 minutes. Transfer to a cutting board and cut the tart lengthwise in half and crosswise to make 12 even slices. Serve hot, with the sauce.

LIME TARTLETS

PREP: 25 minutes COOK: 8 minutes

Makes 12 tartlets

Sweet Pie Crust Pastry (page 231)
1 pomegranate or ¼ cup fresh blueberries
Lime Curd (page 460)

1. Preheat the oven to 400°F. Cut out 12 (2½-inch) rounds of parchment paper. Roll out the pastry on a lightly floured work surface to an ⅛-inch thickness. Cut out 12 (3½-inch) rounds with a cookie cutter and place in 12 (2½-inch) tartlet molds or in the 12 (2½-inch) cups of a regular-size muffin pan. Prick the pastry with a fork, line each with a round of parchment, and fill with enough dry rice or pastry weights to hold the paper against the sides of the tartlet shells. If using tartlet molds, place the 12 filled molds on a baking sheet.

2. Bake the tartlet shells until set, about 4 minutes. Carefully lift the papers and the rice or weights off the pastry and bake the tartlet shells until golden, about 4 minutes longer.

3. Cool the tartlet shells in the pans 5 minutes; carefully remove from the pans. Cool on a wire rack.

4. Cut the pomegranate in half and knock out the seeds into a bowl by hitting the skin side of the pomegranate with the back of a soup spoon. Just before serving, spread the lime curd in the tartlet shells and sprinkle with a few pomegranate seeds or blueberries.

Lemon Curd Tartlets

Spread Rich Lemon Lemon Curd (page 459) or Easy Lemon Curd (page 458) in the tarts instead of the Lime Curd. Garnish with the pomegranate seeds or thinly sliced fresh figs, arranging the slices cut side up.

TINY PECAN TARTS

PREP: 20 minutes   COOK: 25 minutes

Makes 24 tartlets

Cream-Cheese Pastry for Tartlets (page 229)

1 egg

¾ cup brown sugar

1 tablespoon unsalted butter, softened

1 teaspoon vanilla extract

⅛ teaspoon salt

⅔ cup broken pecan pieces

1. Preheat the oven to 325°F. Grease 2 (12-compartment) mini-muffin pans with nonstick cooking spray. Place a pastry ball in each cup and press evenly to line the bottom and side, up to the rim of each.

2. Combine the egg, sugar, butter, vanilla, and salt in a bowl and stir until blended. Stir in the pecans. Spoon the mixture into the lined muffin cups, dividing evenly and filling just to the rim of each.

3. Bake the tartlets until golden, 25 to 30 minutes. Cool before removing from the pans.

DOUBLE-CHOCOLATE TEACAKES

PREP: 20 minutes   COOK: 25 minutes

Makes 12 teacakes

10 ounces bittersweet chocolate, chopped

¾ cup (1½ sticks) unsalted butter,
cut into 1-inch pieces

5 eggs

½ cup sugar

¾ cup all-purpose flour

¾ teaspoon baking powder

Unsweetened cocoa powder for dusting
or Chocolate Glaze (page 463)

1. Preheat the oven to 325°F. Generously grease the 12 (5-ounce) cups of a regular-size muffin pan. Cut 12 rounds of parchment paper to fit the cups; place a round in each cup.

2. Combine the chocolate and butter in a small saucepan and heat over low heat, stirring frequently, until melted and smooth. Remove from the heat and set aside.

3. Combine the eggs and sugar in a medium bowl and beat at high speed with an electric mixer until light and fluffy, about 6 minutes. Combine the flour and baking powder in a sifter and sift over the egg mixture. Gently fold to mix. Add the chocolate mixture and fold to mix. Bake until the tops spring back when lightly pressed with your finger, about 20 minutes.

4. Pour the batter into prepared muffin pan cups. Bake until the tops spring back when lightly pressed with your finger, about 20 minutes.

5. Cool the cakes in the pan 2 minutes; transfer to a wire rack placed over a baking sheet. Dust with cocoa sprinkled through a fine sieve or spread with Chocolate Glaze. Serve warm.

MINIATURE CHEESECAKES

PREP: 25 minutes   COOK: 20 minutes

Makes 24 cheesecakes

A few fresh blueberries or a single raspberry makes a juicy alternative garnish.

Cream Cheese Pastry for Tartlets (page 229)

2 (3-ounce) packages cream cheese, softened

1 egg

2 tablespoons sugar

1 teaspoon vanilla extract

½ cup sour cream

¼ cup grape jelly or other purple or red jelly

1. Preheat the oven to 350°F. Grease 2 (12-compartment) mini-muffin pans with nonstick cooking spray. Place a pastry ball into each cup and press evenly to line the bottom and the side, up to the rim of each.

2. Combine the cream cheese, egg, sugar, and vanilla in a bowl and stir until blended. Spoon the mixture into the prepared muffin cups, dividing evenly and filling just to the rim of each.

3. Bake the tartlets until golden and set, about 20 minutes. Cool before removing from the pan.

4. Spread each cheesecake with sour cream. Melt the jelly in a small saucepan over low heat (or place in a custard cup, cover with plastic wrap, and microwave on high power 20 seconds, stirring after 10 seconds to blend the unmelted parts in with the melted). Drizzle the melted jelly over the cheesecakes and leave as is or feather the jelly into the sour cream using a wooden pick.

BABY FRUITCAKES

PREP: 25 minutes COOK: 15 minutes

Makes about 36 cakes

½ cup (1 stick) unsalted butter, softened

½ cup sugar

2 eggs

¼ cup finely diced candied orange peel

¼ cup finely diced candied lemon peel

¼ cup finely diced candied apricots

¼ cup finely diced candied mango

¼ cup finely diced candied pears

2 tablespoons orange-flavored liqueur

1 ¾ cups all-purpose flour

1 teaspoon baking powder

½ teaspoon ground cardamom

Lemon Glaze (page 464)

¼ cup chopped toasted pistachios

1. Preheat the oven to 350°F. Lightly butter the cups of 3 (12-compartment) mini-muffin pans. (Bake the fruit-cakes in batches if you don't have that many pans.)

2. Combine the butter and sugar in a large bowl and beat until light and fluffy. Beat in the eggs, one at a time, beating well after each addition. Stir in the candied fruits and liqueur.

3. Combine the flour, baking powder, and cardamom in a sifter, and sift the mixture onto a sheet of waxed paper. Gently stir the flour mixture into the batter until blended.

4. Fill each prepared muffin cup two-thirds full with the batter. Bake until the top of the cakes spring back when lightly pressed with your finger, 15 to 20 minutes. Cool the cakes in the pans 5 minutes on wire racks. Remove from the pans and let cool completely. Spread the tops with the Lemon Glaze. Top each with a pinch of pista-chios before the glaze sets.

EASY APPLE TARTLETS

PREP: 15 minutes plus standing   COOK: 25 minutes

Makes 16 tartlets

½ (1-pound) package frozen puff pastry (1 sheet), thawed overnight in the refrigerator

3 tablespoons unsalted butter

5 Granny Smith apples, peeled, cored, and sliced

⅓ cup brown sugar

¼ cup golden raisins

2 tablespoons Calvados (apple brandy) or other brandy (optional)

1 teaspoon ground cinnamon

Chantilly Cream (page 456) or vanilla ice cream for serving (optional)

1. Allow the puff pastry to stand at room temperature for 30 minutes so it can be unrolled without cracking.

2. Meanwhile, melt the butter in a large skillet over medium-high heat. Add the apples and sauté until softened, 4 to 5 minutes. Add the sugar, raisins, Calvados, and cinnamon and stir until the sugar starts to melt. Cook without covering until the juices thicken slightly, about 5 minutes. Set aside to cool completely.

3. Preheat the oven to 400°F. When the pastry is soft enough to unfold easily, roll out on a lightly floured work surface to a 12-inch square. Prick the entire surface evenly with a fork. Cut into 3-inch squares using a sharp knife.

4. Fit each square into a regular-size muffin cup. Fill each with the apple mixture. Bake until the pastry is a rich golden brown and the filling is bubbly, 12 to 15 minutes. Let the tarts cool in the pan 5 minutes; transfer to a wire rack. Serve with Chantilly Cream or ice cream, if you like.

ALMOND TWISTS

PREP: 20 minutes   COOK: 15 minutes

Makes 48 twists

1 cup ground almonds
⅓ cup plus about 2 tablespoons sugar
1 teaspoon ground cinnamon
Quick Flaky Pastry (page 227)
1 egg, beaten

1. Preheat the oven to 400°F. Line a baking sheet with parchment paper. Combine the almonds, ⅓ cup sugar, and the cinnamon in a small bowl and mix well.

2. Sprinkle about 1 tablespoon sugar on the work surface and roll out 1 pastry square to a 12-inch square, dusting the surface with more sugar if needed. (Keep the remaining pastry refrigerated until after the first batch of twists is baked.) Brush the square with the beaten egg and sprinkle with half the nut mixture. Lightly roll with the rolling pin to press the nuts into the pastry.

3. Cut the pastry square into 1-inch-wide strips using a sharp, thin-bladed knife. Cut the strips crosswise in half. Twist each strip 2 or 3 times and place 1 inch apart on the prepared baking sheets. Bake until golden, about 15 minutes. Cool on the baking sheets.

4. Repeat with the remaining pastry and nut mixture.

ELEPHANT EARS (PALMIERS)

PREP: 30 minutes plus chilling   COOK: 15 minutes

Makes 96 palmiers

½ cup plus about 2 tablespoons sugar
1 teaspoon ground cinnamon
Quick Flaky Pastry (page 227)

1. Combine ½ cup sugar and the cinnamon in a small bowl.

2. Sprinkle about 1 tablespoon sugar on the work surface and roll out 1 pastry square to a 12-inch square, dusting the surface with more sugar if needed. (Keep the remaining pastry refrigerated until after the first piece of dough is folded and refrigerated.) Sprinkle evenly with half the cinnamon sugar.

3. Fold over 2 opposite sides of the square so the ends meet in the center of the square. Repeat, folding the folded halves, making a 3- by 12-inch rectangle. Place

the rectangle on a baking sheet, cover with plastic wrap, and refrigerate. Repeat with the remaining pastry and cinnamon-sugar. Refrigerate the pastry rectangles at least 1 hour before rolling out.

4. Preheat the oven to 400°F. Line baking sheets with parchment paper. Place a pastry rectangle on a cutting board and cut crosswise into ¼-inch slices using a sharp, thin-bladed knife. Place the slices, cut side down and 1 inch apart, on the prepared baking sheets. Lightly flatten with the palm of your hand so the sugar mixture sticks to the pastry layers.

5. Bake the pastries until golden, about 15 minutes. Cool on the baking sheets. Repeat with the remaining pastry rectangle and cinnamon sugar.

DOUBLE-ALMOND MACAROONS

PREP: 20 minutes   COOK: 8 minutes

Makes 48 macaroons

1 cup toasted blanched whole almonds

1¼ cups sugar

1 (8-ounce) can or tube almond paste

2 egg whites

1 teaspoon grated lemon zest

3 ounces bittersweet chocolate, melted

3 ounces white chocolate, melted

1. Preheat the oven to 425°F. Line baking sheets with parchment paper. Combine the almonds and ¼ cup of the sugar in a food processor and grind until fine but not oily.

2. Break the almond paste into small pieces in a large bowl. Add the remaining 1 cup sugar, the egg whites, and the lemon zest. Whisk until blended. Whisk in the ground almonds. Place the mixture in a pastry bag fitted with a ½-inch star tip. Pipe rosettes onto the prepared baking sheets. Bake until golden, about 8 minutes. Cool on wire racks.

3. Dip half of each macaroon into one of the melted chocolates and set aside to dry on parchment-lined baking sheets.

DOUBLE-CHOCOLATE WAFER COOKIES

PREP: 20 minutes   COOK: 10 minutes

Makes about 30 cookies

1¼ cups (2 ½ sticks) unsalted butter, softened

1 cup packed light brown sugar

¾ cup granulated sugar

2 eggs

2 teaspoons vanilla extract

1¾ cups all-purpose flour

1 cup unsweetened European-style cocoa powder

1 teaspoon baking soda

½ teaspoon salt

1 (12-ounce) bag mini chocolate chips

1. Preheat the oven to 350°F. Line baking sheets with parchment paper. Combine the butter, brown sugar, and granulated sugar in the bowl of an electric mixer and beat at high speed until light and creamy. Beat in the eggs one at a time, beating after each addition. Beat until light and fluffy. Beat in the vanilla. Combine the flour, cocoa, baking soda, and salt in a sifter placed over a sheet of waxed paper; stir and sift. Add the flour mixture to the butter mixture and beat until blended. Stir in the chips.

2. Drop heaping tablespoons of batter 4 inches apart onto the prepared baking sheets. Bake until firm, about 10 minutes. Cool cookies on sheets 2 minutes. Transfer to wire racks to cool completely.

Triple-Chocolate Cookie Sandwiches

Cover the flat side of 1 wafer cookie with Chocolate Ganache (page 461) that has been chilled enough to be spreadable. Top with another wafer, placing the flat side down. Press gently to hold the cookies together. Repeat with as many wafers and as much ganache as desired.

Chocolate Ice Cream Sandwiches

Spread a ½-inch-thick layer of vanilla ice cream on the flat side of a wafer cookie and top with another wafer, flat side down. Wrap in plastic and freeze until firm or ready to serve.

EASY LEMON TARTLETS

PREP: 10 minutes

Makes 4 servings

8 (3-inch) soft oatmeal cookies
Confectioners' sugar for dusting
½ cup canned lemon pie filling
   or Easy Lemon Curd (page 458)
   or Rich Lemon Curd (page 459)

1. Remove the centers of 4 cookies using a 1-inch round cookie cutter. Sprinkle the tops of the cut cookies with confectioners' sugar placed in a fine sieve.

2. Spread the pie filling over the flat sides of the remaining cookies. Cover each with a sugar-dusted cookie, sugar side up.

JAM TRIANGLES

PREP: 40 minutes   COOK: 15 minutes per batch

Makes 72 triangles

¼ cup sugar plus more if needed

Quick Flaky Pastry (page 227)

¾ cup favorite jam or more if needed

1. Preheat the oven to 400°F. Line baking sheets with parchment paper. Sprinkle about 2 tablespoons sugar on a work surface and roll out 1 pastry square to a 12-inch square, dusting the surface with more sugar if needed. (Keep the remaining pastry refrigerated until after the first batch of triangles is baked.)

2. Cut the pastry square crosswise into 2-inch strips using a sharp, thin-bladed knife. Cut lengthwise at 2-inch intervals to make 36 (2-inch) squares.

3. Spread a generous ½ teaspoon jam over each square to ¼ inch from the edges. Brush 2 opposite corners of each square with water and fold diagonally to form a triangle. Press gently to seal the corners. Press the edges with the tines of a fork to seal and make a decorative edge. Arrange on the prepared sheets. Bake until golden, about 15 minutes.

4. Repeat with the remaining pastry rectangle, sugar, and jam.

RASPBERRY RUGELACH

PREP: 30 minutes   COOK: 10 minutes

Makes 24 rugelach

To make your own cinnamon sugar blend, mix ½ cup of sugar with 1 tablespoon of cinnamon.

1 (1-pound) package frozen puff pastry (2 sheets), or Easy Puff Pastry (page 225) or Quick Flaky Pastry (page 227)

1 cup raspberry jam

½ cup chopped almonds or walnuts

½ cup mini semisweet chocolate pieces

1 egg, beaten

2 tablespoons cinnamon sugar

1. Preheat the oven to 400°F. Line a baking sheet with parchment paper. Thaw the frozen pastry as package label directs. Unfold 1 pastry sheet on a lightly floured work surface and roll to a 12- by 11-inch rectangle. Spread with half the jam and sprinkle with half the nuts and chocolate. Cut in half lengthwise; cut crosswise in thirds. Cut each rectangle diagonally in half.

2. Roll up the triangles starting with the short side. Place on the prepared baking sheet with the point side down.

3. Repeat with the remaining pastry, jam, nuts, and chocolate.

4. Brush the pastry with the egg and sprinkle with the cinnamon sugar. Bake until crisp and golden, about 10 minutes.

CHERRY LINZER BARS

PREP: **30 minutes plus chilling**   COOK: **50 minutes**

Makes 15 to 30 pieces

1 (8-ounce) package cream cheese, softened

1 cup (2 sticks) unsalted butter, softened

2 cups all-purpose flour

1 teaspoon almond extract

1 (21-ounce) can cherry pie filling

2 tablespoons sugar

1. Combine the cream cheese and butter in a food processor and process until blended. Add the flour and almond extract and process until a dough ball forms. Divide in half and shape each half into a ½-inch-thick square. Cover with plastic wrap and refrigerate at least 30 minutes.

2. Pour the pie filling into a bowl and snip the cherries into small pieces using kitchen shears. Set aside.

3. Preheat the oven to 350°F. Roll out 1 piece of dough to a 15- by 10-inch rectangle on a well-floured work surface. Slide it onto a piece of parchment paper. Transfer the paper and dough to a large baking sheet. Spread the pie filling over the dough.

4. Roll out the remaining dough to a 15- by 10-inch rectangle and sprinkle with the sugar. Cut lengthwise into ¾-inch-wide strips using a fluted pastry wheel. Arrange the strips crisscross fashion over the pie filling 1 inch apart, cutting the strips to fit. Arrange the remaining strips around the edges to build a fanciful, high border.

5. Bake until the pastry is golden and the filling is bubbly, about 50 minutes. Cool in the pan on a wire rack. Cut into 3-inch or bite-size pieces.

SPICED SHORTCAKE ROUNDS

PREP: 20 minutes   COOK: 12 minutes

Makes 12 shortcake rounds

These are delicious and dainty enough by themselves with tea, but can also be useful as a substitute for biscuits or cake when it's strawberry season.

2 cups all-purpose flour

¼ cup sugar

1 teaspoon freshly grated nutmeg

¾ cup (1½ sticks) unsalted butter,
cut into pieces and frozen

2 egg yolks

2 tablespoons water

1. Preheat the oven to 375°F. Line a baking sheet with parchment paper. Combine the flour, sugar, and nutmeg in a food processor and pulse to mix. Add the butter and pulse until crumbly. Mix the egg yolks and water in a cup with a fork until blended. With the machine running, add the yolks through the feed tube. Process just until mixed.

2. Turn out the dough onto a lightly floured work surface and roll out to a ½-inch thickness with a lightly floured rolling pin. Cut out rounds with a 3½-inch cookie cutter. Reroll scraps and cut out more rounds to make a total of 12 rounds. Place the rounds on the prepared baking sheet and score decoratively with a fork.

3. Bake until golden, about 12 minutes. Transfer to a wire rack to cool.

Instant Strawberry Shortcake

Place one cake flat side down on a dessert dish and spread generously with crème fraîche. Fan out a sliced strawberry and gently place on top. Dust with confectioners' sugar placed in a fine sieve.

EASY TIRAMISÙ

PREP: 10 minutes
Makes 4 servings

½ cup strong coffee
2 tablespoons confectioners' sugar
2 tablespoons brandy
4 thick slices pound cake
1 cup ricotta cheese
¼ cup mini chocolate chips

Mix the coffee, sugar, and brandy in a cup. Brush the mixture over the cake and place each slice in a goblet. Mix the ricotta and chocolate chips and spoon on top of the cake.

VANILLA MINI CUPCAKES

PREP: 15 minutes   COOK: 15 minutes

Makes 24 cupcakes

½ cup (1 stick) unsalted butter, softened

1 cup sugar

3 eggs, separated

½ teaspoon vanilla extract

1 cup all-purpose flour

½ teaspoon baking powder

¼ teaspoon baking soda

⅛ teaspoon salt

½ cup buttermilk

Prepared frosting and decorations

1. Preheat the oven to 350°F. Grease 24 mini-muffin cups with butter. Combine the butter and sugar in a large bowl; beat with an electric mixer at high speed until light and fluffy. Beat in the egg yolks and vanilla; set aside.

2. Combine the flour, baking powder, baking soda, and salt in a sifter and sift onto waxed paper. Beat the egg whites in a bowl with a mixer at high speed until soft peaks form when the beaters are raised.

3. To the butter mixture, add one-fourth of the flour mixture alternately with one-third of the buttermilk, beginning and ending with the flour mixture (do not overbeat). Fold in the egg whites using a plastic spatula.

4. Spoon the batter into the prepared cups. Bake until the tops of the cakes spring back when lightly pressed with your finger, 15 to 20 minutes. Cool the cakes in the pans on a wire rack 5 minutes. Remove from the pans and cool completely. Frost and decorate as desired.

LACY BENNE (SESAME SEED) WAFERS

PREP: 10 minutes plus chilling   COOK: 16 minutes

Makes about 100 wafers

Serve with tea or to accompany a sorbet or granité.

1 cup white sesame seeds (benne)
1 cup packed light brown sugar
¾ cup (1½ sticks) plus 1 tablespoon unsalted butter
¾ cup all-purpose flour
1 egg
1 teaspoon vanilla extract
¼ teaspoon baking powder
¼ teaspoon salt

1. Preheat the oven to 400°F. Line a rimmed baking sheet with parchment paper. Spread out the sesame seeds on the prepared baking sheet. Bake until golden and toasted, about 10 minutes, stirring every few minutes and monitoring the seeds carefully to make sure they don't scorch. Remove the paper from the pan and place on a wire rack so the seeds can cool.

2. Combine the brown sugar, butter, flour, egg, vanilla, baking powder, and salt in a large bowl and stir until blended. Add the seeds and mix well. Cover and refrigerate the dough until chilled, at least 30 minutes.

3. Preheat the oven to 375°F. Line additional baking sheets with parchment paper. Shape small teaspoonfuls of dough into balls and place 3 inches apart on the prepared baking sheets (you can reuse the one used for toasting the sesame seeds). Press each ball to flatten slightly. Bake until the edges are browned, about 6 minutes. Cool the wafers in the pan and remove carefully as they are fragile. Store in an airtight container.

BOURBON PECAN TRUFFLES

PREP: 20 minutes plus chilling

Makes about 36 truffles

2½ cups sifted confectioners' sugar

½ cup European-style unsweetened cocoa powder
   plus more for dusting

⅓ cup (⅔ stick) unsalted butter, melted

2 tablespoons bourbon

2 tablespoons heavy cream

½ teaspoon vanilla extract

⅛ teaspoon salt

¾ cup chopped toasted pecans

1. Combine the sugar and cocoa in a bowl and mix well. Add the butter, bourbon, cream, vanilla, and salt and mix until blended. Stir in the nuts. Cover with plastic wrap and refrigerate until firm, about 2 hours.

2. Shape the mixture into 1-inch balls (about 1 heaping teaspoon each) using your hands or a melon-ball scoop. Place the balls on a baking sheet and dust with unsweetened cocoa powder, rolling the balls to coat completely. Place in an airtight container and refrigerate until serving.

DIRT CAKE

PREP: 20 minutes
Makes 24 servings

1 store-bought or homemade (from a cake mix
   or scratch) square or sheet cake covered
   in white frosting
5 (8-inch) pretzels
1½ cups crushed store-bought chocolate
   wafer cookies or Double-Chocolate Wafer
   Cookies (page 328, made without the chocolate chips)
   or more if needed
Assorted color round flat lollipops
Green spearmint-leaf jelly candy
Assorted color gummy worms
Green candy decorating sprinkles
Mini pretzels

1. Place the cake on a serving platter or tray. Cut the pretzel into 4 (2-inch) pieces using a sharp knife. Make a pretzel-log square frame in the center, cutting the pretzel to fit using a sharp knife.

2. Fill the frame with crushed-cookie "dirt" to make a flowerbed. Insert lollipops in the "flowerbed" so that they stand up with as much of the sticks showing as possible. Cut leaf-shape candies in half lengthwise and arrange on each side of the lollipop sticks. Poke holes in the "dirt" and stick enough of a worm in each to look like the worm is going into or coming out of the "dirt."

3. Sprinkle green sprinkles on the icing around the "flowerbed" and make a mini-pretzel "fence" around the top edge of the cake by placing the mini pretzels around the sides of the cake with half of the pretzel sticking up above the cake.

PECAN PRALINES

PREP: 25 minutes plus cooling   COOK: 10 minutes

Makes 24 pralines

These extra-sweet treats are best appreciated with hot coffee or tea.

1 cup firmly packed brown sugar

1 cup granulated sugar

½ cup evaporated milk

1 cup pecan halves or pieces

2 tablespoons unsalted butter

1½ teaspoons vanilla extract

1. Combine the brown sugar, granulated sugar, and milk in a large saucepan over medium heat. Cook, stirring constantly to keep it from boiling over, until the syrup registers 228°F on a candy thermometer, about 5 minutes. Add the pecans and butter and continue to cook until the thermometer registers 232°F.

2. Remove the pan from the heat and stir in the vanilla. Cool, stirring occasionally, until the surface of the mixture is dull, not shiny, about 20 minutes.

3. Spoon the pralines onto parchment-lined baking sheets into 24 thin patties. Set aside to cool for at least 30 minutes. Place each praline in a waxed-paper sandwich bag.

COCONUT PRALINES

PREP: 10 minutes   COOK: 10 minutes

Makes about 12 pralines

These loose-cannon shaped sweets make an exciting garnish when inserted into a scoop of sorbet or ice cream.

1 cup sugar
½ cup water
1 cup toasted shredded coconut

Combine the sugar and water in a small saucepan over low heat and cook, stirring, until the sugar is dissolved. Simmer the mixture over medium heat until golden and fragrant, 5 to 7 minutes. Stir in the coconut. Pour the mixture onto a parchment-lined baking sheet. Hold the paper onto the sheet and tilt the sheet to spread the mixture to as thin as possible before it sets. Cool the praline until hard, about 5 minutes. Break into irregularly sized pieces.

GLAZED STRAWBERRIES

1 pint unhulled strawberries, with stems if possible
½ (16-ounce) ready-to-spread cream-cheese
    or dark-chocolate frosting
1 tablespoon orange-flavored liqueur (optional)

1. Gently rinse the strawberries with cold water and pat dry with paper towels. Set aside on a parchment-lined baking sheet.

2. Combine the frosting with the liqueur in a microwave-safe bowl and mix until blended. Cover with plastic wrap and microwave on medium power to soften, about 10 seconds, stirring after 5 seconds.

3. Hold a strawberry by the stem or hull and dip the bottom two thirds of each strawberry into the softened frosting; place on the parchment-lined baking sheet. Repeat with the remaining berries and frosting.

LEMON SORBET

PREP: 10 minutes plus chilling and freezing

COOK: 5 minutes

Makes 10 servings

2¼ cups cold water

1½ teaspoons unflavored gelatin

1 cup sugar

¾ cup light corn syrup

2 teaspoons grated lemon zest

1 cup lemon juice

1. Pour ¼ cup water into a small bowl and sprinkle the gelatin on top. Let soak until spongy and softened, about 5 minutes. Combine the remaining 2 cups water, the sugar, and syrup in a small saucepan and heat to boiling over medium heat, stirring to dissolve the sugar. Add the softened gelatin mixture and stir to melt, about 1 minute. Remove the pan from the heat and pour into a bowl. Add the lemon zest and juice and stir to blend. Cover and refrigerate overnight until cold.

2. Freeze in an ice cream maker as manufacturer directs. Place in freezer container and freeze until serving.

PICK-A-BERRY SORBET

PREP: 15 minutes plus chilling and freezing

Makes 10 servings

1 pound strawberries, raspberries, blackberries,
  or blueberries
½ cup sugar
2 cups Simple Syrup (page 473)
1 tablespoon lemon juice

1. Place the berries in a food processor and sprinkle with the sugar. Pulse until coarsely chopped. Let the sugared berries macerate in the bowl 2 hours.

2. Process the macerated berries until pureed. Strain through a fine sieve placed over a large bowl and press to extract all the juices. Discard the solids. Add the simple syrup and lemon juice to the berry juice and stir to blend. Cover and refrigerate at least 3 hours or overnight.

3. Freeze the berry mixture in an ice cream maker as manufacturer directs. Pack in freezer containers and freeze until serving.

GREEN APPLE SORBET WITH CALVADOS

PREP: 10 minutes plus chilling and freezing

COOK: 3 minutes

Makes 4 to 6 servings

4 cups fresh Granny Smith apple juice

1 cup sugar

2 teaspoons grated lemon zest

4 to 6 ounces Calvados (apple brandy from Normandy)

1. Combine 1 cup apple juice, the sugar, and lemon zest in a small saucepan and heat to boiling, stirring to dissolve the sugar. Place the remaining 3 cups apple juice in a pitcher and stir in the sugar mixture. Refrigerate until very cold, at least 4 hours.

2. Freeze the apple mixture in an ice cream maker as manufacturer directs. Pack in a freezer container and freeze until serving.

3. Scoop the sorbet into glasses and pour some Calvados on top. Serve immediately.

ORANGE-MANGO GRANITÉ

PREP: 10 minutes plus overnight freezing

Makes 8 servings

2 mangoes, peeled, pitted, and chopped,
    plus small slices of mango for garnish
Grated zest of 2 oranges
2 cups fresh orange juice
¾ cup lime juice
¼ cup mango liqueur
Honey-Sesame Cups (optional, page 367)

1. Combine the mangoes, orange zest, and orange juice
in a food processor or blender and process until the mangoes are pureed. Pour into an 11- by 9-inch glass baking
dish and add the lime juice and liqueur; stir to blend.
Freeze until slushy, about 3 hours, stirring occasionally.
Freeze overnight.

2. To serve, let the granité stand 20 minutes at room
temperature to soften slightly. Break the granité into
chunks and process until icy but not slushy in a food
processor. Spoon into Honey-Sesame Cups (if using)
and garnish each serving with slice of mango.

LIMONCELLO-ROSEMARY GRANITÉ

PREP: 10 minutes plus overnight chilling and freezing

COOK: 10 minutes

Makes 12 servings

¼ cup fresh or dried rosemary leaves

5 cups water

2 cups sugar

2 cups dry white wine

6 tablespoons lemon juice

3 tablespoons Limoncello (Italian lemon liqueur)

SUGARED ROSEMARY SPRIGS

2 tablespoons powdered egg whites

¼ cup water

12 (3-inch) fresh rosemary sprigs (tip ends)

½ cup granulated sugar

1. Make the granité: Mix the rosemary leaves with 2 cups of the water and the sugar in a saucepan. Heat to boiling over high heat, stirring to dissolve the sugar. Reduce the heat to medium-low and simmer 5 minutes. Remove the pan from the heat and cool the syrup completely. Pour into a bowl, cover, and refrigerate overnight.

2. Strain the syrup into a bowl and add the remaining 3 cups water, the wine, lemon juice, and Limoncello; mix well. Freeze in an ice cream maker as manufacturer directs. Place in a freezer container and freeze until serving.

3. While mixture freezes, make the Sugared Rosemary Sprigs: Mix the egg whites with the water in a small bowl until blended. Dip the rosemary sprigs into the egg white mixture and lightly sprinkle with sugar. Place on a parchment-lined baking sheet and freeze until serving.

4. To serve, scoop the granité into 12 martini glasses or bowls and garnish with a frozen sugared rosemary sprig.

POMEGRANATE GRANITÉ

PREP: 10 minutes plus freezing   COOK: 5 minutes

Makes 10 servings

1 cup sugar
2 cups water
2 tablespoons grated lemon zest
4 cups pomegranate juice
Mint sprigs for garnish

1. Combine the sugar, water, and lemon zest in a medium saucepan and heat to boiling over medium heat, stirring until the sugar dissolves. Boil 2 minutes. Set aside to steep and cool.

2. Pour the pomegranate juice into an 11- by 9-inch glass baking dish. Pour the sugar syrup through a fine sieve into the pomegranate juice. Stir to blend. Freeze until frozen, about 3 hours, stirring occasionally.

3. To serve, let the granité stand a few minutes at room temperature to soften slightly; if it is hard-frozen, break the granité into chunks and process until icy but not slushy in a food processor. Spoon into wine glasses or juice glasses and garnish each serving with a mint sprig.

HOLIDAY GRANITÉ

1 (6-inch) sprig fresh rosemary
  plus 10 side-sprig clusters for garnish
1½ cups sugar
3½ cups water
1 (12-ounce) package cranberries
¼ cup grated orange zest
2 teaspoons fresh lemon juice

1. Combine the rosemary, sugar, and 1½ cups water in a medium saucepan and heat to boiling over medium heat, stirring until the sugar dissolves. Boil 2 minutes. Set aside to steep and cool.

2. While the syrup cools, combine the remaining 2 cups water, the cranberries, orange zest, and lemon juice in a medium saucepan. Heat to boiling over medium heat.

Simmer until the cranberries are soft, about 20 minutes. Pour the mixture through a sieve placed over a large glass measure. Transfer the cranberry solids to a food processor and puree. Strain the pureed cranberries through the same (unwashed) sieve placed over the glass measure with the cooking liquid. Discard the solids. Set the liquid aside to cool.

3. Strain the rosemary syrup through a sieve into an 11- by 9-inch glass baking dish. Add the cranberry-juice mixture and stir to blend. Freeze until frozen, about 3 hours, stirring occasionally.

4. To serve, let the granité stand a few minutes at room temperature to soften slightly. If it is hard-frozen, break the granité into chunks and process until icy but not slushy in a food processor. Spoon into wine glasses or juice glasses and garnish each serving with a rosemary-sprig cluster.

PICK-A-BERRY GRANITÉ

PREP: 25 minutes plus freezing

Makes 6 servings

1 pound strawberries, raspberries, blackberries, or blueberries plus more berries for garnish

½ cup sugar

1. Place the berries in a food processor and sprinkle with the sugar. Pulse until the berries are coarsely chopped. Let macerate in the bowl 15 minutes, pulsing 2 to 3 times every 5 minutes.

2. Process the macerated berries until pureed. Strain through a fine sieve placed over a bowl and press to extract all the juices. Discard solids.

3. Pour the sieved mixture into a shallow pan or glass baking dish and place in the freezer. Freeze until firm, about 45 minutes. Break up the mixture with a fork to make a slush. Repeat every 30 minutes. The final slush should be able to mound without liquid exuding from it and will take between 2 and 4 hours, depending on the freezer and the size of the pan or dish.

4. Serve the granité when it is the desired consistency or freeze it for later use. If it is hard-frozen, break the granité into chunks and process until icy but not slushy in a food processor. Spoon the granité into wine glasses or juice glasses and garnish with berries.

ESPRESSO GRANITÉ

PREP: 10 minutes plus freezing   COOK: 3 minutes

Makes 6 servings

3 cups boiling water

1 cup sugar

2 cups espresso coffee

½ teaspoon vanilla extract

1. Combine the boiling water and sugar in a heat-safe bowl and stir until the sugar dissolves. Stir in the coffee and set aside to cool.

2. Stir the vanilla into the coffee mixture. Transfer to a metal pan or glass baking dish. Freeze until firm, about 45 minutes. Break up the mixture with a fork to make a slush. Repeat every 30 minutes. The final slush should be able to mound without liquid exuding from it and will take between 2 and 4 hours, depending on the freezer and the size of the pan or dish.

3. Serve the granité when it is the desired consistency or freeze it for later use. If it is hard-frozen, break the granité into chunks and process until icy but not slushy in a food processor. Spoon the granité into wine glasses or juice glasses.

FROZEN LATTES

PREP: 10 minutes

Makes 6 servings

2 cups espresso coffee, chilled
1 (14-ounce) can sweetened condensed milk
½ cup milk

1. Pour the coffee into an ice-cube tray and freeze overnight.

2. Pop out the espresso ice cubes and place in a blender. Add the sweetened condensed milk, rinse out the can with the milk, and add the milk to the blender. Blend until a smooth slush forms. Pour into short glasses and serve immediately.

PREP: 10 minutes
Makes 6 servings

1 quart coffee or other flavor ice cream
¾ cup store-bought or homemade
    (page 471) caramel sauce
½ cup toasted chopped pecans or walnuts
⅓ cup toasted flaked coconut

Scoop ice cream into 6 sundae glasses or dessert bowls and top with caramel sauce. Sprinkle with pecans and coconut.

ICE CREAM CONES

PREP: 25 minutes   COOK: 8 minutes

Makes 6 to 8 cones

Use a melon-ball scoop or small ice cream scoop to fill these delicate cones with sorbet, granité, or ice cream.

3 egg whites, at room temperature

1 cup all-purpose flour

¾ cup confectioners' sugar

6 tablespoons unsalted butter, melted

1. Preheat the oven to 350°F. Line baking sheets with parchment paper. Combine all the ingredients in a bowl and whisk until blended. Let stand 10 minutes.

2. For each cone, spread 2 tablespoons batter in a thin round on a prepared baking sheet. Repeat to make 6 or 8 rounds. Bake until the wafers are set and beginning to brown around the edges, 8 to 10 minutes.

3. Quickly remove the wafers from the parchment using a thin metal spatula and shape each into a cone (with the top of the wafer on the outside). Place the cones seamside down on a parchment-lined sheet. Wad small pieces of aluminum foil into balls and insert in the cones to hold them open while they cool.

HOT CRANBERRY SUNDAES

PREP: 10 minutes   COOK: 12 minutes

Makes 6 servings

2 cups (10 ounces) fresh or frozen cranberries,
    coarsely chopped
⅔ cup sugar
½ cup orange juice
Vanilla frozen yogurt or ice cream
Chopped nuts (optional)

1. Combine the cranberries, sugar, and orange juice in a medium saucepan and heat to boiling over medium-high heat, stirring until the sugar dissolves. Simmer over low heat until the mixture thickens, stirring occasionally, 10 minutes.

2. Scoop frozen yogurt into serving dishes or stemmed heat-safe glasses and spoon the hot cranberry mixture on top. Sprinkle with nuts, if you like.

STEAMED SPICED CUSTARD CUPS

1 star anise
1 (3-inch) cinnamon stick
3 cups half-and-half
½ cup strong-flavored honey
4 eggs

1. Combine the star anise, cinnamon, half-and-half, and honey in a small saucepan and heat to simmering over low heat, whisking to dissolve the honey. Simmer 5 minutes.

2. Place the eggs in a medium bowl and whisk until blended. Gradually whisk the hot spice mixture into the eggs. Strain the egg mixture through a sieve into a heat-safe glass measure.

3. Spoon the batter into 8 ramekins or Chinese teacups. Place in a bamboo or metal steamer placed in a wok or pan of simmering water. Cover and steam over gently boiling water until set, about 25 minutes, adding more boiling water to the wok or pan as needed. Serve the custards warm or at room temperature.

STEAMED COCONUT CAKES

PREP: 15 minutes COOK: 15 minutes

Makes 6 servings

4 eggs

¾ cup Simple Syrup (page 473)

1¼ cups all-purpose flour

1¼ teaspoons baking powder

3 tablespoons finely shredded coconut

1. Combine the eggs and syrup in a medium bowl and beat with an electric mixer at high speed until light and thick, about 8 minutes. Place the flour and baking powder in a large bowl and mix well. Add the coconut and mix well. Add the egg mixture and fold gently until mixed.

2. Spoon the batter into 6 ramekins or Chinese teacups. Place in a bamboo or metal steamer placed in a wok or pan of simmering water. Cover and steam over gently boiling water until firm and puffed, about 15 minutes. Serve warm or at room temperature.

FROZEN TORTONI CUPS

1 cup frozen nondairy whipped topping, thawed

1 pint vanilla ice cream, slightly softened

¼ cup mini semisweet chocolate pieces

2 tablespoons almond-flavored liqueur (Amaretto)
   or ½ teaspoon almond extract

¼ cup crushed Italian almond cookies (amaretti)

1. Place 10 paper or foil liners in muffin-pan cups and set aside.

2. Combine the whipped topping and ice cream in a medium bowl and fold together until blended using a plastic spatula. Stir in the chocolate pieces and liqueur. Spoon into the prepared muffin cups, dividing evenly. Sprinkle with the crumbs. Freeze until serving, at least 30 minutes.

CREAMY PEANUT-CHOCOLATE CUPS

PREP: **15 minutes plus freezing**

Makes 12 servings

½ (8-ounce) package cream cheese, softened
½ cup chunky peanut butter
½ cup confectioners' sugar
½ teaspoon vanilla extract
1 cup heavy cream
12 small Chocolate Cups (page 366)
Unsweetened cocoa powder for dusting

1. Combine the cream cheese and peanut butter in a medium bowl and beat with an electric mixer at medium speed until blended. Beat in the sugar and vanilla until blended.

2. Beat the cream in a bowl or glass measure until stiff peaks form when the beaters are raised. Fold the cream into the cream-cheese mixture until no white streaks remain. Spoon or pipe the cream-cheese mixture into the Chocolate Cups, transfer to a freezer container, cover, and freeze until firm, about 2 hours.

3. Remove the cups from the freezer about 10 minutes to soften before serving. Dust with cocoa powder placed in a fine sieve just before serving.

CHOCOLATE CUPS

These are perfect containers for sorbets and granités because they won't get soggy like pastry containers.

1 (6-ounce) package semisweet or milk chocolate chips
1½ teaspoons shortening or vegetable oil

1. Combine the chocolate and shortening in the top of a double boiler or in a bowl set over (not in) hot (not boiling) water. Heat, stirring, over medium heat until the chocolate melts.

2. Line a muffin pan with 6 large (2½-inch) paper liners or a mini muffin pan with 12 small paper liners. Brush or spoon the chocolate into the paper liners to coat. Refrigerate until the chocolate sets.

HONEY-SESAME CUPS

PREP: 15 minutes plus chilling   COOK: 4 minutes

Makes about 12 cups

Use these glamorous containers to hold scoops of mousse or sorbet.

½ cup (1 stick) unsalted butter, softened
1 cup confectioners' sugar
¼ cup honey
½ cup (4 to 5) egg whites
1 cup sifted all-purpose flour
2 tablespoons black sesame seeds

1. Combine the butter and sugar in a medium bowl and beat until smooth. Beat in the honey. Beat in the egg whites until smooth. Add the flour and sesame seeds and stir until blended. Refrigerate 30 minutes.

2. Preheat the oven to 300°F. Line a baking sheet with parchment paper. Grease the outsides of 12 upside-down cups or the cups of an inverted muffin pan.

3. Spread the batter into four 5- to 6-inch rounds using a wet finger or back of a spoon onto the prepared baking sheet. Bake until browned around the edges and golden in the center, about 4 minutes. Slide a metal spatula under a tuile to release it and quickly shape into a cup by placing over the prepared muffin cups. Repeat with remaining baked tuiles.

4. Repeat 3 times with the remaining tuile batter.

PLATTERS

ANTIPASTI DE SALUMI

PREP: 20 minutes
Makes 16 servings

16 slices prosciutto di Parma or serrano ham

16 slices bresaola

16 slices Genoa salami or soppressata

16 slices mortadella

8 ounces green beans, blanched

4 leaves radicchio

Marinated Cipollini Onions (page 372) or 1 (10-ounce)
   jar marinated grilled cipolle onions, drained

1 (6-ounce) jar marinated artichoke hearts, drained

1 (8-ounce) piece Parmigiano-Reggiano cheese,
   cut into rough chunks

8 ounces small marinated balls fresh mozzarella cheese

1 (8-ounce) chunk Gorgonzola cheese,
   cut into rough chunks

4 leaves green leaf lettuce

1 cup mixed olives

1 (9-ounce) jar Tuscan peppers, drained

1 (7-ounce) jar sliced roasted red peppers, drained

1 pint cherry tomatoes

1. Arrange the prosciutto and bresaola in rosettes on
a large platter. Roll the salami and mortadella into cones
and arrange point side down in a group on the same
platter. Arrange the green beans next to the meat in
a line.

2. Arrange the radicchio leaves on the platter to form
cups and fill one with the onions, one with the artichoke
hearts, one with the Parmigiano-Reggiano, one with the
mozzarella balls, and one with the Gorgonzola. Arrange
the lettuce leaves in the remaining spaces on the platter
and place a small glass bowl on the platter. Fill with
the olives. Place the tomatoes, Tuscan peppers, and red
peppers over the meats and around the platter.

MARINATED CIPOLLINI ONIONS

PREP: 20 minutes plus standing   COOK: 5 minutes

Makes 8 servings

1 pound small mixed red and white cipollini onions
   or large pearl onions (about 20), peeled and trimmed
5 tablespoons extra-virgin olive oil
2 tablespoons red wine vinegar
1 tablespoon sugar
2 bay leaves
¼ teaspoon salt
¼ teaspoon freshly ground black pepper

1. Prepare a grill for barbecue or preheat the broiler. Blanch the onions in 2 quarts boiling, salted water 3 minutes. Drain in a colander.

2. In a large bowl, combine 2 tablespoons of the oil, 1 tablespoon of the vinegar, the sugar, and bay leaves and stir to dissolve the sugar. Add the onions and toss to coat. Transfer to a wire grill basket or foil-lined baking sheet. Grill or broil 6 inches from the heat until the onions are browned and tender, about 5 minutes.

3. Transfer the onions to a bowl and drizzle with the remaining 3 tablespoons oil and 1 tablespoon vinegar. Add the salt and pepper and toss to coat. Let stand 2 hours, stirring occasionally.

AÏOLI AND CRUDITÉ PLATTER

PREP: 10 minutes

Makes 12 to 16 servings

Aïoli (page 429), Anchovy and Black Olive Aïoli
(page 430), and/or Chipotle Aïoli (page 431)
1 large red pepper, cut into strips
1 large yellow pepper, cut into strips
1 head Belgian endive, leaves separated
1 pound raw pencil-thin asparagus
1 pound fingerling potatoes, cooked and halved lengthwise
1 pound broccoli florets, blanched and chilled
1 pound baby carrots with a little green stem attached,
    blanched and chilled
8 ounces green beans, blanched and chilled
8 ounces raw button mushrooms, trimmed

Spoon the aïoli into a bowl or into separate bowls and
place in the center of a large rimmed platter. Arrange the
vegetables in groups or in an interesting pattern of mixed
vegetables around the platter.

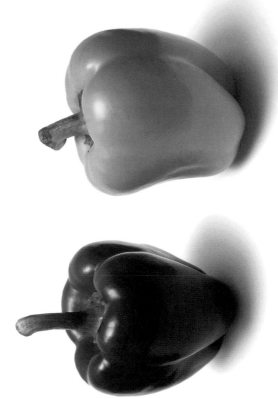

GRILLED VEGETABLE PLATTER

PREP: 15 minutes plus marinating

COOK: 2 minutes per batch

Makes 12 servings

¼ cup dark sesame oil

¼ cup rice vinegar

2 tablespoons minced garlic

2 tablespoons minced fresh cilantro

½ teaspoon salt

½ teaspoon red pepper flakes

8 ounces Japanese eggplant,
cut lengthwise into ½-inch slices

8 ounces green zucchini, cut lengthwise
into ½-inch slices

8 ounces yellow zucchini or summer squash,
cut lengthwise into ½-inch slices

12 medium green onions

1 small red pepper, quartered lengthwise

½ cup pine nuts

½ cup fresh purple basil leaves, torn if large

1. Combine the sesame oil, vinegar, garlic, cilantro, salt, and pepper flakes in a large bowl and mix well. Add the eggplant, green and yellow zucchini, green onions, and red pepper and toss to coat with the marinade. Marinate for 1 hour.

2. Preheat a grill to high heat. In batches, remove the vegetables from the marinade and place flat in a vegetable grilling rack or on the grill. Grill, turning once, until marked, about 2 minutes. Transfer with tongs to a serving platter to cool slightly. Sprinkle the vegetables with the pine nuts and basil and serve.

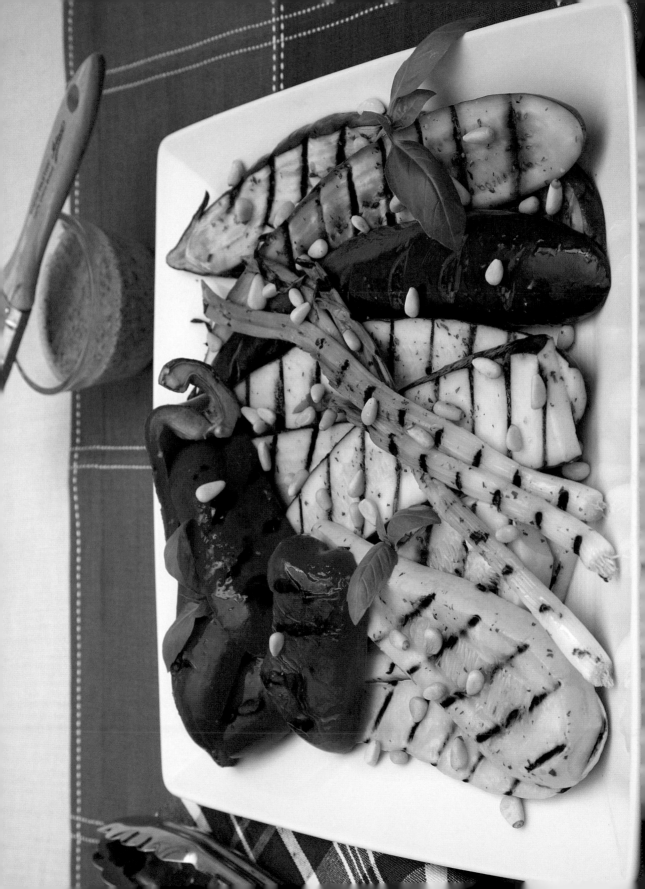

CHICKEN LIVER PÂTÉ PLATTER

PREP: 40 minutes

Makes 12 to 16 servings

Chicken Liver Pâté (page 59)

Crostini (page 166)

Matzoh

Red and yellow pear tomatoes

Chopped hard-cooked eggs

Small brined or salted capers, rinsed and patted dry

Onion Confit (page 168)

Belgian endive leaves

Radicchio leaves

1. Invert the pâté onto a large serving platter. Let stand at room temperature at least 30 minutes but not more than 1 hour. Set a spreading knife alongside or in the pâté.

2. Place the crostini and matzoh in napkin-lined baskets. Spoon the tomatoes, eggs, capers, and confit into cups of endive and radicchio and arrange around the pâté with small spoons. Have guests spread the crostini and matzoh with the pâté and top with choice of toppings.

SHRIMP COCKTAIL PLATTER

PREP: 1 hour 30 minutes COOK: 5 minutes

Makes 10 servings

You can, of course, buy cooked, shelled, and deveined shrimp with the tails intact. This is a "from scratch" recipe in case you want to give your guests the sweet fruits of your labor—not to mention the best flavor.

2 pounds headless large unshelled shrimp,
tails intact
4 cups beer or cold water
2 teaspoons salt
5 black peppercorns
Cocktail Sauce (page 445)
Ice
Lime wedges

1. Cut each shrimp vertically about halfway up the curve, leaving the other half intact. Slit the wide end with the tip of a paring knife and pull out the vein. If it doesn't all come out, finish cleaning the shrimp after cooking.

2. Up to 4 hours ahead of serving (it will take about an hour to shell the shrimp), cook the shrimp: Combine the beer, salt, and peppercorns in a large saucepan and heat to boiling over high heat. Add the shrimp and stir to spread them evenly. Cover and cook until pink and barely cooked through. Drain immediately. Place the shrimp in a bowl of ice and water to stop the cooking and cool through; drain again. Remove the shells and any veins from the shrimp and place in a bowl. Cover and refrigerate until cold.

3. To serve: Place the Cocktail Sauce in a bowl and place in the center of a large, shallow bowl of ice. Pile the shrimp on the ice around the sauce bowl. Garnish with lime wedges and serve immediately.

SKEWERED FRUIT ANTIPASTO PLATTER

PREP: 20 minutes

Makes 6 servings

12 small shrimp, cooked, shelled, and deveined

12 seedless green grapes

6 small balls mozzarella cheese, halved

12 seedless purple grapes

12 (¾-inch) cubes cream havarti cheese
    or sweet muenster cheese

6 plump candied apricots, halved crosswise

6 paper-thin slices prosciutto di Parma, halved crosswise

3 ripe fresh black figs, quartered lengthwise

1. Thread a shrimp and then a green grape onto each of 12 short wooden picks and place in a row on a large platter. Thread a piece of mozzarella and then a purple grape onto each of 12 short wooden picks and place in a row next to the shrimp skewers. Thread a cube of havarti and then a piece of apricot onto each of 12 short wooden picks and place in a row next to the mozzarella skewers.

2. Weave a slice of prosciutto back and forth on each of 12 short wooden picks so they make ribbons about 1½ inches long. Thread a fig quarter, flesh side first, onto each pick. Place on the platter next to the apricot skewers.

3. Serve immediately or cover and refrigerate until serving.

SCANDINAVIAN SALMON PLATTER

PREP: 25 minutes plus marinating

Makes 8 to 10 servings

Gravlax (salmon marinated in a dill brine) is the star of this pretty platter. If the dill is hot-house grown or not very pungent, coarsely chop the bunch to release the flavor and sprinkle it over the fish.

GRAVLAX

1 (3- to 3½-pound) center-cut fresh
    salmon fillet with skinned

1 large bunch fresh dill

¼ cup kosher salt

¼ cup sugar

2 tablespoons white or black peppercorns, crushed

2 bunches fresh dill or green-leaf lettuce leaves

Cherry tomatoes and/or cucumber slices

Mustard-Dill Sauce (page 453)

Scandinavian crackers

1. Make the gravlax: Check the salmon to make sure all the pin bones are removed; remove any with tweezers or needle-nose pliers. Cut the fillet crosswise in half (try to be exact) and place one-half in a glass baking dish with the skin side down. Wash the dill, shake it dry, and place it on the salmon in the dish.

2. Combine the salt, sugar, and pepper in a small cup and mix well. Pat the mixture evenly over the dill onto the fish. Top with the other half of the fish, skin side up. Cover the dish tightly with plastic wrap and top with a heavy platter, quarter-sheet pan, or small baking sheet; weight it evenly with about 2 pounds of canned foods or things you may have in the refrigerator.

3. Let the fish marinate at least 48 hours or up to 3 days in the refrigerator. Every 12 hours, remove the weights and plastic wrap, turn the fish over, and baste with the marinade that accumulates (separate the halves to baste between them). Replace the plastic wrap each time and make sure the weights are distributed evenly.

4. When the gravlax is finished marinating, scrape away the dill and seasonings from each half. Place the separated halves skin side down on a cutting board and cut diagonally across the grain into thin slices, detaching them from the skin by sliding the knife between the flesh and the skin but keeping all the slices in place on the skin.

5. Create the platter: Arrange a bed of dill or lettuce leaves on a large platter so the fern/curly ends face the sides. Place a whole half of gravlax slices (on the skin) onto the bed (reserve remaining gravlax slices). Garnish the platter with cherry tomatoes and cucumber slices.

6. Serve with a basket of Scandinavian crackers and a bowl of Mustard-Dill Sauce. Have guests smear the sauce on the crackers before using a fork to lift a slice of salmon on top.

PREP: 10 minutes
Makes 6 servings

Crushed ice
Fresh seaweed
Fresh parsley sprigs
Fresh dill sprigs
12 oysters, shucked and on the half-shell
12 clams, shucked and on the half-shell
Mignonette Sauce (page 454)
½ cup store-bought cocktail sauce
¼ cup prepared horseradish
Lemon and lime wedges

Line a large rimmed platter with the crushed ice and top with the seaweed, parsley, and dill. Arrange the oysters and clams on top. Fill small bowls or empty oyster and clam shells with Mignonette Sauce, cocktail sauce, and horseradish and set them alongside the platter. Tuck lemon and lime wedges around the seafood.

NACHO PLATTER

PREP: 10 minutes

Makes 16 servings

Black Bean and Hominy Nachos
(page 280)
Ham and Chayote Nachos
(page 282)
Scallop Seviche and Mango Nachos
(page 277)

Arrange some of each of the nachos on a platter, mixing up the color of the corn chips. Have the remaining nachos ready to replenish the platter or make up a second platter to put out while replenishing the first one.

SUMMER FRUIT PLATTER WITH ALMOND CREAM

PREP: 25 minutes plus chilling

Makes 12 servings

4 large egg yolks

1 cup confectioners' sugar

¼ cup almond-flavored liqueur

¾ cup heavy cream

6 ripe fresh green figs, quartered lengthwise

6 medium ripe but firm Italian prune plums, halved lengthwise and pitted

1 pint ripe small unhulled strawberries

1 pint red cherries, with stems

1 pint yellow cherries, with stems

1. Combine the egg yolks, sugar, and liqueur in a heat-safe bowl placed over a pan of simmering water. Whisk or beat with a portable electric mixer over medium heat until the mixture is warm and has tripled in volume. Pour into a large bowl, cover, and refrigerate until thickened, about 2 hours.

2. Before serving, whip the cream until stiff in a cold bowl. Fold the whipped cream into the egg-yolk mixture until blended. Transfer to a serving bowl and place on a platter. Surround with the fruits, in groups. Serve with picks for dipping the fruit into the almond cream.

DRIED FRUIT AND NUT PLATTER

PREP: 10 minutes
Makes 12 servings

1 pound mixed nuts in the shell
4 cups Trail Mix (page 154)
8 ounces dried figs
8 ounces medjool dates
8 ounces deglet noor dates, each split and
    stuffed with 1 teaspoon pineapple-flavored
    cream cheese
8 ounces dried apricots

Place the mixed nuts in a wooden bowl in the center
of a large serving platter. Divide the Trail Mix between
2 small wooden bowls and place them on opposite sides
of the bowl of nuts. Arrange the dried fruits in piles
between the bowls. Place 6-inch skewers in thin vases
near the platter for skewering the fruit pieces.

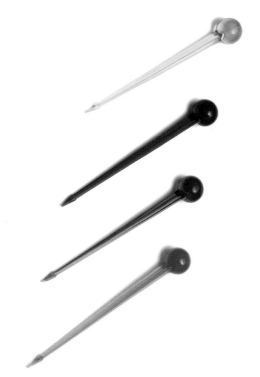

DESSERT CRÊPES-TO-ORDER BAR

PREP: 15 minutes

Makes 24 crêpes with leftover fillings

Warm Crêpes (page 233) cooked or prepared batter

Granulated sugar for sprinkling

Hazelnut-chocolate spread

Hot Fudge Sauce (page 468)

Vanilla Custard Sauce (page 469)

Caramel Sauce (page 471)

Rich Lemon Curd (page 459)

Lime Curd (page 460)

Spread and roll up jelly-roll fashion or fold over the crêpes and serve on a warmed platter. Fill the warmed crêpes to order, or cook the crêpes and fill to order.

TROPICAL FRUIT BOWL WITH CITRUS CREAM

PREP: 15 minutes
Makes 8 servings

4 mangoes, pitted, peeled, and sliced

2 star fruit, cut crosswise into ¼-inch-thick stars

2 prickly pears, quartered lengthwise

1 pound seedless watermelon chunks

1 pound pineapple chunks

1 pint small unhulled strawberries

1 cup nonfat lime yogurt

2 tablespoons honey

1 tablespoon minced crystallized ginger

1 teaspoon grated orange zest

Combine the mangoes, star fruit, pears, watermelon, pineapple, and strawberries in a large bowl and mix gently. Combine the yogurt, honey, ginger, and orange zest in a bowl and mix well. Transfer to a small, decorative bowl and place in the center of a large shallow bowl. Spoon the fruit around the small bowl. Serve with picks for dipping the fruit into the citrus cream.

CHOCOLATE-DIPPED
FRESH-FRUIT PLATTER

PREP: 15 minutes

Makes 12 servings

Chocolate Ganache (page 461)

12 long-stemmed, unhulled strawberries

12 yellow cherries with stems

12 red cherries with stems

12 bite-size chunks fresh pineapple,
 on skewers or wooden picks

12 orange segments, on skewers or wooden picks

12 mango slices, on skewers or wooden picks

12 red seedless grapes, on skewers or wooden picks

12 green seedless grapes, on skewers or wooden picks

12 purple seedless grapes, on skewers or wooden picks

If you like, dip the fruits in the chocolate ahead of time, let the chocolate harden, and arrange on a platter.

Place the Chocolate Ganache in a warmed earthenware pot or a fondue pot over a flame and place on a heat-safe plate in the center of a platter. Surround with bowls of the various fruits, arranged separately or mixed, with plates and napkins alongside, so guests can dip at will.

PLATTER OF PASTRIES AND OTHER ASSORTED IRRESISTIBLES

PREP: 10 minutes

Makes 12 servings

12 Fruit Fool Shots (page 302)
12 Fresh Fruit Cheesecake Tartlets (page 313)
12 Mini Cream Puffs (page 305)
12 Mini Chocolate Éclairs (page 307)
12 Lime Tartlets (page 319)
12 Bourbon Pecan Truffles (page 341)

Place each irresistible in a small fanciful paper or foil mini-muffin cup liner and arrange on one or more trays for easy access to temptation.

DRINKS

FRESH LEMONADE

2½ cups Simple Syrup (page 473)
2½ cups freshly squeezed lemon juice
    (from 10 to 12 large lemons)
Ice cubes
Lemon slices
Fresh mint sprigs

Combine the syrup and lemon juice in a large pitcher and stir to blend. Pour into ice-filled tall glasses and add a lemon slice and a mint sprig in each.

LIMEADE

PREP: 5 minutes

Makes 6 servings

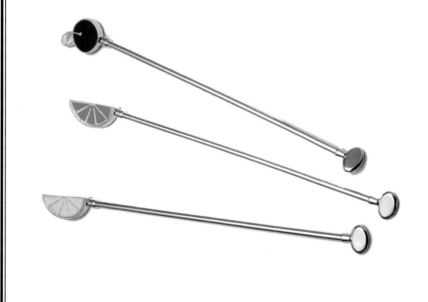

1½ cups freshly squeezed lime juice
  (from about 12 large limes)
1 cup Simple Syrup (page 473)
Crushed ice
Club soda, chilled
2 limes, ends trimmed, sliced crosswise

Combine the lime juice and syrup in a pitcher and stir
until blended. Pour into ice-filled glasses to fill halfway.
Top off each glass with club soda and add a swizzle stick
for stirring. Add a lime slice to each glass.

FRUIT SPRITZERS

PREP: 5 minutes   **COOK: 4 minutes**

Makes 8 to 12 servings

1½ cups water

¾ cup sugar

3 lemons, zested and juiced

3 limes, zested and juiced

1 quart pink grapefruit juice

Ice cubes

Club soda or seltzer, chilled

1. Combine the water, sugar, lemon zest, and lime zest in a small saucepan and stir until the sugar dissolves. Heat to boiling and boil 1 minute. Let cool.

2. Strain the mixture through a sieve into a large pitcher. Add the lemon juice, lime juice, and grapefruit juice and stir to blend. Refrigerate until serving.

3. To serve: Pour into tall ice-filled glasses to fill halfway. Top off each glass with club soda and add a swizzle stick for stirring.

ELLIOT'S SPRITZERS

PREP: 15 minutes

Makes 8 servings

3 large ripe peaches

¾ cup chilled fresh orange juice

¼ cup lemon juice

2 tablespoons grated peeled fresh ginger

1 (23-ounce) bottle peach-flavored sparkling water, chilled

Ice cubes

1. Peel, pit, and cut 2 peaches into 1-inch chunks. (Reserve the third peach for garnish.)

2. Combine the peach chunks, orange juice, and lemon juice in a blender or food processor. Place the ginger in a fine sieve and press out the juice over the peach chunks; discard the ginger solids. Blend or process the peach mixture until smooth. Pour into a large pitcher, cover, and refrigerate until serving.

3. To serve: Halve and pit the remaining peach; cut lengthwise into 8 slices. Stir the peach mixture and add the sparkling water. Gently stir to blend. Pour the spritzer into ice-filled glasses and add a peach wedge to each.

STRAWBERRY FLIPS

PREP: 10 minutes

Makes 4 to 6 servings

2 cups frozen whole strawberries (unsweetened)

2 cups chilled milk

¼ cup grenadine syrup

1 cup chilled club soda or more if needed

8 fresh mint sprigs

Combine the strawberries, milk, and grenadine in a blender and puree until smooth. Pour the mixture into tall glasses to within 1 inch of the top. Slowly pour the soda into the center of each glass to form a generous head. Garnish with mint sprigs.

RUBY FRUIT SLUSHIE

PREP: 20 minutes plus freezing

Makes 12 servings

8 cups cubed seedless watermelon
1 tablespoon sugar
2 cups fresh ruby-red grapefruit juice
Fresh mint sprigs

1. Place half of the watermelon in a food processor and sprinkle with half of the sugar. Process until pureed. Strain through a fine sieve placed over a shallow glass baking dish. Repeat with the remaining watermelon and sugar. Gently press on the solids in the sieve to extract all the juice; discard the solids.

2. Pour the grapefruit juice into the dish and stir to blend. Freeze until firm and slushy, 1 to 2 hours. To serve, spoon into tall cordial glasses and garnish each with a mint sprig.

PINEAPPLE-GRAPEFRUIT FROST

PREP: 15 minutes plus freezing

Makes 8 servings

2 cups fresh pineapple cubes
6 cups chilled grapefruit juice

1. Reserve 4 cubes of pineapple for garnish. Combine the remaining pineapple and 2 cups of the grapefruit juice in a blender or food processor; blend or process until pureed. Pour into ice-cube trays and freeze until hard, 4 hours or overnight.

2. To serve: Cut the reserved pineapple cubes in half and impale each piece on the end of a 6-inch bamboo skewer. Set aside. Combine half of the fruit ice cubes and 2 cups of the remaining grapefruit juice in a blender and blend until slushy. Pour into champagne flutes. Repeat with remaining fruit cubes and grapefruit juice. Garnish with the pineapple skewers so the pineapple chunk leans on the edge of the glass.

ICY GINGER TEA

PREP: 15 minutes plus chilling

Makes 6 servings

4 bags peppermint tea or 4 tablespoons
   loose peppermint tea

½ cup grated peeled fresh ginger
   plus unpeeled slices for garnish

½ cup packed fresh mint leaves
   plus sprigs for garnish

⅔ cup honey

6 cups boiling water

1 cup lemon juice

Ice cubes

1. Place the tea, ginger, mint, and honey in a heat-safe
bowl or glass measure and add the boiling water. Stir to
dissolve the honey; steep 6 minutes.

2. Strain the mixture through a sieve into another heat-
safe bowl or glass measure and cool. Pour into a pitcher
and stir in the lemon juice. Refrigerate until chilled,
about 2 hours. Pour into ice-filled glasses and garnish
with ginger slices and mint sprigs.

WHISKEY FRAPPÉS

PREP: 15 minutes

Makes 6 servings

1 orange
1 lemon
1 (6-ounce) can frozen lemonade concentrate
¾ cup orange juice
¾ cup bourbon whiskey
2 cups crushed ice

1. Trim the ends off the orange and lemon and cut the fruits crosswise into ¼-inch rounds. Cut the orange slices in half.

2. Combine the frozen lemonade concentrate, orange juice, whiskey, and ice in a blender and puree to a slushy consistency. To serve, pour into tall glasses and add a slice of orange and lemon to each glass.

MANGO PUNCH WITH STRAWBERRY ICE RING

PREP: 10 minutes

Makes 12 servings

4 cups mango nectar or puree, chilled

2 cups fresh, strained orange juice
   or store-bought pulp-free orange juice, chilled

2 cups apple juice, chilled

1 (32-ounce) bottle club soda, chilled

Strawberry Ice Ring (page 406)

Check the size of your punch bowl. The fruit-juice part of the punch is 8 cups, the club soda will add another 4, and the ice ring will displace about 4 more cups. If you don't think your bowl will hold 16 cups (4 quarts), combine just half of the juices and club soda in the bowl, add the ice ring, then replenish the punch as needed.

1. Combine the mango nectar, orange juice, and apple juice in a pitcher and mix to blend. Keep cold in the refrigerator until needed.

2. Pour the punch into a large punch bowl; add the club soda and ice ring. To serve, ladle into punch cups or other glasses.

STRAWBERRY ICE RING

PREP: 10 minutes plus freezing

Makes 1 ice ring

1 quart distilled water
12 large unhulled strawberries
1 lemon, sliced into wedges
1 lime, sliced crosswise into ¼-inch-thick rounds

1. Pour 1 inch of water into a 2-quart ring mold and arrange the strawberries, lemon wedges, and lime rounds in the mold. Freeze until the fruit is firm, about 2 hours. Add enough cold water to the mold to fill it three-fourths up the height of the fruit. Freeze until solid, several hours or overnight.

2. When the ring is frozen, unmold by dipping the bottom of the mold in a bowl of warm water and holding it just until the ice begins to loosen from the mold. Transfer the mold to a parchment-lined pie plate and store the ring in the freezer until ready to use.

SPICED CRANBERRY PUNCH

PREP: 15 minutes plus steeping   COOK: 10 minutes

Makes 16 servings

This punch can be made ahead and stored in the refrigerator. If serving it cold, garnish with orange slices and fresh cranberries. You can also serve with ice cubes made from cranberry-juice cocktail with an orange slice and a few cranberries in each.

1 cup sugar

4 cups water

12 whole cloves

4 (3-inch) cinnamon sticks

2 tablespoons grated peeled fresh ginger

8 cups cranberry-apple juice cocktail

2 cups fresh, strained orange juice
   or store-bought pulp-free orange juice

1 cup lemon juice (from 6 lemons)

1½ cups spiced or dark rum
   or additional cranberry-apple juice cocktail

1. Combine the sugar, water, cloves, cinnamon, and ginger in a large saucepan and stir until the sugar dissolves. Heat to boiling over medium-high heat; simmer over low heat 10 minutes. Remove the pan from the heat, cover, and let steep 1 hour.

2. Strain the sugar mixture through a fine sieve into a punch bowl or large pitcher. Stir in the cranberry cocktail, orange juice, and lemon juice. Chill or serve hot, stirring in the rum just before serving.

RED SANGRIA

PREP: 10 minutes plus standing COOK: 5 minutes

Makes 4 to 6 servings

1 cup Simple Syrup (page 473)
2 peaches, peeled, pitted, and cut lengthwise
   into thin slices
1 lime, thinly sliced crosswise
1 orange, thinly sliced crosswise
1 (1.5-liter) bottle Chilean red wine
16 ice cubes

1. Heat the syrup in a medium saucepan until simmering. Add the peaches, lime, and orange; remove from the heat. Cover and let steep at room temperature for 4 hours.

2. Pour the mixture into a large pitcher and add the wine. Stir to mix, cover, and let stand at room temperature at least 2 hours before serving.

3. To serve, add the ice and pour the sangria into glasses, including some ice and fruit in each.

White Sangria

Use Chilean white wine instead of red and substitute slices of honeydew, cantaloupe, and casaba melon for the peaches, lime, and orange.

GAME, SET, AND MATCH PIMM'S PUNCH

PREP: 10 minutes

Makes 6 servings

½ cup freshly squeezed lemon juice
½ cup freshly squeezed lime juice
½ cup freshly squeezed orange juice
½ cup Simple Syrup (page 473)
½ cup Pimm's No. 1
Ice cubes
2-inch center chunk of an unpared
  European cucumber, thinly sliced
  crosswise into 6 rounds
12 fresh borage or mint leaves
About 2 cups chilled tonic water

Combine the lemon, lime, and orange juices with the syrup and Pimm's in a pitcher and stir to blend. Place a few ice cubes in each of 6 tall glasses, along with a cucumber slice and 2 borage leaves. Add the Pimm's mixture, dividing equally and to at most 2 inches from the top. Top off each glass with tonic water.

WATERMELON PUNCH BOWL

PREP: 25 minutes

Makes 12 servings

1 watermelon or, if using a punch bowl,
    15 cups watermelon, seeds removed
1 cup superfine sugar or more to taste
¾ cup ffresh lime or lemon juice or more to taste
Ice cubes

1. Make the watermelon punch bowl (if you like): Place the watermelon on a cutting board and cut off a slice from the flattest side so the melon doesn't rock when placed with the cut side down. Cut off the top fourth of watermelon, making consecutive and connecting zigzag or curved cuts. Remove the top and scoop out the insides to make 15 cups of watermelon flesh. Remove the seeds from the flesh.

2. In batches, combine the watermelon, sugar, and lime juice in a blender and puree. Taste and add more sugar and/or juice if needed. Blend again if adding more. Strain through a sieve into a large pitcher without pressing the solids. Skim off any foam from the punch and refrigerate until cold.

3. To serve: Pour the punch into the watermelon punch bowl or other punch bowl and add the ice. Ladle into punch cups or other glasses.

HOT CITRUS PUNCH

10 cups sweetened store-bought or homemade (page 394)
    lemonade

1 (7-ounce) bottle sweetened lime juice

1 lemon, ends trimmed, cut crosswise into thin slices

1 lime, ends trimmed, cut crosswise into thin slices

3 (3-inch) cinnamon sticks

1. Combine the lemonade, lime juice, lemon and lime slices, and cinnamon in a large saucepan and mix to blend. Heat to boiling over medium-high heat. Pour into a heat-tempered punch bowl or deep food-safe pottery bowl. (Warm the bowl first by filling it with hot water and letting it stand 5 or 10 minutes before adding the punch.)

2. To serve, ladle the punch into heat-tempered mugs or glasses, including a few slices of fruit in each.

PARTY-ON EGGNOG

PREP: 15 minutes plus standing and chilling

COOK: 10 minutes

Makes 6 to 8 servings

3 cups whole milk
1 cup sugar
½ vanilla bean, split lengthwise
6 egg yolks
¾ cup bourbon whiskey
Freshly grated nutmeg for sprinkling

1. Combine 1½ cups of the milk, the sugar, and vanilla-bean halves in a small heavy saucepan. Cook over medium heat, stirring constantly to dissolve the sugar, until small bubbles form around the edges of the milk. Remove from the heat, cover, and let steep 30 minutes.

2. Scrape the seeds from the vanilla-bean halves into the steeped-milk mixture; discard the pods. Place the egg yolks in a medium bowl and beat lightly. Reheat the steeped milk until hot. Gradually whisk 1 cup of the steeped milk into the yolks, whisking until blended. Whisk the egg-yolk mixture back into the remaining steeped milk. Cook the custard over medium heat, stirring, until it registers 150°F on a candy thermometer or coats the back of a metal spoon (do not boil), about 5 minutes. Strain the hot custard through a sieve into a heat-tempered pitcher and stir in the remaining milk and the bourbon. Cover and refrigerate at least 8 hours or overnight.

3. To serve: Pour into a punch bowl and sprinkle with nutmeg. Ladle into punch cups or short glasses and sprinkle nutmeg over each serving.

HOT SPICED TEA

PREP: 40 minutes   COOK: 5 minutes

Makes 6 to 8 servings

1 orange

16 whole cloves

4 cups boiling water

4 bags black tea such as English breakfast

1 (3-inch) cinnamon stick

½ cup sugar or more to taste

2 cups fresh, strained orange juice
or store-bought pulp-free orange juice

½ cup lemon juice

1. Punch 2 lines of 8 small cuts each, evenly spaced, around the center of the orange with the tip of a paring knife; insert the cloves into each slit. Cut the orange into 8 wedges so that each wedge contains 2 cloves. In a heat-safe pitcher or glass measure, pour the boiling water over the tea bags. Add the orange wedges and the cinnamon sticks to the tea. Let steep 5 minutes.

2. Remove the tea bags (do not squeeze them or it will make the tea bitter) and place the tea in a saucepan. Add the sugar and stir until dissolved. Heat over low heat until hot; remove from heat and let steep 15 minutes. Add the orange juice and lemon juice and stir to blend. Taste and add more sugar if needed. Heat over low heat until hot.

3. Remove the cinnamon stick and pour the tea into heat-safe cups. Include an orange wedge in each cup.

SPIRITED COFFEE

PREP: 5 minutes   COOK: 10 minutes

Makes 6 servings

4 cups freshly brewed coffee
1 cup brandy, bourbon, or Irish whiskey
½ cup fresh, strained orange juice
    or store-bought pulp-free orange juice
⅓ cup honey
¼ teaspoon ground cardamom
About ¾ cup Chantilly Cream (page 456)
    or whipped cream

Combine the coffee, brandy, orange juice, honey, and cardamom in a saucepan and heat until hot. Ladle into mugs or heat-tempered glasses and top with a dollop of Chantilly Cream or whipped cream.

EXTRA-SOOTHING MULLED WINE

PREP: 15 minutes   COOK: 20 minutes

Makes 12 servings

4 cups store-bought or homemade (page 394)
  sweetened lemonade

½ cup sugar

12 whole cloves

2 allspice berries

2 (3-inch) cinnamon sticks

½ nutmeg, crushed into small pieces

8 chamomile tea bags

1 (1.5-liter) bottle red or white wine

1. Combine the lemonade, sugar, cloves, allspice, cinnamon, and nutmeg in a medium saucepan. Heat to boiling, stirring to dissolve the sugar. Simmer over medium-low heat 5 minutes. Add the tea bags and remove the pan from the heat; cover and steep 5 minutes.

2. Heat the wine in a large saucepan to boiling over medium-high heat. Strain the tea mixture through a sieve into the wine and stir to blend. Let heat but not boil about 5 minutes.

3. To serve, ladle the mulled wine into heat-tempered mugs or glasses.

HOT BUTTERED RUM

PREP: 15 minutes

Makes 16 servings

1 pint best-quality vanilla ice cream, softened

1 cup (2 sticks) unsalted butter, softened

1 cup brown sugar

2 teaspoons ground cinnamon

1 teaspoon freshly grated nutmeg

Dark or light rum

Boiling water

Long cinnamon sticks or licorice sticks for serving

1. Combine the ice cream, butter, brown sugar, ground cinnamon, and nutmeg in a food processor and pulse to combine. Scrape into a freezer container and freeze until serving.

2. For each serving: Pour about 2 tablespoons rum into a 12-ounce mug or heat-safe glass and add ¼ cup of the ice-cream mixture. Fill the mug with about 1 cup boiling water. Add a cinnamon stick to use for stirring the ice-cream mixture until melted.

MEXICAN HOT CHOCOLATE

2½ cups milk or water
1 cup (about 5 ounces) chopped Mexican
    or other semisweet chocolate
4 (3-inch) sticks cinnamon,
    preferably Mexican

1. Combine the milk, chocolate, and cinnamon in a
saucepan and heat, whisking, until the chocolate melts.
Fish out the cinnamon and set aside.

2. In batches, blend the hot chocolate in a blender until
frothy. Pour into cups, place a cinnamon stick on top of
the froth in each, and serve immediately.

BRANDY CHOCOLATE CREAM

PREP: 10 minutes plus chilling

Makes about 3¼ cups

1 (14-ounce) can sweetened condensed milk
1 cup brandy
1 cup ultra-pasteurized heavy cream
3 tablespoons chocolate syrup
Ice and chilled club soda (optional)
Freshly brewed coffee (optional)

1. Combine the milk, brandy, cream, and chocolate syrup in a 1-quart jar. Seal and shake to combine. Refrigerate until cold, about 2 hours. Shake the jar to recombine before using.

2. To serve: Pour the brandy cream over ice in tall glasses, filling the glasses only halfway, and top them off with club soda. You can also pour ¼ cup of the brandy cream into mugs or heat-tempered glasses and add ¾ cup freshly brewed coffee to each. Store the remaining brandy cream in the refrigerator.

BLOODY MARY SLUSHES

PREP: 20 minutes plus overnight freezing

Makes 8 servings

1 medium onion, quartered
1 (46-ounce) can vegetable juice
3 tablespoons Worcestershire sauce
1 tablespoon lemon juice or more to taste
2 cups pepper-flavored vodka
Lime slices

1. Place the onion in a blender with 2 cups of the vegetable juice, the Worcestershire sauce, and lemon juice. Blend until the onion is pureed into the juice. Pour the mixture into a shallow 2½-quart glass baking dish and stir in the remaining vegetable juice. Cover and freeze overnight.

2. One hour before serving, remove the frozen juice mixture from the freezer and let stand at room temperature 30 minutes.

3. Break the mixture into small chunks using a fork. Place half in a blender or food processor. Add 1 cup vodka and blend or process until smooth. Spoon into 4 large stemmed glasses. Repeat with the remaining frozen mixture and vodka. Garnish each glass with a lime slice.

SAUCES, SYRUPS, CREAMS & GLAZES

TOMATO-PEPPER SAUCE

PREP: 10 minutes   COOK: 12 minutes

Makes about 1 cup

1 tablespoon butter

½ cup finely chopped green pepper

¼ cup finely chopped onion

1 small garlic clove, peeled

½ teaspoon Spanish bittersweet (smoked) paprika
  or a pinch of cayenne

2 (3-ounce) ripe plum tomatoes, seeded and chopped

½ teaspoon salt or more to taste

¼ teaspoon freshly ground black pepper
  or more to taste

½ cup sour cream

1 tablespoon chopped fresh flat-leaf parsley

Melt the butter in a skillet over medium heat. Add the green pepper, onion, and garlic and sauté until soft, about 7 minutes. Add the paprika and sauté 1 minute. Stir in the tomatoes, salt, and pepper and sauté until the tomatoes are softened and sizzling, about 3 minutes. Stir in the sour cream and heat thoroughly. Taste and add more salt and pepper if needed. Stir in the parsley.

CLASSIC BASIL PESTO

PREP: 10 minutes

Makes about 2 cups

2 large garlic cloves, halved

2 cups firmly packed stemmed fresh basil leaves

¾ cup grated Parmigiano-Reggiano cheese

2 tablespoons pine nuts

¾ cup extra-virgin olive oil or more if needed

Place the garlic, basil, cheese, and nuts in food processor or blender. Cover and blend until evenly smooth. With the machine running, pour in the oil in a thin, steady stream through the feed tube and process until a thick, smooth paste forms, stopping to scrape the sides and adding a little more oil if the mixture is stiff.

MIXED MUSHROOM PESTO

PREP: 15 minutes   COOK: 30 minutes

Makes about 2 cups

8 ounces shiitake mushrooms, caps only

8 ounces sliced button mushrooms

⅓ cup olive oil

1 garlic clove, crushed through a press

½ teaspoon kosher salt or more to taste

¼ teaspoon freshly ground black pepper

½ cup pine nuts, toasted

½ cup freshly grated Parmigiano-Reggiano cheese

⅓ cup chopped fresh flat-leaf parsley

1 tablespoon lemon juice

1. Preheat the oven to 375°F. Line a baking sheet with foil. Combine the shiitake mushrooms and button mushrooms on the prepared baking sheet. Mix the oil, garlic, salt, and pepper in a cup and pour over the mushrooms. Toss to coat. Bake until the mushrooms are tender, about 30 minutes.

2. Transfer the mushrooms to a food processor and pulse until finely chopped. Add the pine nuts, cheese, parsley, and lemon juice and process until a rough paste forms. Taste and add more salt and pepper if needed.

AÏOLI

PREP: 5 minutes

Makes about 1¹/₂ cups

1 large egg or 2 egg yolks

1 tablespoon freshly squeezed lemon juice or more to taste

¹/₂ teaspoon salt or more to taste

¹/₄ teaspoon ground white pepper or more to taste

1 to 1¹/₂ cups extra-virgin olive oil or more if needed

2 large garlic cloves, crushed through a press

1. Combine the egg, lemon juice, salt, pepper, and 2 tablespoons of the oil in a food processor and blend until smooth, about 1 minute.

2. With the machine running, pour in enough of the remaining oil in a thin, steady stream through the feed tube to make a creamy and smooth sauce that is thick but not stiff. Stop the machine and scrape the sides. Add the garlic and process until blended, about 30 seconds. Taste the sauce and add more salt, pepper, and lemon juice if needed.

ANCHOVY AND BLACK OLIVE AÏOLI

PREP: 5 minutes

Makes about 1½ cups

1 large egg or 2 egg yolks

1 tablespoon freshly squeezed lemon juice
or more to taste

4 anchovy fillets

¼ teaspoon ground white pepper
or more to taste

1 to 1½ cups extra-virgin olive oil
or more if needed

2 large garlic cloves, crushed through a press
or more if needed

¼ cup finely chopped pitted oil-cured black olives

1. Combine the egg, lemon juice, anchovies, pepper, and 2 tablespoons of the oil in a food processor and blend until smooth, about 1 minute.

2. With the machine running, pour in enough of the remaining oil in a thin, steady stream through the feed tube to make a creamy and smooth sauce that is thick but not stiff. Stop the machine and scrape the sides. Add the garlic and process until blended, about 30 seconds. Stir in the olives. Taste the sauce and add more salt, pepper, and lemon juice if needed.

CHIPOTLE AÏOLI

PREP: 10 minutes

Makes about 1½ cups

1 large egg or 2 egg yolks

*1 tablespoon freshly squeezed lemon juice
or more to taste*

½ teaspoon salt or more to taste

*¼ teaspoon ground white pepper
or more to taste*

*1 to 1½ cups extra-virgin olive oil
or more if needed*

*1 canned chipotle chile in adobo sauce
plus 1 teaspoon or more of the adobo sauce*

2 large garlic cloves, crushed through a press

1. Combine the egg, lemon juice, salt, pepper, and 2 tablespoons of the oil in a food processor and blend until smooth, about 1 minute.

2. Coarsely chop the chipotle and blend with 1 teaspoon of the adobo sauce. Stir into the mixture. With the machine running, pour in enough of the remaining oil in a thin, steady stream through the feed tube to make a creamy and smooth sauce that is thick but not stiff. Stop the machine and scrape the sides. Add the garlic and process until blended, about 30 seconds. Taste and add more salt, pepper, lemon juice, and/or adobo sauce if needed.

SWEET AND SOUR DIPPING SAUCE

PREP: 5 minutes   COOK: 5 minutes

Makes about 2 cups

½ cup rice vinegar

1 tablespoon sugar

2 tablespoons slivered hot red chile pepper
 (wear gloves when handling) or
 ½ teaspoon red pepper flakes

½ cup water

½ cup lemon juice

¼ cup fish sauce (Vietnamese nuoc mam
 or Thai nam pla)

1 tablespoon soy sauce

Heat the vinegar in a small saucepan until hot, remove from the heat, and add the sugar (and pepper flakes if using). Stir until the sugar dissolves. Stir in the chile (if using), water, lemon juice, fish sauce, and soy sauce.

LIME DIPPING SAUCE

PREP: 5 minutes

Makes 3/4 cup

2 teaspoons grated lime zest

½ cup lime juice

¼ cup fish sauce (Vietnamese nuoc mam or Thai nam pla)

1 jalapeño chile pepper (taste to make sure it is hot), finely chopped (wear gloves when handling)

1 garlic clove, crushed through a press

1 teaspoon sugar

Combine all the ingredients in a small bowl and whisk until the sugar dissolves.

CUCUMBER-CHILI DIPPING SAUCE

PREP: 10 minutes plus chilling

Makes about 3/4 cup

1 lime, zested and juiced

1 garlic clove, minced

¼ cup fish sauce (Thai nam pla
or Vietnamese nuoc mam)

2 tablespoons sugar

2 tablespoons rice vinegar or more to taste

1 teaspoon sambal oelek (Indonesian pepper paste)
or 1 thin red chile pepper (taste to make sure
it is hot), sliced crosswise into thin rings
(wear gloves when handling) or more to taste

½ cup water or as needed

¼ cup grated cucumber

2 tablespoons julienned carrot

Combine the lime zest and juice, garlic, fish sauce, sugar,
vinegar, and sambal oelek in a bowl and stir until the
sugar dissolves. Stir in enough water to thin the sauce
to a dipping consistency but still have a very perky flavor.
Stir in the cucumber and carrot. Cover and refrigerate
at least 1 hour or up to 8 hours. Taste and add more
vinegar and/or sambal oelek or chile pepper if needed.
Serve at room temperature.

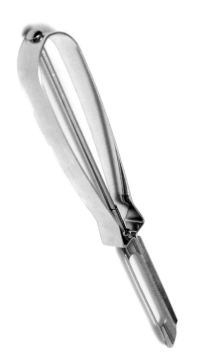

EASY GREEN ONION DIPPING SAUCE

PREP: 5 minutes

Makes about ³/₄ cup

2 green onions, minced

½ cup rice wine vinegar

2 tablespoons soy sauce

2 teaspoons grated fresh ginger

Combine all the ingredients in a bowl and mix well.

CUCUMBER-BUTTERMILK SAUCE

PREP: 15 minutes

Makes about 2 1/2 cups

1 (8-ounce) package cream cheese, softened

1 1/4 cups buttermilk

1 European cucumber

2 tablespoons lemon juice

1 tablespoon finely snipped fresh chives

1/2 teaspoon salt or more to taste

1/4 teaspoon freshly ground white pepper
or more to taste

1. Combine the cream cheese and buttermilk in a blender and pulse until blended. (To do this in a food processor, use 1 cup of the buttermilk.) Pour into a glass measure (stir in the remaining buttermilk if using a food processor).

2. Peel the cucumber and cut in half lengthwise. Drag a teaspoon down the middle to remove the seeds. Shred the cucumber into short pieces, squeeze gently to remove the liquid, and add to the cream-cheese mixture. Add the lemon juice, chives, salt, and pepper. Taste and add more salt and pepper if needed.

SPICY TOMATO SAUCE

PREP: 5 minutes COOK: 15 minutes

Makes about 3 cups

3 tablespoons olive oil
1 medium red onion, coarsely chopped
2 garlic cloves, crushed through a press
2 teaspoons finely grated orange zest
1 teaspoon sugar
1 habanero chile pepper, finely chopped
  (wear gloves when handling)
  or ½ teaspoon red pepper flakes
3 pounds plum tomatoes, cored and cubed
2 tablespoons chopped fresh basil

1. Heat the oil in a large nonstick skillet over medium-high heat. Add the onion and sauté 3 minutes. Stir in the garlic, orange zest, sugar, and habanero; sauté 2 minutes. Reduce the heat to medium. Stir in the tomatoes and basil; cook 10 minutes, stirring occasionally.

2. Pass the sauce through a food mill set over a bowl.

LEMON-WATERCRESS BUTTER SAUCE

PREP: 10 minutes   COOK: 7 minutes

Makes about 1¼ cups

½ cup (1 stick) unsalted butter

2 shallots, minced

1 teaspoon all-purpose flour

1 bunch fresh watercress, rinsed, spun dry,
   tough stems removed

¼ cup lemon juice

¼ teaspoon salt

¼ teaspoon freshly ground black pepper

1. Melt the butter in a large skillet over medium heat. Add the shallots and sauté until softened, about 2 minutes. Stir in the flour until blended and cook, stirring, 1 minute. Add half of the watercress and sauté until wilted.

2. Scrape the sautéed watercress mixture into a blender or food processor. Add the remaining watercress, the lemon juice, salt, and pepper and puree.

YOGURT-HORSERADISH SAUCE

PREP: 5 minutes

Makes about 1½ cups

1 cup plain whole-milk yogurt
½ cup mayonnaise
2 tablespoons creamed white horseradish
   (from a freshly opened jar) or to taste

Combine the yogurt, mayonnaise, and horseradish in a bowl and mix well. Cover and refrigerate until serving.

MOROCCAN CILANTRO SAUCE

PREP: 10 minutes
Makes about 1½ cups

½ cup extra-virgin olive oil

1 garlic clove, crushed through a press

1 (2-inch) piece fresh ginger, peeled and thinly sliced

1 teaspoon red pepper flakes

7 cups packed fresh cilantro leaves, rinsed and dried

2 tablespoons lemon juice

2 teaspoons ground cumin

1 teaspoon kosher salt or more to taste

In a food processor, combine ¼ cup of the olive oil, the garlic, ginger, and pepper flakes. Pulse to finely chop the garlic and ginger. With the machine running, add handfuls of cilantro through the feed tube until about 3 cups are left. Scrape down the sides of the bowl and add the lemon juice, cumin, and salt. With the machine running, add the remaining ¼ cup oil and the remaining cilantro in handfuls. Process until the sauce is smooth. Taste and add more salt if needed.

INDONESIAN PEANUT SAUCE

PREP: 5 minutes COOK: 35 minutes

Makes about 3 cups

3 tablespoons peanut oil

2 cups shelled peanuts (not dry-roasted)

6 Thai bird chiles, finely chopped

3 large shallots, sliced

2 garlic cloves, sliced

2 cups water

1 cup coconut milk

6 fresh kaffir lime leaves, stems removed,
  leaves sliced

2 tablespoons Indonesian kecap manis
  (sweet soy sauce)

1 lemon, juiced

1 teaspoon salt or more to taste

½ teaspoon freshly ground pepper
  or more to taste

1. Heat 1 tablespoon of the oil in a medium skillet over medium heat. Add the peanuts and sauté until golden brown, 4 to 6 minutes. Transfer with a slotted spoon to a paper towel–lined baking sheet to drain.

2. Add the remaining 2 tablespoons oil to the same skillet, along with the chiles, shallots, and garlic. Sauté until fragrant and softened, about 2 minutes. Add the water, coconut milk, lime leaves, and kecap manis and heat to boiling.

3. While the sauce heats, grind the peanuts in a food processor. Add to the sauce. Simmer over low heat until thickened to a coating consistency, 15 to 20 minutes. Add the lemon juice, salt, and pepper and mix well. Taste and add more salt and pepper if needed. Serve at room temperature.

QUICK PEANUT SAUCE

PREP: 10 minutes

Makes about 1 cup

1 large garlic clove, crushed though a press

½ cup unsweetened peanut butter

¼ cup rice vinegar

2 tablespoons chopped fresh cilantro

1 tablespoon soy sauce or more to taste

2 teaspoons light brown sugar

1 teaspoon chile oil or paste or more to taste

¼ teaspoon salt or more to taste

½ cup warm water or more as needed

Combine the garlic, peanut butter, vinegar, cilantro, soy sauce, brown sugar, chile oil, and salt in a bowl and stir until blended. Gradually stir in the warm water so that the mixture doesn't get lumpy. Stir in enough additional water if needed to make a consistency good for dipping, not too thick or thin. Taste and add more soy sauce, chile oil, and/or salt if needed.

CHUNKY PINEAPPLE-PEANUT SAUCE

PREP: 5 minutes   COOK: 5 minutes

Makes 1¹/₂ cups

1 (8-ounce) can crushed pineapple, undrained

¹/₂ cup chunky peanut butter

1 tablespoon roasted garlic teriyaki sauce or more to taste

1 tablespoon brown sugar

¹/₄ teaspoon cayenne

2 tablespoons chopped fresh cilantro

2 tablespoons finely chopped green onions

Combine the pineapple and its juice, the peanut butter, teriyaki sauce, brown sugar, and cayenne in a small saucepan and mix well. Heat to boiling over medium heat and simmer 3 minutes. Stir in the cilantro and green onions. Taste and add more teriyaki sauce if needed.

PINEAPPLE CHUTNEY

2 cups (½-inch) chunks fresh pineapple
1 tablespoon chopped fresh mint
1 tablespoon sugar
1 teaspoon grated lime zest
2 tablespoons lime juice
1 teaspoon minced fresh red or green hot chile
(taste it to make sure it is hot; wear gloves
when handling)

Place the pineapple in a food processor and pulse until coarsely chopped. Add the mint, sugar, lime zest, lime juice, and chile and pulse to combine.

COCKTAIL SAUCE

PREP: 5 minutes

Makes 1¼ cups

1 cup ketchup

1 tablespoon dark brown sugar

1 tablespoon minced shallot

1 tablespoon prepared horseradish
or more to taste (you will need
more if the jar was not opened recently)

½ teaspoon grated lime zest

1 teaspoon lime juice

½ teaspoon hot pepper sauce or more to taste

¼ teaspoon freshly ground black pepper

⅛ teaspoon salt

Combine all the ingredients in a medium bowl and stir until blended. Taste and add more horseradish and/or hot sauce if needed. Serve immediately or cover and refrigerate up to 4 hours before serving.

HONEY-BOURBON MUSTARD SAUCE

PREP: 5 minutes   COOK: 10 minutes

Makes about 2 cups

1 cup bourbon whiskey
1 cup honey
¼ cup Dijon mustard

Combine the bourbon, honey, and mustard in a small saucepan and mix until blended. Heat to boiling over medium heat, stirring frequently. Simmer over low heat until thickened, 4 to 5 minutes. Serve hot, warm, or at room temperature.

BLUE CHEESE DIPPING SAUCE

PREP: 10 minutes

Makes about 1 1/2 cups

1 cup mayonnaise
1 cup plain low-fat yogurt
3 tablespoons lemon juice
6 ounces blue cheese, crumbled
1 tablespoon minced fresh flat-leaf parsley

Combine all the ingredients in a bowl and whisk until blended. Cover and refrigerate until ready to serve.

HERBED TOMATO DIPPING SAUCE

PREP: 5 minutes
Makes about 2 cups

1 (14½-ounce) can pizza-style chunky tomato sauce
1 tablespoon red wine vinegar
½ teaspoon red pepper flakes
½ teaspoon dried oregano

Combine the tomato sauce, vinegar, pepper flakes, and oregano in a food processor or blender and puree until smooth. Pour into a small saucepan and heat until hot.

LEMONY GREEN ONION DIPPING SAUCE

PREP: 5 minutes   COOK: 8 minutes

Makes 1½ cups

1 tablespoon vegetable oil
2 garlic cloves, crushed through a press
2 green onions, finely chopped
2 lemons, zested and juiced
4 teaspoons cornstarch
1 cup chicken broth or water

Heat the oil in a small saucepan over medium-high heat. Add the garlic, green onions, and lemon zest and sauté until the onions are tender, about 3 minutes. Mix the cornstarch with ¼ cup of the lemon juice in a cup until blended and add to the onion mixture. Add the broth and heat to boiling. Cook, stirring constantly, until the sauce is thickened and clear, about 1 minute. Taste and add more lemon juice to make a balanced sweet-and-sour sauce. Serve hot.

CIDER-HONEY BARBECUE SAUCE

PREP: 10 minutes   COOK: 15 minutes

Makes about 1/2 cups

2 tablespoons canola or vegetable oil
1 medium onion, chopped
4 garlic cloves, chopped
1 cup apple cider
½ cup ketchup
¼ cup honey
½ teaspoon dry mustard

Heat the oil in a small skillet over medium-high heat.
Add the onion and sauté until softened, about 4 minutes. Add the garlic and sauté until fragrant, 1 minute.
Add the cider, ketchup, honey, and mustard and whisk
until blended. Simmer over medium-low heat until
thickened, about 10 minutes, whisking occasionally.

KENTUCKY BARBECUE SAUCE

PREP: 5 minutes COOK: 25 minutes

Makes 3 to 4 cups

2 cups ketchup
1 cup packed brown sugar
1 cup bourbon whiskey
¼ cup Worcestershire sauce
¼ cup cider vinegar
¼ cup soy sauce
2 teaspoons dry mustard
½ teaspoon cayenne

Combine all the ingredients in a medium saucepan and mix until blended. Heat to boiling over high heat, stirring occasionally. Simmer over low heat until thickened, 20 to 25 minutes, stirring occasionally.

BALSAMIC-SOY BARBECUE SAUCE

PREP: 5 minutes   COOK: 15 minutes

Makes about 3¹/₂ cups

2 cups ketchup
¹/₂ cup balsamic vinegar
¹/₄ cup soy sauce
3 tablespoons brown sugar
1 tablespoon dry mustard
1 tablespoon grated peeled fresh ginger
6 garlic cloves, crushed through a press
1 cup Scotch whiskey

Combine the ketchup, vinegar, soy sauce, sugar, mustard, ginger, and garlic in a small saucepan and mix well.
Cook over medium-high heat, stirring, until boiling.
Simmer over low heat until thickened, 10 to 15 minutes.
Stir in the whiskey.

MUSTARD-DILL SAUCE

The sauce can be covered and refrigerated for several days. Re-stir before using.

¼ cup store-bought or homemade (page 455) mustard

1 teaspoon dry mustard

3 tablespoons sugar

2 tablespoons white wine or distilled vinegar

⅓ cup canola or grapeseed oil

3 tablespoons chopped fresh dill

Combine the mustards, sugar, and vinegar in a small bowl and mix to form a paste. Gradually whisk in the oil, whisking until the sauce is blended and the texture of mayonnaise. Stir in the dill.

MIGNONETTE SAUCE

PREP: 5 minutes
Makes about 3/4 cup

⅓ cup olive oil or canola oil
¼ cup red wine vinegar
1 small plum tomato, finely chopped
1 small shallot, minced
1 tablespoon small capers, packed in salt,
  rinsed, drained, and patted dry
1 teaspoon grated lemon zest

Combine the oil and vinegar in a small bowl and whisk until blended. Whisk in the tomato, shallot, capers, and zest.

HOMEMADE MUSTARD

PREP: 10 minutes plus standing and chilling

COOK: 20 minutes

Makes about 2 cups

1 cup hot water
⅔ cup dry mustard
6 tablespoons yellow mustard seeds
1 cup white wine vinegar
¼ cup small capers, packed in salt, rinsed, drained, patted dry
2 teaspoons kosher salt
2 teaspoons sugar

1. Combine the hot water, dry mustard, and mustard seeds in a small bowl and mix well. Cover and let stand 3 hours.

2. Place the vinegar in a small saucepan and heat to boiling. Stir the vinegar into the mustard-seed mixture. Stir in the capers, salt, and sugar, and mix well. Pour into a blender or food processor and puree.

3. Pour the puree into the same (unwashed) saucepan used to heat the vinegar and heat over medium heat until fragrant. Reduce the heat to low and cook, stirring frequently, 10 minutes. Pour the mustard into a jar and let cool. Cover and refrigerate at least 24 hours before using.

CHANTILLY CREAM

2 1/4 cups heavy cream
1 1/2 tablespoons sugar
1 teaspoon vanilla extract
Pinch of salt

Combine the cream, sugar, vanilla, and salt in a large chilled bowl and beat at high speed until soft peaks form when the beaters are raised. Use immediately or cover and refrigerate up to 1 hour. After that, rewhip slightly before serving.

PASTRY CREAM

PREP: 15 minutes   COOK: 8 minutes

Makes 2 cups

1½ cups half-and-half
½ vanilla bean, split lengthwise in half
⅓ cup sugar
2 tablespoons all-purpose flour
2 tablespoons cornstarch
⅛ teaspoon salt
4 egg yolks
2 tablespoons unsalted butter, in pieces,
     softened
¼ cup heavy cream

1. Combine the half-and-half and vanilla bean in a saucepan and heat to simmering over medium heat. Keep warm.

2. Combine the sugar, flour, cornstarch, and salt in a medium bowl. Add the egg yolks and whisk until blended. In a thin, steady stream, whisk in the hot half-and-half and the vanilla bean. Pour the mixture back into the same saucepan and cook over low heat, whisking constantly, until boiling, 3 to 5 minutes. The mixture will start to form lumps as it cooks so whisk vigorously to keep it smooth.

3. Remove from the heat and whisk in the butter. Strain through a sieve into a clean bowl. Place plastic wrap directly on the surface to keep a skin from forming and refrigerate until cold.

4. Beat the cream in a glass measure with a portable electric mixer until soft peaks form when the beaters are raised. Gently fold the whipped cream into the pastry cream using a rubber spatula.

EASY LEMON CURD

PREP: 5 minutes   COOK: 6 minutes

Makes about 2 cups

3 eggs, lightly beaten
2 large lemons, zested and juiced
1 cup sugar
½ cup (1 stick) unsalted butter,
    in ½-inch pieces, softened

Combine the eggs, lemon zest and juice, sugar, and butter in a heavy saucepan and whisk constantly over medium heat until thickened, about 6 minutes. Lift the pan off the heat and whisk vigorously if the mixture starts to curdle. Scrape into a heat-safe bowl and cool.

RICH LEMON CURD

PREP: 5 minutes COOK: 15 minutes

Makes about 1¼ cups

5 egg yolks

2 large lemons, zested and juiced

¾ cup sugar

½ cup (1 stick) unsalted butter,
  in ½-inch pieces, softened

Combine the eggs, lemon zest and juice, sugar, and butter in the top of a double boiler set over simmering (not boiling) water. Whisk or stir with a wooden spoon until thick and light, about 15 minutes. Scrape into a heat-safe bowl and cool.

LIME CURD

PREP: 5 minutes   COOK: 15 minutes

Makes about 1¼ cups

2 *eggs, beaten*

6 *tablespoons unsalted butter, in ½-inch pieces,*
softened

¾ *cup sugar*

½ *cup freshly squeezed lime juice*

Combine the eggs, butter, sugar, and lime juice in the top of a double boiler set over simmering (not boiling) water. Whisk or stir with a wooden spoon until thick and light, about 15 minutes. Scrape into a heat-safe bowl and cool.

CHOCOLATE GANACHE

PREP: 5 minutes plus chilling COOK: 10 minutes

Makes about 1¹/2 cups

6 ounces semisweet chocolate chips
   or chopped squares
²/3 cup heavy cream

Combine the chocolate and cream in a small saucepan and cook over low heat, stirring constantly, until the chocolate melts and the mixture is smooth. Refrigerate until thick but still pourable, about 1 hour.

CRÈME FRAÎCHE

PREP: 5 minutes plus standing and chilling

COOK: 3 minutes

Makes 2 cups

2 cups heavy cream
2 tablespoons buttermilk or sour cream

Heat the cream in a small saucepan over low heat to 100°F. Add the buttermilk and mix well. Pour into a jar, cover, and let stand at room temperature for 6 to 8 hours. Refrigerate at least 24 hours before using.

CHOCOLATE GLAZE

PREP: 5 minutes COOK: 10 minutes

Makes about 1 cup

½ cup water

¼ cup sugar

4 ounces semisweet chocolate chips
  or chopped squares

Combine the water and sugar in a small saucepan and heat to boiling over medium heat, stirring until the sugar dissolves. Add the chocolate and stir until the chocolate melts and the mixture is smooth. Simmer until thick enough to coat the back of a spoon, about 1 minute. Cool 30 minutes before using.

LEMON GLAZE

PREP: 5 minutes
Makes about 1/3 cup

1 cup sifted confectioners' sugar
1 tablespoon Limoncello (Italian lemon liqueur)
1 teaspoon grated lemon zest

Combine the sugar, liqueur, and zest in a small bowl and stir until blended. Cover with plastic wrap until ready to use.

APRICOT GLAZE

PREP: 10 minutes   COOK: 13 minutes

Makes about 1³/₄ cups

1 (1-pound) jar apricot preserves or jam
¼ cup water
2 tablespoons lemon juice

1. Combine the preserves, water, and lemon juice in a small saucepan. Slowly heat to boiling over medium-low heat, stirring occasionally to blend as the preserves melt. Simmer 5 minutes, stirring occasionally.

2. Strain the glaze through a sieve into a heat-safe bowl. Scrape back into the (cleaned) saucepan and simmer until the glaze is a thin coating consistency, about 5 minutes (depending on the quality of the preserves).

RED CURRANT GLAZE

PREP: 5 minutes   COOK: 8 minutes

Makes 1/2 cup

½ cup red currant jelly
1 tablespoon water
1 to 2 tablespoons Kirsch (cherry-flavored brandy)
   or other brandy or liqueur (optional)

Melt the jelly, water, and Kirsch (if using) in a small
saucepan over medium heat, stirring until smooth.
Heat to boiling. Use when hot to glaze fruit.

QUICK AND EASY CHOCOLATE SAUCE

PREP: 5 minutes   COOK: 10 minutes

Makes about 1¼ cups

4 (1-ounce) squares unsweetened chocolate

1 cup sugar

½ cup half-and-half

¼ cup (½ stick) unsalted butter, in chunks

1 teaspoon vanilla extract

Combine the chocolate, sugar, half-and-half, and butter in a small saucepan. Heat to boiling over medium-high heat, stirring until the sugar dissolves and the butter and chocolate melt. Stir in the vanilla. Serve hot, warm, or at room temperature.

HOT FUDGE SAUCE

PREP: 5 minutes   COOK: 5 minutes

Makes about 1¹/₂ cups

½ cup unsweetened cocoa powder

½ cup packed dark brown sugar

½ cup heavy cream

¼ cup (½ stick) unsalted butter

3 tablespoons coffee-flavored liqueur (optional)

Combine all the ingredients in a small heavy saucepan and heat to boiling over medium-high heat, stirring constantly. Boil 1 minute. Remove from the heat and keep warm.

VANILLA CUSTARD SAUCE

PREP: 40 minutes COOK: 10 minutes

Makes 1 1/2 cups

1 1/2 cups milk

1/2 (3-inch) cinnamon stick

1/2 vanilla bean, split lengthwise in half

1 egg

3 tablespoons sugar

1. Combine the milk, cinnamon stick, and split vanilla bean in a small heavy saucepan. Heat over medium heat until small bubbles form around the edges. Remove from the heat, cover, and let steep 30 minutes. Remove the cinnamon stick and vanilla-bean halves; reserve the bean halves.

2. Combine the egg and sugar in a medium bowl. Pour the steeped milk into the egg mixture. Scrape in the seeds from the vanilla-bean halves; discard the pods. Return the milk mixture to the (cleaned) pan. Cook the custard over medium heat, stirring until thickened (do not boil), about 5 minutes. Strain the hot custard through a sieve into a bowl. Use immediately, or place plastic wrap directly on the surface to prevent a skin from forming and refrigerate until using.

BRANDIED HARD SAUCE

PREP: 40 minutes
Makes about 1 1/2 cups

½ cup (1 stick) unsalted butter, softened
1 cup confectioners' sugar
1 tablespoon brandy (or more to taste)
3 tablespoons heavy cream (optional)

1. In a medium bowl, whisk the butter until fluffy. Gradually whisk in the sugar until blended. Whisk in the brandy until blended and fluffy. If desired, gradually whisk in the cream until blended.

2. Pile the butter mixture into a serving bowl, cover with plastic wrap, and refrigerate. Let stand at room temperature for about 30 minutes before serving.

CARAMEL SAUCE

PREP: 5 minutes   COOK: 15 minutes

Makes 1¼ cups

1 cup sugar
¼ cup water
1¼ cups heavy cream
⅛ teaspoon salt
2 teaspoons vanilla extract

1. Combine the sugar and water in a deep, heavy 1½-quart saucepan and heat to boiling over high heat, swirling the pan frequently to dissolve the sugar (do not stir) and brushing any crystals from the sides of the pan using a wet pasty brush. Boil until a dark caramel forms, about 6 minutes. Remove the pan from the heat.

2. Carefully pour in the cream (the mixture will sputter) and return the pan to the heat. Cook, stirring constantly, until the caramel dissolves and the sauce is smooth. Stir in the salt and vanilla.

MOCHA RUM SAUCE

PREP: 5 minutes   COOK: 10 minutes

Makes 1 1/4 cups

½ cup packed dark brown sugar

¼ cup unsweetened European-style cocoa powder

2 teaspoons instant espresso-coffee powder

½ cup heavy cream

2 tablespoons unsalted butter, cut into bits

2 ounces bittersweet chocolate, chopped

1 tablespoon dark rum

½ teaspoon vanilla extract

Combine the brown sugar, cocoa powder, and coffee powder in a small saucepan and mix well. Gradually whisk in the cream and whisk until blended. Add the butter and cook over medium-low heat, whisking constantly, until the butter is almost melted. Add the chocolate and whisk until the chocolate melts and the sauce is smooth. Whisk in the rum and vanilla. Serve hot or warm.

SIMPLE SYRUP

PREP: 5 minutes   COOK: 5 minutes

Makes 2¹/₂ cups syrup

2 cups sugar
1¹/₂ cups water

Combine the sugar and water in a small saucepan and heat to boiling over medium-high heat, stirring to dissolve the sugar. Boil 1 minute, remove from the heat, and let stand until cool.

INDEX

METRIC MEASUREMENTS

Liquid Ingredients by Volume

1/4 tsp=			1 ml
1/2 tsp=			2 ml
1 tsp=			5 ml
1 tbls=	1/8 cup=	1/2 fl oz=	15 ml
2 tbls=	1/4 cup=	1 fl oz=	30 ml
4 tbls=	1/3 cup=	2 fl oz=	60 ml
5 1/3 tbls=		3 fl oz=	80 ml
8 tbls=	1/2 cup=	4 fl oz=	120 ml
10 2/3 tbls=	2/3 cup=	5 fl oz=	160 ml
12 tbls=	3/4 cup=	6 fl oz=	180 ml
16 tbls=	1 cup=	8 fl oz=	240 ml
1 pt=	2 cups=	16 fl oz=	480 ml
1 qt=	4 cups=	32 fl oz=	960 ml
		33 fl oz=	1000 ml= 1 l

Length

(To convert inches to centimeters, multiply the number of inches by 2.5.)

1 in=			2.5 cm
6 in=			15 cm
12 in=	1 ft=		30 cm
36 in=	3 ft=	1 yd=	90 cm
40 in=			100 cm= 1 m

Cooking/Oven Temperatures

	Fahrenheit	**Celsius**	**Gas Mark**
Freeze Water	32° F	0° C	
Room Temperature	68° F	20° C	
Boil Water	212° F	100° C	
Bake	325° F	160° C	3
	350° F	180° C	4
	375° F	190° C	5
	400° F	200° C	6
	425° F	220° C	7
	450° F	230° C	8
Broil			Grill

Dry Ingredients by Weight

(To convert ounces to grams, multiply the number of ounces by 30.)

1 oz=	1/16 lb=	30 g
4 oz=	1/4 lb=	120 g
8 oz=	1/2 lb=	240 g
12 oz=	3/4 lb=	360 g
16 oz=	1 lb=	480 g